TROWEL LOVE
Essays on the Sociology of American Archaeology

Lawrence E Moore

In Memory of my parents

Robert E Moore (1932 – 2012)

Clara D Moore (1933 - 2011).

CONTENTS

CONTENTS CONT.

ACKNOWLEDGMENTS

This book is a collection of essays written over a 28 year period. Literally, hundreds of people have influenced me in that time. However, good friends stand out: Bill Long (1958-1999), Mike Johnson, Sue Artt, Gary Houston, and Wally Haussamen. All require mention as they provided some of the longest conversations over time. Mentors, known and never met, include Frank Bessac (1922-2010), James Deetz (1930-2000), and Bill Gardner (1935-2002), and, Robert Murphy (1924-1990), William Strauss (1947-2007) and Neil Howe; from them I have drawn the most inspiration.

The Chapters 2 through 28 previously appeared in several venues. A full citation is given at the end of each chapter. Many come from my blog The Age of Intuition (http://ageofintuition.blogspot.com) that has been ongoing since fall 2010. The journals I pulled from include the *North American Archaeologist*, the *Journal of Middle Atlantic Archaeology*, and the *European Journal of Archaeology*. Several essays came from the *SAA Archaeological Record*, the newsletter of the Society for American Archaeology. Another one came from the newsletter for the Society for Historical Archaeology, and two from a book in the Worldwide Archaeology Series published by the Avebury/Ashgate Publishing Company. Lastly, one chapter is a slightly condensed version of my master's thesis done at the University of Montana. Only Chapter One is new.

The last couple of years have been hard due to the passing of my parents. Both were great readers who respected all forms of literature; I wish I had done something like this sooner. This book is done in their memory; they are greatly missed.

To my daughter Meghan, a shining star: there are many road trips yet to come.

L Moore
December, 2013
Broken Arrow, Oklahoma.

1 A GOOD WALK SPOILED

About thirty years ago, I was sitting on an upturned plastic bucket watching a crew of archaeologists. It was a warm summer morning, a pleasant Monday with birds chirping and cows grazing nearby. We were on an old plantation in the South. I was taking ethnographic notes about life in a field school. The crew was excavating the remains of an alleged slave quarter dating to the antebellum nineteenth century. Under the top soil were four small piles of bricks in a rectangular pattern, brick piers as corner supports for a frame building that once stood there. Broken bricks, glass, ceramics, and metals were scattered around. The crew was "exposing" it all so that it could be mapped and then collected. Exposing meant they were carefully removing the grass and top soil to reveal the architecture and artifacts below, and they did so in neat little square excavation units. It was more like sculpting, shaving, and carving the soil, not really digging.

The crew of eight was a mixture of college students and other adults, mainly teachers, who had paid to work on a summer archaeology project. Participants could sign up for two, four, or six weeks of the school. We had just begun the third week and the crew had three new workers. The crew chief was a man in his mid twenties and a graduate student at a prominent university working on the site from which his dissertation later emerged. He had opened the day by giving simple instructions to the crew, and had placed new workers to assist those who had worked the first two weeks.

One new worker was a teenage college student. She pulled a shiny new large mason trowel out of her bag. The crew chief asked to see it, looked at it, and tossed it over the fence into the cow pasture, proclaiming, "this isn't a trowel". Everyone was surprised and the girl was some put out. He laughed it off and gave her a trowel from his bag, saying, "this is a real trowel". He elaborated a little by discussing how important trowels were to archaeologists and that they joked about having Trowel Love. The day went

1

on without further incident and no one recovered the tossed trowel.

Later I would learn that archaeologists take great pride in their tools, especially the trowel. But not just any trowel. In the United States, the proper archaeological trowel has to be from The Marshalltown Company, located in Marshalltown, Iowa. It must be a mason's trowel, never a garden trowel, triangular (pointy) and 4.5 inches in length. As long as you have that trowel, you can have others, pointy or rectangular, and never longer than six inches, and shorter ones are for "detailed" work. While in the field some carry their trowel like a pistol, maybe in a tool holster or belt, often stuck in a back pocket (handle or blade down, it doesn't matter), but always handy.

Great debates, even mock duels, have been fought about the care of and qualities of Marshalltown trowels. Some prefer to sharpen and oil their tools regularly. The big concern is whether to sharpen both top and bottom of an edge to make a sharp bevel, or to sharpen just the top so that the edge has a wedge shape. Others contend that sharpening is not needed, all one needs to do is "sharpen through use" and let the sweat of your hand be the oil. A trowel worn down to a nubbin is a piece of art. The tool is a universal one; it can be a knife to cut watermelon or cake, and a spatula to serve it. I've seen one man try to pick his teeth with one. Some believe that "Marshalltowns" never break and are balanced perfectly. Archaeologists with international experience may counter that the Goldblatt trowel is better because it is common among international archaeologists. (Ironically, the Goldblatt Tool Company is another American manufacturer). An archaeologist with a Goldblatt in her field bag, or box, will likely be questioned about her presumed international fieldwork.

The trowel is the symbol of a professional field archaeologist. Knowing how to use it suggests great competency and character. The highest award an archaeologist can aspire to is to receive a gold plated Marshalltown trowel, pointy 4.5-inch, mounted on a plaque from an archaeological organization in acknowledgement of one's lifetime of archaeological accomplishments. One of the most famous essays of the late twentieth century, printed near the end of the great debates over the New Archaeology of the 1960s and 1970s, was "The Golden Marshalltown" (Flannery 1982). Of course, other tools are beloved because of long use and familiarity. Many a shovel has had the same care as a trowel. Field vehicles are old friends who get you there and back. The loving touch is even given to computers and cameras. Only the trowel, however, represents a commitment to a profession. Its image adorns many logos of archaeological societies, and tee shirts and coffee mugs, like a badge of honor.

I would eventually learn these things as I switched from being the student of ethnography to a working archaeologist. After a few years of itinerant work, I settled into the Fairfax County, Virginia, heritage resource program, and became a "public" archaeologist. Working with volunteers, students, interns, and other archaeologists, I directed several projects and administered a few others. Nevertheless, my experience as an ethnographer never left me. I was always the participant observer, slight emphasis on observer, wondering, "what the heck is this profession?" I wrote several argumentative papers in those years.

In the mid 1990s, I left Fairfax County, and the profession, having had enough of the politics of the Washington DC area and of historic preservation. My family and I moved to Denver and I went to work for a mutual fund company. Starting at the bottom in sales, I rose quickly into sales management. Having settled into that industry, and thinking I was there for the long term, I re-engaged with archaeology in late 1999 as a volunteer and directed some fieldwork through the Denver Chapter of the Colorado Archaeological Society. It was a rewarding time. I also wrote the "Misplaced Trowel" essay in those years (Moore 2001b) never thinking I would soon return as a professional.

In June 2002, near the end of that recession, I was laid-off as my company shrank due to declining assets under management. Hustling for another job, and in competition with dozens of younger and recently laid off sales managers in the Denver area, I chose to go into the consulting industry based upon environmental compliance and its associated historic preservation compliance industry known as "cultural resource management" (CRM), which is the applied archaeology and history business.

My years in financial services were useful. I crafted a business style of writing and I learned much about marketing and human behavior that I would not have considered had I stayed in public archaeology. Ideas such as generational theory, the falsity of rationalism, and a different perspective on reflexivity became thoroughly developed. I also discovered that science was no longer revered as it had been when I was younger. Although I had a bachelor's degree in economics, and had trouble completing that, I liked finance a lot. It was fun and exciting. I also learned that both were shallow, their theoretical models were nothing but conduits for big business to steal from others, and neither was about helping average people. The 1990s were the last years that personal financial planning had any credibility. In 1999 I had earned the vaunted CFP credential (Certified Financial Planner) and it was worthless. By the early 2000s, it was clear (to me) that both economics and finance had left the path of integrity and had completely sold out to big money interests and corruption. I didn't mind leaving it behind as a career because I used my new knowledge to improve my personal finances, a satisfying effort.

In mid 2002, the question before me was "if it happened there could it happen to other professions?" As I re-entered the world of archaeology and CRM I set out to analyze the status of CRM and archaeology in general.

That effort led to several essays, a renewed commitment to the profession, and a growing realization that everything had changed. American archaeology was nothing like I had remembered from the 1980s and 1990s. I felt like a new kid on the block. Many people I had worked with for years were retired, deceased, or working outside the profession, replaced by a new brand of archaeologists--and a new ethos had fully captured the profession, Historic Preservation, as a form of a new Romanticism.

I too had changed. It turns out, surprisingly, I enjoy the new Romanticism, what I call twenty first century Romanticism. I began to write about it on a blog called The Age of Intuition. The name is, obviously, a reminder that we are no longer in an Age of Reason. America's second Enlightenment, the years of Modernism and scientism, circa 1890 to 1990, was over. Scientists and other thinkers are now hustling harder than ever to make a living because American society does not privilege their work as was done under Modernism. Money and power has corrupted many. The pursuit of knowledge as an end unto itself, an ideal of late Modernism, is not enough in a Romantic era. The process of research and its results have to be entertaining and/or useful to others who use it for their own ends, and not necessarily scholarly ends, such as American Indians appropriating archaeology for their own purposes (promoting their sovereignty and their ethnic heritage as they see fit). While I'm not much for the preservation ethos, other Romantic ethos's are available. I think the development of numerous strong public and community focused archaeology programs with a democratic penchant (a revival of the Gemeinschaft perspective) is the way to go. There already have been some successes in the right direction; but, alas, not enough. Given the current poor economic environment, defending the status quo of CRM is the profession's focus.

The essays in this volume convey the journey just briefly outlined. Chapters two through six, and the last three, are statements of my current view of archaeology and its American parent, anthropology. The essays in between demonstrate my wanderings on getting there. I reserve the right to change my opinions as I choose. What will likely not change are my methods and attitudes toward analysis and reasoning. I have long been a pragmatist, in the philosophical sense, and a user of dialectics. Human beings are successful and fallible, regularly under achieving their potentials. Both archaeologists and the products of their efforts, "archaeological knowledge", fit that description well. This not a criticism--archaeologists deserve our admiration because they keep trying (economists and evolutionary biologists have given up, for different reasons).

The essays do seem a bit random or disjointed. Many were written as responses to specific issues and other writers. Numerous themes run through them. I list the important ones here so that they will not be completely new when encountered elsewhere.

Science is a human endeavor. Scientists do not transcend their host society through claims of objectivity; one cannot be absolutely value neutral. Science entails much normative culture, so the specters of relativity or "anything goes" chaos are not relevant. American archaeologists and anthropologists are people embedded in the culture of the host society, "America". They are a partial microcosm of the host society (i.e. they do not fully represent it), and the events that they create are partially synchronized with the events of the broader society. Studying them does inform us about America. But the part does not equal the whole; understanding archaeologists says little about politicians or baseball players, for example.

American culture history has cyclical cultural patterns. The broadest is an alternation between Apollonian and Dionysian cognitive framing, taking those concepts from Nietzsche (1967), and as used by Ruth Benedict (1934); the two patterns are, respectively, the same as Low Context Culture and High Context Culture as described by Hall (1976). Nietzsche recognized the alternation in ancient Greek culture; Benedict and Hall did not, viewing cultures as fixed, which they are not.

Awakenings are the transitional eras when America switches from one cognitive framing to the other. They are creative and intense cultural and intellectual eras, and the culture is full of confidence. The "sixties and seventies" was the last Awakening, known as the Fourth. The Third Awakening was the Progressive Era (circa 1890 to 1920) that initiated twentieth century Apollonian Modernism and spread science and the ideology called "scientism" into most corners of American society; science was also given a privileged leadership status in society. The Fourth Awakening initiated the return of Dionysian Romanticism, a reassertion of many ideas of nineteenth century Romanticism; it also led to the demise of scientism in popular culture and within the professions (with surviving pockets of believers); science itself lost its privileged status and now operates in a supporting role across American culture. In American archaeology, the confident New Archaeology ran its course during the Fourth Awakening.

In the 1950s, like most of American culture, American archaeology was mostly Apollonian and Modernist, pursuing and controlling its own research agenda. By 1990 both were mostly Dionysian and Romantic. Today, archaeology operates in a mixed environment (academic, museum, applied) with most practitioners working in the CRM venue, supporting historic preservation compliance. Archaeologists do have other Romantic options open to them, such as expanding community archaeology programs (the ideal High Context Culture type of program), but they lack confidence to make a change.

A four part sub-cycle in America culture history is the rotation of cultural "seasons"; they are: awakening (summer), unraveling (autumn), secular crisis (winter), and the cultural high (spring). Each lasts between twenty to twenty four years. Secular crisis is the opposite of awakening. It is a dangerous era and total war is very possible; the culture lacks confidence and is in an identity crisis. Significant status quo changes occur during cultural winters.

America is in secular crisis, entering sometime in the early 2000s; the credit crisis of 2008-2009 verified it. The real unemployment rate of the nation, the U6 number, has been at mild depression levels, above ten percent, since mid 2007. A substantial portion of the nation lacks confidence in its elected leaders. In popular culture, survivalism and escapism-through-fantasy is widespread. The identity crisis to resolve is: "is America still number one?" Conceptually, we are in the same place as the American Revolution, the Civil War-Reconstruction era, and the Great Depression-World War II era. This is a dangerous era and it will last into the 2020s. There is plenty of time for dramatic and quick cultural change to occur.

American archaeology is in secular crisis. Archaeologists have lost much control of their profession and feel as if they have no or less influence with the general public. Two strong forces are undermining archaeologist's ability to do focused research. The preservation ethos has diminished excavations nationwide and emphasizes pedestrian surveys, site record keeping, and site avoidance attitudes; archaeologists have enabled this process. Second, American Indian tribes, individually not united, are asserting more control over portions of the archaeological record; archaeologists are no longer the sole authorities about American "prehistory". Economic issues also plague archaeologists but they could be mitigated if other decisions were made.

The cultural high season is when the culture rebuilds, consolidates, and refocuses after surviving the secular crisis; a stronger sense of unity and confidence pervades the culture. For America, this was the post World War II era, phasing into the Fourth Awakening. For American archaeology, this was the era of expanding academic departments and the development of Salvage Archaeology programs.

The unraveling cultural season is a period of culture wars. In America this was the early 1980s into the early 2000s, the period when the country ultimately polarized politically into the "Red and Blue states". A dozen moral topics were debated. Scientism was destroyed nationwide and science demoted to a supporting role in society. In archaeology this played out as the processual versus post-processual debate; CRM replaced Salvage Archaeology in the 1980s.

American archaeologists divide themselves into prehistorians and historical archaeologists. Prehistorians have controlled the profession since the beginning of American professional archaeology in the Progressive Era, and they control its main organization, the Society for American Archaeology (SAA), since its inception in the early 1930s. Most American historical archaeologists have long felt as second class citizens within the profession, having little power or influence on the direction of the profession. They organized in 1968 into their own society (Society for Historic Archaeology). Resolution of the current secular crisis will likely switch the power roles of the two groups or equalize them; most archaeologists will also have to negotiate a compromised outcome with numerous tribes. Prehistorians have much to lose. (This book is not about American archaeologists who work outside America).

A second sub-cycle in American culture history is the rotation of generations. The four generational types are: idealists, reactives, heros, and artists; they rotate about every 22 years. They correspond to living generations as: idealists (Baby Boomers), reactives (Generation X), heros (elderly GI and younger Millennials), and artists (elderly Silent and very young New Progressives). Each generation leaves its mark on American culture and archaeology.

The reactive generational archetype is a powerful symbol in American culture that transcends the generational cycle. It is that of the rebel, the pirate, the cavalier, it is the patriot who yells "don't tread on me"; it is the icon of the American revolutionary or pragmatic survivor. In real life it is George Washington and Paul Revere. In American fiction it is Natty Bumpo (aka Deerslayer, Hawkeye), Tom Sawyer and Huck Finn, the cowboy, and, the popular Indiana Jones. Through Indy, archaeologists represent a cherished American ideal, as a pathfinder, adventurer, survivor, and sometimes, a tragic hero. More recently, we have the similar character of Daniel Jackson from the popular series *Stargate SG-1*; as an archaeologist and adventurer, he is the moral voice putting the brakes on an aggressive military and nation. From the perspective of our entertainment industry, archaeologists, as a class, have not lost their integrity.

I agree, regardless of the temptations, failures, and gratuities found in CRM. In the midst of a culture sold out to consumerism and immediate gratification, archaeologists, while doing their jobs, have continued their perspective of the long term and have sought the wisdom that comes with tough experiences. (I can't speak to what they do outside their profession). For a moral person, it is a better place to be than economics or finance.

The phrase "a good walk spoiled" is, of course, associated with golf. Among golfers, which I occasionally include myself, it is common to hear claims of "a bad day of golf is better than a good one at work". Most archaeologists, especially those in CRM, would agree--a bad day of fieldwork is better than a good day in the office. Beyond the pleasures of being out and about, the phrase also reflects the fallibility of humans because golf is such a humbling game. Archaeology is so much like this. For all its successes, it is often a swing away from failure. It, along with all the social sciences, has not delivered any eternal truths or social or historical laws. Mostly, what we get are interesting stories, and some of those are trickster "Coyote" tales. As a pragmatist, I am skeptical of claims about social truths and laws but I know there are people, many archaeologists included, who do believe in such things and they strive to discover them. In addition, if they have any success, it often quickly becomes spoiled. But-- hey--they likely had a good time getting there.

The truth is, for most human endeavors, that which is successful will contain within it that which will bring it down. For archaeology, in this current era, the success of the preservation ethos that drives CRM is undermining the whole profession. Moreover, there is not much archaeologists can do about it without external help, such as revising heritage laws and regulations (which they fear to initiate because any proposed change is viewed-feared as an opportunity to cut the whole program), or a significant change within American culture, which is also possible. Maybe the tribes can band together (unlikely, but try anyways) and push for a national heritage law that supports their interests in natural, cultural, and ethnic conservation.

This is where we stand in late 2013. A swing away from failure, holding on by our fingertips, and emphasizing good pedestrian field events.

Objective knowledge, so called Truth, is such fun stuff. It is always paradoxical. As an unobservable, you cannot measure it or standardize it. And yet, its quality is revealed, exposed, when you see it.

What, or who, is an American archaeologist? It's an unobservable. Measuring or standardizing them (c.f. Zeder 1997) is meaningless unless it is done frequently to document historical changes within categories. And even if that was done one should be skeptical of any strong conclusions because statistical surveys hide as much as they reveal. Basically, there is no pattern other than a useless one: "deteriorating middle class" people, mostly of a Caucasian appearance.

However, as is often said among themselves, "I know one when I see one". We can know something about their qualities. For that reason alone, as a class of human beings partially representative of the Human Condition, they deserve their own sociology (and philosophy). This book is a humble move toward that moving target.

2 THE LAMENESS OF OTHERNESS

I recently read the book *Reversed Gaze: An African Ethnography of American Anthropology* by Mwenda Ntarangwi (2010). I encourage serious anthropologists to use it in graduate seminars as a discussion piece.

The book describes Ntarangi's maturation in anthropology from graduate school to being an associate professor. Along the way, he discusses racism, class, and power structures in anthropology. One of his main points is that American anthropology is focused on studying the Other, or Alterity. You learn much about Ntarangwi and that it must be hard to come to America from Africa and then write about Americans. It makes one wonder about the validity of all ethnography. It's not that Ntarangwi is 'wrong' so much as his *culture critique* perspective misdirects his understanding of American anthropology. I have several comments.

First, I'm not bothered by being reminded that racism exists in America and in anthropology. I was surprised that Ntarangwi seemed surprised (or disappointed) by this fact. Did he buy into all the equality mumbo jumbo our culture throws out to the world? I guess he had a rude awakening similar to Rabinow's in Morocco (1977) who was told by a Muslim friend that Jews (i.e. Rabinow) will always be seen as inferior by Muslims. Chinese born and raised Francis L. K. Hsu lived with it too (Hsu 1973; 1979; Claes 1996). American history is incomplete without the racism discussion. Our American Civil War with 600,000 dead may have ended slavery but not racism.

In addition, it seems that Ntarangwi came to the US with an exalted view of American anthropologists and scholars in general. It seems he expected them to be pillars of collegiality and equality; and, that they, somehow, could be above it all. Unfortunately, academic tribes (Adams 1988; Becher and Trawler 2001) are not paragons of virtue. They can be as low as any other aspect of our culture. Anthropologists, and all scholars, are human beings. They have all the virtues and vices, all the grace and pettiness, of the class. In typical human fashion, they make we/they distinctions that are not always fair or socially graceful. It is nice to think well of others--but ethnography requires deeper insight than that.

Americans can be very judgmental of each other and hard on themselves. While anthropology should be used as a mirror to assess our own culture and individual lives (Kluckhohn 1959) I never fully bought into the in-your-face "anthropology as culture critique" perspective that began in the mid 1980s (Marcus and Fisher 1986). In my ethnography of archaeologists (Moore 1986) I tentatively used the *culture critique* framing, thinking it was still a "mirror-for-man" perspective. But I rejected other harsh criticisms of anthropology because I viewed them as "self flagellation," something I was not then, or now, interested in doing. My judgment then was that *culture critique* seemed overly judgmental rather than constructively critical; later publications from that group would confirm this. Trencher (2002) views it as having been obstructive as well.

Today, I view *culture critique* as one expression of Baby Boomer henpecking and politicking that is so divisive. This style of communication did appear in American popular culture in the 1980s. The best example is in comedy. When the Johnny Carson show was running the humor was always about Carson (Silent generation) making fun of himself, and there was a classiness about it. He made his guests look good. Then came the David Letterman and Jay Leno shows, both of which provided Boomer henpecking, with guests verbally slapped around and made to look stupid. *Culture critique* demeans and damages what it studies. It also forces people to take sides.

Ntarangwi plays this too. On page 42 he describes how he enjoys having his students read Horace Minor's 1956 essay on the body rituals of the Nacirema (American spelled backwards). He doesn't tell them until afterwards that the study is about 1950s America. So, he gets frustrated comments from his class. This is him playing a gotcha moment and putting the class at a psychological disadvantage. I would rather have seen him tell the class what the essay is about up front and that they should write an essay on how they think things have changed. This would send the message that America has culture that can be studied, and you also make the students engage it.

The *culture critique* folks acted like anthropologists had not done enough research on American culture. I suspect that Marcus and Fisher, and others of their ilk, underestimated, or ignored, the depth and breadth of anthropological research into *self* and American culture. Mead (1942) and Gorer (1964) had already provided idealized versions of Middlebrow culture, and Henry (1965) provided heavy hitting constructive criticism. By the early 1980s there were excellent readers available on the anthropology of American culture (Spradley and Rynkiewich 1975; Messerschmidt 1981). In 1992 Moffett was able to review over 160 anthropological monographs that had been done the previous decade about American culture. The process continues: Gusterson (1997) updated the idea of Studying Up and today we have Karen Ho (2009) writing about Wall Street. By having bought into the *culture critique* perspective, I suspect that Ntarangwi also underestimates or ignores the vastness and quality of this literature.

Culture critique and its obsession with self/otherness is not a good foundation from which to study another culture or even some aspect of one's own culture because it is demeaning to those studied. *Culture critique* is always a "gotcha" mentality, a game of one-upmanship. The *culture critique* crowd love to say "gotcha America" and "gotcha anthropologists" for being the hypocrites you are. The title of the book says "gotcha" from my "reversed gaze." One should never fall in love with a phrase.

When I was in graduate school in the early 1980s some of us joked about the "we have met the Others and they are us" phrase that was then popular. Everyone knew it was a spin-off of the old saying "we have met the enemy and they are us." Unfortunately, the *culture critique* crowd fell hard for it. They are the ones who escalated Otherness into a poplar term in anthropology. They missed the joke and took it seriously—we are the enemy, shame on us, take sides.

Figure 2-1: Google Ngram for "Otherness" in American English, 1900-2008.

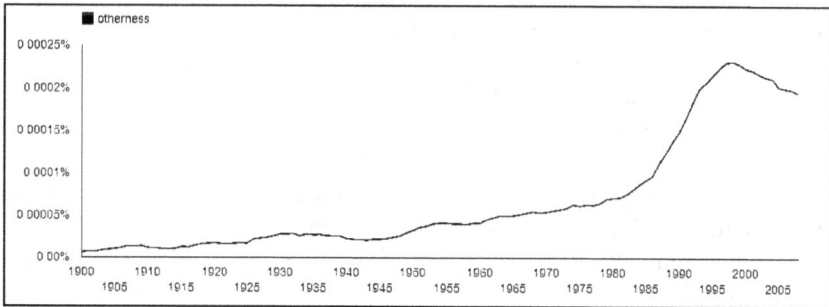

Otherness and anthropology come together in American anthropology with the work of Levi Strauss. In 1963 his *Structural Anthropology* was released in English and by the 1970s structuralism was the new fad in the social sciences and literary circles. In 1983 Fabian published his famous *Time and the Other* and many went gaga about it [I suspect he would take some of it back if he could (Fabian 2006, 2011)]. Next, came Marcus and Fisher (1986) and the pump was primed much further. On Figure 2-1 it's clear that Otherness takes off as a popular idea in the 1980s and then peaks in the late 1990s with a subsequent fall off.

The duality "Reflexivity/Otherness" is the post modern version of the old "we/they" duality. American anthropology is interested in it because all of Western Civilization debates it. The *culture critique* crowd use the we/they binary to demean American culture and it institutions; they criticize to tear down. The alternative *professional stranger* (Agar 1996) approach offers constructive criticism with the intent of no further action (a take it or leave it attitude) or seeks to improve American culture. As they used to say: "America-love it or leave it". The *culture critique* crowd won't leave.

Fortunately, as Figure 2-1 suggests, the study of Otherness, and by extension the *culture critique* approach, is a dying trend. When you have researchers comparing the elderly to others (Hazan 2009) you know that the silly point has been reached. Also, it never became universal across the profession or across cultural anthropology. Marvin Harris and Otherness don't go together and historical archaeologists would give you a blank stare if you asked them about it. Otherness is just a weird contemporary Western idea and many non-Western cultures would not understand it (cf. Gruen 2010). There are other ways to conceive of anthropology and ethnography. I prefer the ethnographer as professional stranger concept.

Figure 2-1 actually reveals more than I have suggested. It is a depiction of word usage in American English not just anthropological works. Prior to 1960 Otherness was mostly a theological, philosophical and ethical concept. It remains so today. The most common usage of Otherness is in theology, usually with reference to the Otherness of God.

American Christians are very interested in discovering the Otherness of God and they know that you find God in other people. The best example of this is Martin Buber's (1971 [1923]) *I and Thou*. It plays out as I/you, we/they, and civilized/savage in Western culture. In 1979 Giles Gunn published *The Interpretation of otherness: Literature, Religion, and the American Imagination*, a nice analysis of how Americans are focused on identity issues, especially the self/society conflict, as portrayed in fiction. But, it's not just that they want to be rugged individuals in society they also want fellowship with others. The quest for fellowship is the quest for God. Finding God in another culture is no different (Headley 1983; priest and anthropologist). Any theologian or mystic would recognize that the post modern anthropologists studying Otherness are basically looking for some version of God. Very few are reflexive enough to know that they are.

As an observer of all this I have to say that American culture is pervaded by Christian beliefs and values. Americans who become anthropologists also carry with them these basic perspectives even if they themselves are atheists. Christianity is embedded in American anthropology at a meta level. The big bubble on Figure 2-1 indicates that Americans used the term Otherness as they lived out the Fourth Great Awakening that spanned 1960 to 1990. Certainly, there was some hangover that made it last a little longer. This is what one should expect as the fundamentalist mentality of modernist anthropological scientism was replaced by the fundamentalist post modern democratic anthropology during those same years. Now that post modernism is the norm in anthropology the aggressive henpecking of the *culture critique*-ers need not continue; Figure 2-1 suggests it is waning.

As one who lives at the intersection of agnosticism and mysticism, I was never looking for God. To me the whole Otherness issue is lame.

Ntarangwi is lucky. America is a land of people reinventing themselves all the time. He can do this too; he can have a Do Over. It's part of his personal evolution. I suggest he restart the project from a different perspective. He said many times that he is interested in the holistic approach of anthropology. Therefore, he should actually take such an approach because the part he is most familiar with, *cultural critique* as anthropology, is not the whole. He'll also find that the "ethnography of archaeology" literature (Edgeworth 2006; Sandlin and Bey 2006) is useful, providing parallel discussions. Further, he needs to embrace applied anthropology because 70 percent of all newly minted PhDs end up working outside of academia. The profession is not really an academic one when most of its students end up doing applied work. He should also read the basic references in the anthropology of anthropology genre that he ignored (Herzfeld, 1989; Khare 1990; Kim 2002; Sangren, 2007; and Trencher 1993, 2000).

Lastly, I do think that Ntarangwi is on a good path. He seems inquisitive and willing to persevere as he struggles to define his own identity. Good ethnographers are always monitoring the cultural landscape, they have situational awareness, and they know when to take a break from it all. Reminiscent of Nash's (1964) idea that ethnographers are always *strangers* Robert Murphy (1980:11) wrote:

> ...the agonizing process of ethnography is always incomplete; we skim off the top and come away, if we have done our jobs properly, with a sense of loss and unfulfilment.

You will never find yourself if ethnography is your sole means of searching, and, your identity is greater than the part called *anthropologist*.

from: The Age of Intuition, April 24, 2011.

3 ANTHROPOLOGY'S ROTTEN EGG

A while back I commented on the book *Reversed Gaze: An African Ethnography of American Anthropology* by Mwenda Ntarangwi (2010). It is time to follow up on a problem he identifies.

As he introduces the book, and his motivations for doing it, Ntarangwi writes (2010: vii):

> It is also a story hemmed within a specific discourse and views about anthropology that can be best represented by remarks from fellow graduate students who wondered what I was doing in a "racist" discipline...I became quite disturbed by the "racist" label placed on anthropology by fellow graduate students in other disciplines, particularly those in sociology and political science.

Later, I discover that this is not a rare problem. Hawaiian native Ty Tengan (2005: 247) writes:

> When I entered the anthropology graduate program at the University of Hawai'i at Ma͞noa (UHM) in 1998, I was dismayed to find that I was forced to justify my positionality as both an 'O͞iwi (Indigenous Hawaiian) and an anthropologist...Those I met were shocked that I was in anthropology and told me that it was 'an evil white discipline' that was 'racist towards Hawaiians'.

Okay, no argument, anthropology, a profession found in many countries, is tainted with racism. Among others, Hsu (1973; 1979), a Chinese born scholar, pointed it out years ago.

In a land full of racism such as America, you must assume that people born and raised here will likely bring their cultural baggage with them as

14

they enter anthropology. So, American anthropology is tainted with racism, although many anthropologists are not racists, and many are trying to lessen the problem. The point here is that anthropology has an image problem within the American academy. The issue above was found at universities in Illinois and Hawaii. Apparently, graduate students in other disciplines don't worry about the racist label, and, they are happy to sling it at anthropology. Thus, anthropology students do have to worry about it. Anthropology seems like a scapegoat.

When and why has this stinky image cast its pall over anthropology within the American academy? When did anthropology become the poster child of scientific racism and colonialism? It's hard to imagine that political science, economics, sociology, or any other discipline, had no part in the expansion of American capitalism and imperialism after World War II. And, if they exist on American soil, they too will be tainted with racism. Have you ever seen a black economist or a Native American sociologist? I suppose there are a few but they are not common.

American anthropologists have to fix this image and identity problem. Third party intervention is needed using savvy marketing consultants. No amount of anthropology of anthropology can fix it. Navel gazing is not the answer. The brand of anthropology needs to be re-invented. I know the racist discussion has been out there ever since Boas fought the issue at the beginning of the twentieth century. However, as a graduate student in the 1980s I don't ever remember anything like this, especially since I did an ethnography of anthropology in those years.

Was it the political correctness of the late 1980s and 1990s that led to this image? Did so many people inside anthropology piss on the discipline such that other professions noticed the stink and took advantage of it? Maybe so, maybe the fears of Herbert Lewis (1999: 716) about Misrepresentation and its Consequences have come to fruition:

> This article deals with several of the most common charges leveled at anthropology, notably that it has regularly and necessarily exoticized "Others," has been ahistorical, and has treated each culture as if it were an isolate, unconnected to any other. It demonstrates how inaccurate and easily falsifiable such claims are and recommends a critical reevaluation of these unexamined and destructive clichés…

Maybe anthropologists painted "racist" on their foreheads in their never ending desire for self destruction. I don't know.

I do know that no graduate student in any discipline should ever have to worry about such a label.

from: The Age of Intuition, May 16, 2011.

4 LEWIS BINFORD AND JAMES DEETZ AS INNOVATORS

Earlier this week archaeologist Lewis Binford (1930-2011) passed away. He was famous in the 1960s-1980s era due to his innovations in theory and method. While I never cared much for his work I do enjoy thinking about people's careers. Also, Binford is a nice contrast to James Deetz (1930-2000), who did influence me. Both were cast as rivals in the 1970s and 80s.

These two archaeologists can be compared using David Galenson's (2006) two categories, Young Geniuses and Old Masters. Galenson identified two types of innovators, Conceptual Innovators and Experimental Innovators. (Reminder--most people are not innovators.)

Conceptual Innovators are young geniuses whose work communicates discoveries and ideas. They are deductive, plan their work carefully, have clear ideas in mind, work quickly to complete a project, and know when they are done. Conceptual innovators peak early in their careers, before age 35, and their later work is less inspiring. Conceptual painters regard experimental types as mere artisans, lacking in intelligence. Conceptual innovators are "rationalists" who disregard other forms of thought as being useless; they view themselves as exceptional.

Binford was a young genius and he peaked in the years 1962-1972. He did a lot of work after that time that was very un-interesting (although his disciples can't get enough of it). His writing style was also hard to follow so many folks preferred not to read him. He undertook many projects but never really changed much theoretically. He had a conceptual hammer and everything was a nail. Here is a list of his important papers that started an intellectual movement in archaeology:

- Archaeology as Anthropology, *American Antiquity* 28(2):217-225,

16

1962

- A Consideration of Archaeological Research Design, *American Antiquity* 29(4):425-441, 1964.
- Archaeological Systematics and the Study of Culture Process, *American Antiquity* 31 (2): 203-210, 1965.
- Smudge Pits and Hide Smoking: The Use of Analogy in Archaeological Reasoning, *American Antiquity* 32 (1):1-12, 1967.
- *New Perspectives in Archaeology*, Chicago, Aldine Press (edited with Sally Binford), 1968.
- *An Archaeological Perspective*, New York, Seminar Press. 1972.

He became the most famous advocate of the New Archaeology that followed a strict form of hypothetico-deductive model based in logical positivism. He advocated one type of science and did not deviate from it, even while the profession moved beyond his ideas. The stuff he wrote in 2001 could easily have been done in 1962. Galenson's description of unbridled arrogance describes Binford very well.

Experimental innovators become Old Masters; they work inductively; planning is unimportant because they make their important decisions while working; they stop a project only when they cannot see how to continue it; they view their enterprise as research, they need to accumulate personal knowledge and require that their techniques emerge from careful study; they distrust theoretical propositions as facile and unsubstantiated; they work at an incremental slow pace; they have total absorption in the pursuit of ambitious, vague, and elusive goals, and they are frustrated with self perceived lack of success, and fear they may not live long enough to attain their realization. Their career is an evolution. Their best work is done later in life, usually after age 40. Experimental painters consider conceptualists as intellectual tricksters, lacking in artistic ability and integrity. Old Masters are intuitive thinkers who have learned to appreciate and integrate other types of thought.

James Deetz was an experimental innovator. His career was a collection of interesting projects from slightly different perspectives, suggesting he was constantly changing and refining his own ideas and methods. He seems to have gone through several phases, as reflected in various publications.

Phase 1. A broad based anthropological archaeologist and artifact analyst willing to try new approaches to artifact analysis; he worked in both historic and prehistoric archaeology:

- An Archaeological Approach to Kinship Change in Eighteenth Century Arikara Culture. Ph.D. dissertation. Department of

Anthropology, Harvard University, Cambridge, MA., 1960.

- A Datable Chumash Pictograph from Santa Barbara County, California. *American Antiquity* 29(4):504-506, 1964.
- The Dynamics of Stylistic Change in Arikara Ceramics. *Illinois Studies in Anthropology*, No. 4. University of Illinois Press, Urbana, Il., 1965.
- *Invitation to Archaeology.* Natural History Press [Doubleday] for The American Museum of Natural History, Garden City, NJ., 1967.
- Archaeology as a Social Science. In "Current Directions in Archaeology" *Bulletin of the American Anthropological Association* 3(3), pt. 2:115-125, 1970.

James Deetz and Edwin S. Dethlefsen

- The Doppler Effect and Archaeology: A Consideration of the Spatial Aspects of Seriation. *Southwestern Journal of Anthropology* 21(3):196-206, 1965.
- Death's Head, Cherub, Urn and Willow. *Natural History* 76(3):29-37, 1967.

Phase 2. Master Historical Archaeologist; he focuses on European settlement in North America:

- Late Man in North America: Archaeology of European Americans. In *Anthropological Archaeology in the Americas*, Betty J. Meggers, editor, pp. 121-130. Anthropological Society of Washington, Washington, D.C., 1968.
- Ceramics from Plymouth, 1620-1835: The Archaeological Evidence. In *Ceramics in America*, Ian M. G. Quimby, editor, pp. 15-40. University Press of Virginia, Charlottesville, 1972.
- A Cognitive Historical Model for American Material Culture, 1620-1835. In Reconstructing Complex Societies: An Archaeological Colloquium, Charlotte B. Moore, editor, pp. 21-29. *Supplement to the Bulletin of the American Schools of Oriental Research*, 20, 1974.
- *In Small Things Forgotten: The Archaeology of Early American Life.* Doubleday, Anchor Press, New York, 1977.

Phase 3. Negotiator; he merges and reworks ideas from different perspectives, and becomes an emissary for historical archaeology in South Africa under and after apartheid:

- Scientific Humanism and Humanistic Science: A Plea for Paradigmatic Pluralism in Historical Archaeology. In Historical Archaeology of the Eastern United States: Papers from the R.J. Russell Symposium, Robert W. Neuman, editor. *Geoscience and Man*

23: 27-34, 1983.

- Harrington Histograms versus Binford Mean Dates as a Technique for Establishing the Occupational Sequence of Sites at Flowerdew Hundred, Virginia. *American Archaeology* 6(1):62-67, 1987.
- History and Archaeological Theory: Walter Taylor Revisited. *American Antiquity*53(1):13-22, 1988.
- American Historical Archaeology: Methods and Results. *Science* 239:362-367, 1988.
- Archaeography, Archaeology, or Archeology? *American Journal of Archaeology* 93(3):429-435, 1989.

Patricia E. Scott and James Deetz

- Building, Furnishings and Social Change in Early Victorian Grahamstown. *Social Dynamics* 16(1):76-89, 1990.

Margot Winer and James Deetz

- The Transformation of British Culture in the Eastern Cape, 1820-1860. *Social Dynamics* 16(1):55-75, 1990.

Phase 4. The Old Master, at the top of his game:

- *Flowerdew Hundred: The Archaeology of a Virginia Plantation, 1619-1864.* University Press of Virginia, Charlottesville, 1993.
- Foreword. In *A Chesapeake Family and Their Slaves: A Study in Historical Archaeology*, by Anne Elizabeth Yentsch, pp. xviii-xx. Cambridge University Press, Cambridge, 1994.
- Discussion: Archaeologists as Storytellers. In Archaeologists as Storytellers, Adrian Praetzellis and Mary Praetzellis, editors. *Historical Archaeology* 32(1):94-96, 1998.
- Archaeology at Flowerdew Hundred. In *"I, Too, Am America"*: *Archaeological Studies of African-American Life*, Theresa A. Singleton, editor, pp. 39-46. University Press of Virginia, Charlottesville, 1999.

Phase 5. Folklorist; reflecting on a life well lived:

James Deetz and Patricia Scott Deetz

- *The Times of Their Lives: Life, Love, and Death in Plymouth Colony.* W.H. Freeman, New York, 2000.

Deetz started out as a modernist archaeologist, a blend of cultural historian and structuralist, a doer of science. He became a raconteur, banjo player, and humanist.

from: The Age of Intuition, April 13, 2011.

5 SOCIAL CHANGE AND
OKLAHOMA PUBLIC ARCHAEOLOGY

Across the United States (US) many local archaeological societies are struggling to keep their fires burning. Editors need journal and newsletter submissions. Memberships are down or flat. The average age of members is increasing. Some states that once had many chapters have lost a few. What's going on? Is archaeology in decline or lost its soul as some have suggested (Bouchard 2004; Moeller 2000)?

While archaeology probably has lost some luster it's not in decline, at least in terms of the number of people employed. The volume of fieldwork is certainly down, replaced by more administrative and planning tasks. Overall, professional archaeology has been flat for many years due to the late-cycle historic preservation orientation of the profession that is aimed at compliance to legislation rather than conducting research. Avocational societies, like the Oklahoma Anthropological Society, are feeling the pinch because they are centered on activities dependant on a certain level of ongoing research: educational lectures, field and lab work, and archaeological tourism. And there just aren't enough projects ongoing to sustain these activities.

Fortunately, this is all going to change in the near future. There are exciting opportunities on the horizon that all have to do with Public Archaeology, a new cycle coming our way.

The new Public Archaeology will be much different from the version outlined years ago by McGimsey (1972). The mechanics of archaeology will be much the same. It's the interaction with the public that will be different. In the old version emphasis was on doing archaeological research that archaeologists considered to be important. In the new version the goal will be offering multiple venues for educational entertainment on many topics that interest the public.

Public Archaeology is also an international concept these days with foreigners at the cutting edge of the discipline (Merriman 2004). There is even a new professional journal, *Public Archaeology*, published in Europe. American archaeologists from the US and Canada started the trend but no longer lead because they have been preoccupied with historic preservation issues. But this too will change in the near future. As historic preservation oriented archaeology concludes its cycle the new Public Archaeology will arise to replace it, triggering a growth spurt in American archaeology. Oklahoma professionals and avocationalists can ride this new wave. The process begins about 2009.

Social Issues Effecting American Archaeology

Numerous changes in North America are influencing when, where, and why archaeology gets done (Moore 2005a, 2006a). Two changes are important, generational changes associated with the Baby Boomers and the changing status of archaeology within American society. These both apply to the US and Canada. The demographic issue is not present in Mexico but that country will benefit from these changes via tourism.

The Baby Boomer generation has had a huge impact on US archaeology because of its size. These folks were born during the years 1946 through 1964. They entered the US workforce when they were about 21, years 1967 through 1985. During the years 1966-1976 memberships in the Society for American Archaeology increased by 180 percent while the previous decade (1956-1966) had an increase of only 74 percent (Moore 2006a). Archaeology didn't suddenly become more popular as a career choice. The entire US workforce expanded to accommodate the extra number of workers and the increase in US archaeology was its participation in that expansion. The Baby Boomer generation is about 2.4 times the size of its parent's generation.

Years later, the great wave of Baby Boomer retirements begins about 2009. In that year 70 percent of the current senior management in US federal service will be eligible to retire. Fifty percent of all current (2005) US federal employees will be eligible to retire by 2010 (Partnership for Public Service 2005:5). State, provincial, and local governments, and much of corporate America have similar statistics.

Baby Boomers will pursue retirement by running not sitting (Dychtwald and Kadlec 2005). This idealistic generation will continue its search for meaning in life and personal satisfaction. They will also revive their desires to implement significant social changes in society. One change will be their creation of the greatest leisure industry North America has ever seen because they will be seeking meaningful recreation and entertainment opportunities while in retirement.

When the retirement wave begins the US workforce will once again accommodate the demographics, this time by contracting because there will be no need to keep so many people employed. Currently, nearly 50 percent of all working US archaeologists are Baby Boomers. As this group retires it follows that the workforce of US archaeology will contract too. Only a small portion of cultural resource management (CRM) will survive this transformation (Moore 2006a) because it is not positioned to take advantage of the growing leisure industries.

To avoid this coming labor contraction American archaeology has to reposition itself to take advantage of growth opportunities developing within leisure industries. The best way to do this is for archaeology to become far more popular with Americans than ever before. To accomplish this, archaeologists need to focus on what is popular within American society and work archaeology into it. They need to focus on topics appealing to large numbers of Americans rather than focusing on topics that are important to a small clique of archaeologists.

This may seem like the commercialization of archaeology. Purists may decry the tainting of a fine social science with vulgar popularity and economics. The reality is that CRM archaeology went commercial 30 years ago. The rest of the profession has been slow to follow. Just like the commercialization of sports has been good for athletes of all ages and both genders, all archaeology needs to benefit from this as well.

Diversification and Commerce

While there are several venues in which archaeology can be done, in the future there will be even more. The history of US archaeology is one of increasing diversification in terms of the number of places and ways in which archaeology gets done. The process will continue and the next level of expansion needs to be attained.

US archaeology has had four major cycles of federal involvement and leadership. The first cycle dated roughly 1847-1930 when the Smithsonian Institution and the Bureau of American Ethnology led US anthropology, with archaeology subsumed under that label. Many other museums also began expanding their collections and exhibits as well. During those years several mound builder studies were done and a superficial understanding of prehistoric America was achieved.

Next was the New Deal Era of archaeology, 1933-1942. As a response to the economic crisis of 1929-1933 several legislations were passed triggering huge civil works projects in the US. Along with these work-relief (relief from unemployment) and construction projects were large archaeological studies. This era has sometimes been considered the greatest revolution in American archaeology because so much fieldwork was done. It was also the era that many universities and colleges initiated their academic archaeology programs. Numerous archaeological societies were started then as well, including the Society for American Archaeology in 1934.

The third cycle was the Salvage Archaeology era, roughly 1945-1980. During those years Reservoir Salvage and Highway Salvage programs led US archaeology. Using the Historic Sites Act of 1935, and later the Federal Aid Highway Act of 1956 and the Reservoir Salvage Act of 1960, archaeologists extended their presence within governmental construction projects to conduct research. Academic archaeology matured and expanded with the post World War II boom as numerous universities took advantage of the contracts that were funneled through the Department of Interior for these programs. Many states created their Archaeological Surveys then as well, with State Archaeologist positions at the helm.

The fourth cycle has been CRM. The National Historic Preservation Act was passed in 1966. Its impact on US archaeology was not really felt until the early 1970s. The late 1970s were full of strife as the National Historic Preservation Act and the Moss-Bennett Act of 1974 (an amendment to the 1960 Reservoir Salvage Act) were both being invoked. This eventually led to the 1980 amendment to the National Historic Preservation Act that made it the new centerpiece legislation and marginalized Moss-Bennett. It also launched US archaeology fully into the applied archaeology direction away from research. Archaeology no longer served itself but served another master, historic preservation (Moore 2001a). Over the course of this cycle, archaeology penetrated deeper into federal and state agencies and into corporate America. It became compliance oriented and commercialized.

These four cycles all represent accumulating phases in the growth of US archaeology. Each cycle added more venues where archaeology gets done. From initially being a museum endeavor in the 19th century, then being an academic profession devoted to scholarship, archaeology is now a complex system that includes museums, colleges, universities, most federal agencies, several state agencies, tribes, and for-profit corporations where the vast majority of the work is applied archaeology serving historic preservation.

Obviously, the big vacuum that needs to be filled is archaeology done through local venues (municipalities and local businesses) serving something else. The new Public Archaeology cycle will fill this need. It will be a leisure industry devoted to serving the needs of a growing leisure class willing to volunteer their time and commit money to issues in which they believe strongly. While many government agencies will shift from historic preservation compliance concerns to recreation projects, the backbone of the new Public Archaeology will be localized programs offering projects in most areas of America. Archaeology has a chance to become the next big hobby and social past time.

In several states there have been municipal programs for many years. For example, both Fairfax and Alexandria counties in Virginia started volunteer Public Archaeology programs in the 1980s. There are similar programs in Arizona, California, Florida, and Maryland. Today, such programs are very much under-represented. There are 3,142 counties and 239 large cities in the US and yet there are maybe only 50 municipal archaeology programs nationwide.

Half of all municipalities can afford to sponsor archaeologists running volunteer programs. In ten years there should be 1,000 such programs across the US. In Oklahoma the larger municipalities such as Oklahoma City, Tulsa, Lawton, and Norman all should have programs. Mid size cities such as Bartlesville, Broken Arrow, Edmond, Enid, Midwest City, Muscogee, Ponca City, Shawnee, and Stillwater also should seriously consider the idea. There is plenty of room to grow archaeology in Oklahoma.

These new programs will have a better chance of success if they are set up as public partnerships between government agencies, universities, colleges, museums, for-profits, or nonprofits, including the local archaeological chapter. They don't have to actually be run by municipalities. One example is the University of West Florida in Pensacola that has had a Public Archaeology center for many years. It blends volunteer opportunities with student field schools. This university recently received a new mandate to expand the Public Archaeology program to as many as seven cities across Florida. In these new cities it is very likely that a mixture of local colleges, nonprofits, and municipalities will be working together to sponsor the new programs.

Additional partnerships need to be arranged within the local business communities. Local Public Archaeology programs need to be integrated into regional efforts at economic development and heritage tourism. If anything, they need to be advertised by tourism planners and local chambers of commerce. Also, the concept of National Heritage Areas (including Heritage Trails and Heritage Rivers) needs to be utilized. These area designations provide National Park Service support for regional economic development and heritage tourism.

This type of expansion is a logical growth pattern for archaeology. Having moved beyond its museum and academic roots by becoming a means to accomplish historic preservation, archaeology cannot retreat to those roots. Now, it's time to branch out further and put archaeology on Main Street America. This can easily be done because Americans want entertainment (Fagan 2002) and archaeology provides excellent educational entertainment. All archaeologists have to do is reach out and fully engage with the American public.

Public Archaeology and Popular Culture

American archaeologists have to recognize and except the fact that archaeology has become part of American popular culture (Holtorf 2005; Russell 2002). This transformation is due largely to the movie *Raiders of the Lost Ark* (1981) and its Indiana Jones sequels. This image has been furthered along by novelists such as Barbara Mertz (writing as Elizabeth Peters and Barbara Michaels) and Tony Hillerman who wrote numerous popular mystery novels with archaeological themes, and by the successful Canadian-made cable television series *Stargate SG-1*, that also has a strong archaeological theme.

Another important issue is that entertainment is changing. It is becoming more interactive. The above items all suggest a passive form of entertainment if they are only thought of as movies and books. But their spin-offs are interactive in terms of video and computer games, amusement park rides, fan clubs, and inter-net chat rooms. If bingo and karaoke can be successes with the American public, so can cataloging artifacts and digging units.

To be effective at Public Archaeology the interests of the general American public must be considered. Archaeologists have to identify what is "hot" or "cool" (Darvill 2004: 57) that will motivate large numbers of Americans to fund archaeology and volunteer their time. Simple market analysis provides a short list of topics suitable for Oklahoma, presented in order of significance:

The Civil War

Within US history the Civil War is the 800-pound gorilla of the profession. More books get published every year on this topic than all other topics combined. This will increase as the 150th anniversary arrives, years 2011-2015. The Civil War in the West is an excellent topic suitable for Oklahoma archaeology as there are battlefields, encampments, military posts, and possibly military earthworks that could be investigated. Social history is also important, focusing on the war's impact on Oklahoma residents. A local twist to this theme would be to investigate the Native American units that served during the war.

Topics that have regional appeal

In this category are numerous themes of Oklahoma heritage that can be investigated archaeologically. Modern material culture studies could be done such as investigating the material culture aspects of oil and gas exploration and production, or of Route US 66. As Oklahoma is well known for its Native American population, studies about the relocation of Native Americans to Indian Territory or their life afterward likely has regional appeal. The Western theme could also be researched, as in the archaeology of outlaws or Cowboy culture. These themes are currently being considered at the national level, as there are bills in the House and Senate to establish a Trail of Tears National Trail for Oklahoma and another National Trail devoted to the Chisholm and Great Western Cattle Trails.

Firsts

American's are obsessed with knowing about the first occurrence of any type of event or process, and the persons associated with them. Americans want to know about the first settler, the first schoolhouse, bank, oil well, etc., in a county or region. In this category is the common archaeological interest in Paleo-Indians and early European colonists and explorers in Oklahoma. Native Americans have picked up on this concept by calling themselves First Americans and First Nations. Oklahoma tribes are likely to initiate their own Public Archaeology projects so that they can interpret their own past in the way that they wish it to be told. Their goal is to control the interpretation of their heritage.

Genealogy

Genealogy is the most popular hobby in the US. One in four adults dabbles in genealogy every year, and, one in twenty is a dedicated hobbyist. Every public library system in the US caters to this hobby. Archaeologists can tap into this by doing projects where living descendants can provide oral history for the project or actually participate in the research. This category is associated with the Firsts category, in that living descendants desire to control the interpretation of their own past.

Exotic-Spectacular-Rare

Anything that is considered exotic, spectacular, or rare is of interest to Americans. It satisfies their emotions about the mystery and romance of the past. For Oklahoma archaeology this includes any site with a rich collection of artifacts and features that can be displayed well. An Oklahoma Buffalo skull with a spear point stuck into it fits this category, as was recently discussed on the television show History Detectives.

All of these topics fit into broader aspects of American popular culture and can draw more people into Public Archaeology programs. If pursued aggressively these topics can double the size of archaeology in Oklahoma in just a few years. Individual Public Archaeology programs probably should be structured to study just one of these themes, thereby ensuring a greater likelihood of success. In some areas of the state there could be multiple programs running simultaneously if they focus on different themes and do not compete with one another for volunteers. Foster diversity instead of being repetitive in the themes.

Finally, the above themes could be interpreted as if historic archaeology has a stronger appeal to Americans than prehistoric archaeology. That would be a misinterpretation of the market research. To Americans, archaeology is just archaeology. They don't get hung up on silly distinctions that professionals perpetuate. Whether one is sifting through the rubble of the World Trade Center for body parts after 9-11-2001 or digging grid units across a prehistoric village, Americans understand that this is archaeology because they see it on television all the time. The goal of the new Public Archaeology is to focus on the interests of the American public, not the profession.

Into the Public Domain

Holtorf (2005), in his interesting book *From Stonehenge to Las Vegas*, argued that the performance of archaeology is what the general public cares about rather than the mundane observations that professionals generally provide. He is probably correct if we view it as a statement about priorities. The process of discovery is more important than the results because it's a metaphor about the journey of life, of self-discovery. It's the journey that is important not the destination. This means that archaeologists need to seriously increase the number of field projects that they are doing.

The results of archaeology still have importance, of course. They are secondary. And in this area, archaeologists need to hedge their bets, if you will, for success. Focus on topics that interest Americans. If archaeology has become an aspect of popular culture then use it to investigate several other themes of popular culture.

Also recognize that this new perspective means that archaeologists have to share control of archaeology, both the process and results of it, with other interested parties. When something is given over to the public domain it is no longer yours to completely control.

Certainly, this proposition appears to take archaeology a long distance from its scholarly roots. This is desired. Archaeology isn't losing its roots; it's blossoming and others are enjoying it. Enable the process instead of resisting it.

from: Social Change and Oklahoma Public Archaeology. *North American Archaeologist* 26(4): 389-397, 2005.

6 ANCIENT ALIENS: FACTS ABOUT THE SHOW

Like many, I sometimes watch the *Ancient Aliens* show on the History Channel. Here are some facts about it.

Fact 1: It doesn't bother me that it is all a farce--I know that it is and treat it as just that. It is mindless entertainment, and *that* is its usefulness to me. A good laugh is always welcome.

Fact 2: The show informs us much about who we are. I'll return to that shortly.

Fact 3: Some archaeologists and historians get upset about these types of misinformation being broadcast across our culture. To them we should only portray "truths." But, philosophers don't even agree what "truths" are; so said "truths" are just academic consensus about certain ideas. Academics are often wrong, just look at current economists.

Fact 4: I despise academic believers as much as I do religious zealots.

Fact 5: A good academic is a skeptic and/or a cynic, i.e. is not a believer.

Fact 6: Some researchers have made good careers out of debunking the ideas and arguments of the "wackoes". Thus, the wackoes have usefulness because they exist so that others can live to debunk them.

Fact 7: Here is an excellent website about debunking the show and its back-story, http://ancientaliensdebunked.com/. They provide an excellent 3-hour video correcting many of the wrong assertions of the show. Enjoy it; it is very well done. (By the way, the video also demonstrates how earlier histories spread non-truths, supporting Fact 3).

Fact 8: The History Channel is a business trying to make a profit. They know that their audience isn't going to hang out to watch endless streams of pure documentaries. They have to jazz it up and *Ancient Aliens* does that quite well. Without such a show, the channel may perish. Do not berate them.

Fact 9: The proponents of the ancient alien theory are con-men. They will do anything and everything to sell their books and videos. Lying is common. They are laughing all the way to the bank.

Fact 10: In our contemporary Dionysian culture, the main trend is that the distinction between fact and fiction is blurred. Fact or "truth" is less important than the appeal of the argument or story. The few debunkers out there are behaving within a counter trend.

Fact 11: To Americans, *Ancient Aliens* is appealing because:

- Fiction 1: We are an advanced culture. We are smarter, better, than those ancient brutes that needed alien help to get by. Our technology proves it--and, if aliens come here, today or in the past, then they must be advanced beyond us.

- Fiction 2: Our culture is superior; it is okay for us to judge other cultures, especially ancient ones, by our contemporary standards. It's okay to interpret the past using contemporary complex metaphors. Why should I take the time to learn their complex metaphors? If I look at an ancient fresco and see an image that reminds me of a light bulb then it must be an image of a light bulb.

- Fiction 3: When two species interbreed you often get bigger, "giant," offspring like ligers and Nephilim.

In our Dionysian culture, a compelling story is more powerful than a fact. Welcome to 21st century romanticism.

from: The Age of Intuition, January 20, 2013.

7 REVIEW OF *ETHNOGRAPHIES OF ARCHAEOLOGICAL PRACTICE*

For several years now there has been growing interest in the ethnography of archaeological settings. Some of this work has been done as the ethnography of science, some as applied ethnography integrated with archaeological research, and some as reflexive archaeology, as this profession, like many others (Beck et al 1994; Bousquet 2004; Scheuerman 2001), has taken a reflexive turn. In *Ethnographies* Matt Edgeworth (2006) brings together fifteen essays that represent the current status of this young genre. The contributors are an international group equally divided between professional ethnographers and archaeologists doing ethnographic studies. I found this diversity appealing and think that readers will too.

In the Preface Edgeworth summarizes what ethnography is and why one would do the ethnography of archaeology. Additionally, in the Introduction, he provides a brief history of the genre, situating these contributions into current discussions about archaeological practices and reflexivity.

The next several essays are about the daily work environment of archaeologists. Based on a United Kingdom study, Thomas Yarrow argues that archaeological sites are created by the actions of those associated with them; in turn, aspects of these same people are created by the material properties of sites. David Van Reybrouck and Dirk Jacobs expand this concept as they argue that socialization of archaeologists cannot be detached from the objectification of archaeological observations into data (based on Jacob's experience at a project in the Netherlands). Jonathan Bateman furthers this discussion by focusing on archaeological draftsmanship, arguing that the drawings and photographs created at sites are the visual lingua franca of the profession. Charles Goodwin also explores the relationship between objects and human communication by summarizing numerous studies of archaeologists in the United States and South America. One example he elaborates on is how archaeologists use various forms of communication to collect data in the field, specifically using verbal communication, gestures, Munsell charts, and standardized forms.

The next few essays continue the daily issues of archaeology. John Carman discusses how archaeology is embedded within the social and political economy of the host countries. He argues that archaeological projects in the United Kingdom are separated from other activities occurring around them, field crews have internally focused social relations, and are focused on immediate tasks. Cornelius Holtorf describes a multinational project in Italy and how several research teams work together. He also discusses two purposes of field schools, as training centers for emerging practitioners and as educational vacations for students not pursuing archaeology as a career. Blythe E. Roveland analyses journal entries from a crew that had worked in Germany, discussing their daily concerns. She also addresses the difficulty of holding two roles simultaneously, field director and ethnographer. Oğuz Erdur narrates his experience doing ethnographic observation on a Turkish project. While he describes minor conflicts among the crew, he also offers insights on ethnography, itself full of conflict and constant negotiations.

The last papers discuss archaeology's engagement with non-professionals, mostly, the locals of host communities. Michael Wilmore discusses how social status and class of participants at a project in the United Kingdom influence decisions made in the field, and how people present themselves on a project. He argues these decisions are mediated by considerations about what might happen out of the field, back at the office, and across academic networks. Angela McClanahan argues that heritage management in Britain is often done without close communication with locals, who often understand their local heritage differently than do outsiders; locals often feel that their values and opinions are impinged upon or ignored by outsiders. Håkan Karlsson and Anders Gustafsson discuss how heritage management in Sweden is controlled by heritage management professionals. They argue that interpretive signs used by heritage managers reflect a closed system that reinforces the power of the managers and limits open communication with the public. Denise Maria Cavalcante Gomes describes how a Brazilian community uses local archaeological information negatively to shape their own identity. In this case the locals did not claim connection to the local archaeological record and did not want archaeologists to make such associations. Similarly, Timoteo Rodriquez discusses a Mayan community in Mexico that stalled an archaeological project because their control of the land and its cultivation was based on events dating to fairly recent history; whereas, archaeologists, seeking to foster tourism by advocating a museum development, tried to emphasize the local's associations with Pre-Columbian Mayan culture. The locals were successful in asserting their claim that their more recent history was more important to them than archaeologist's opinions about prehistoric Mayan culture. Lisa Braglia concludes the book by discussing the complicit agendas between archaeology, ethnography, and local communities. She finishes with a call for ethical ethnographies of archaeology that bridge the chasm between multiple scholarly agendas and the needs and values of local communities.

Ethnographies is an excellent book and important characteristics about archaeology are learned. For example, it becomes more evident that archaeologists should be more sensitive to the needs of locals, whether at home or abroad. Ethnographers are useful in mediating the diplomatic interplay that must occur between all groups. It also appears most archaeologists have to learn the hard way that most non-professionals have completely different understandings of and interests in archaeology and the past; basically, it seems archaeologists are constantly surprised that non-archaeologists don't think like archaeologists.

Ethnographies has some shortcomings. First, Archaeologists are clearly the target audience rather than ethnographers and archaeologists. AltaMira Press doesn't even cross list it with its own social science categories. This emphasis is possibly related to the book's lack of an extended discussion of how ethnography of archaeology relates to ethnographies of science, work, tourism, student and academic cultures, and to reflexive ethnography. This separation supports Carman's analysis.

Ethnographies perpetuates one stereotype: archaeology is about fieldwork. No contribution describes lab work, doing research, or writing archaeological literature. This fieldwork image is consistent with the popular culture image of archaeology that Holtorf described elsewhere (2005). Fieldwork is also described as a rite of passage, a common description about the induction of novices into many professions (Adams 1988; Head 1992; Roth and Bowen 2001). Its accuracy is debatable (Richard 2001). In American archaeology this depiction has been anecdotal since educational ethnographies began; for example, Solon Kimball regularly made this observation (Burns 1983).

Ethnographic and reflexive perspectives can improve archaeology, as vectors of change instead of continuity. Many researchers in *Ethnographies* (Yarrow, Jacobs, Holtorf, Roveland, Carman, Erdur, Gomes, and Rodriquez) seem to have worked from overly compromised roles, leaving them unable or unwilling to speak freely about social relations between colleagues, mentors, and students. Discussions about power relations between professors and students, between professors, and between schools are not taboo (Adams 1988; Becher and Trowler 2001; Pelias 2003), and without them, social change in the profession and a balanced, more complete, reflexivity cannot be achieved.

Short-comings aside, the essays in *Ethnographies* are well written and each has something to offer. *Ethnographies* examines many well known issues about archaeological practices, and does so in a fresh and genuine way. Some of the younger scholars discover that fieldwork may be a rite of passage, that ethnography is hard, challenging work, and that archaeology, also hard work, occasionally resembles its romantic and adventuresome stereotypes. The reader becomes a witness to these self discoveries, and that is reason enough to enjoy the book. Hopefully, more people will also become interested in being ethnographers of archaeological settings because the profession needs to continue the reflexive process.

from: book review of *Ethnographies of Archaeological Practice: Cultural Encounters, Material Transformations* edited by Matt Edgeworth. *European Journal of Archaeology* 8(3): 306-308, 2005.

8 PATTERNS WITHOUT RHYTHM

Preface

This thesis is an ethnography of some historical archeologists living in a field camp. These people were excavating a group of archeological sites and I observed them during their work and free time. I lived with these people for the duration of two field seasons and considered myself a member of the camp community. The main topic of this thesis is a conflict that occurred during one of these seasons and it is presented as a fractionation of the camp community due to tensions between subgroups. However, the reader will also note that I describe the community as having had unity. The discussion does, then, focus on contradictions between ideals, expectations, and conduct, unity and disunity, and equality and inequality. The conflict is described in a synchronic and diachronic context. Thus, the theoretical discussion is one of culture change. The people observed all belong to the fuzzy category "American", which does have its limitations, especially if one likes to atomize the world. But since atomization is one of the generalizations made about American world view, this thesis is a case study in this category.

Some people have asked whether this study is a critique of anthropology or of archeology. No, it is not. This thesis is a discussion of social structure and world view, and it is not self flagellation in the tradition of Hymes (1974), Fabian (1983), or Freeman (1984). I have no guilt pains for what anthropologists do, and the observations made by the above people are obvious to some of us from the younger generation of anthropology.

Moreover, my study has not been inspired by the work of Sellers (1973) or Butler (1976). These papers are interesting, but my work began long before I became familiar with theirs. My idea came from Duane Metzger of the University of California, Irvine, who said it would be interesting to read about people digging. And so, I hope it is.

Everyone involved on the archeological project knew what I was doing. I was not confronted with any objections to my plans, although I did receive several jokes to the effect that the ethnographer should be studied too. But, nonetheless, the names of all people and sites involved are omitted or vaguely described. Those with intimate knowledge of this project will probably recognize people in the report and they may conclude that I have made some people look good or bad. But I did not intend to judge and would argue that any such judgments are the creations of the reader. However, there is one exception to this point: all the people involved should look good because the confidence that they displayed in letting me do this project reflects well upon themselves and me. I thank them for their willingness to be patient and humorous with me.

Introduction

I was involved in a certain archeological project for five years, the first three as a volunteer excavator and the last two as an ethnographer observing the project. The excavations were located on a farm in a rural area of the United states. Excavations were seasonal, occurring in early summer. While there, field crews lived in a tent camp. This is an ethnography of some of the social life in that camp during the year 1984.

The archeological project has changed over the years. Starting from a small field school lasting two weeks in 1980, it expanded to a nine-week season consisting of two field schools in 1984 and 1985. I took notes in 1983 and 1984. The directing archeologist of the project allowed me to do this, and I will refer to him as the Old Timer as he fits Flannery's (1982) characterization of an old time archeologist quite well. The year 1984 marked a turning point in the project. It was the first time that two field schools were offered on the project. These two schools ran contiguously, contrasted in organization and in intent. They will be referred to as Program A and Program B. The addition of the second field school, Program B, was a structural change within the project. And this change readjusted the social structure, the status and role relations between people (Nadel 1957), in the camp such that they became ambiguous, and the differences between power and authority, achieved and ascribed status, and the ages of participants were highlighted. This ambiguity did, then, allow the camp community to divide into factions and this thesis explores the nature and causes of these divisions.

Archeologists are indefinable characters and I doubt if any modal personality could or should be created to describe them. So we must describe them by what they do. Archeology is the study of extinct peoples and the origins of present peoples as manifested in the cultural materials left behind by these people and recovered by archeologists. By analyzing these materials, explicitly, artifacts and features, archeologists infer culture, "the acquired knowledge people use to interpret experience and generate behavior" (Spradley 1980: 6).

But more importantly, for this study at least, an archeologist in charge of a project is a manager. He must plan a project and carry these plans through to completion. This, of course, involves acquiring labor, considering the time period, distance away from home, transportation, and financing. Also, he is a public relations person representing his profession to the public and to his crew. And, internally, the key to a successful project is keeping people happy and motivated to work in the field. Thus, crew members' immediate needs may take precedence over the short term goals of the project. People working and living together must cooperate with each other and let their behavior be guided by the explicit and tacit norms of the overall society and those particular to the project which may conflict with the former.

And if the norms of the project and those of the overall society conflict then the differences between culture and conduct become even more salient. As I am using the concepts, culture and behavior, although interdependent, are not the same and never match exactly. Culture is a system of labels and conceptions about behavior and other cultural forms. As such, cultural forms remain inherently multivocal, that is, open to variable use and interpretation, and cannot be mapped directly onto experience. So, people are frustrated when their ideals and expectations are not met.

This difference between culture and conduct is one way of looking at the fractionation of the camp community. In section two I describe the camp setting, the two programs, and the routine of work. It will be pointed out that the application process for each program led applicants to expect that they would have a certain status in camp and that the two programs had different intentions expressed in their routines. Simply, one was excavation oriented and the other, excavation-lecturing oriented. In section four, the fractionation is described with emphasis on status and authority, status and power, and female and male participation. Since the status relations in camp were ambiguous, one group created new terms to classify people. In section five I use American world view to interpret these terms, which I refer to as class labels, not in the socio-economic sense, but as moral taxonomies. In doing this, the participation of the women in the conflict will be seen as their using their roles as the upholders of American morality to protect their social status. Thus status recognition became an important factor in the tensions in camp because it hindered people from making friends. And I see this paradox of status recognition hindering friendship as an aspect of American world view too.

In a more abstract sense the conflict is seen as a result of a structural change. The reorganization of the project changed status relations between staff and crew members. Instead of a simple field school as Program A had been, a special training field school was set up, Program B. In Program A the primary relationship was that between the teachers of archeology and students of it. But in Program B, the primary relationship was between professional archeologists and professional historians, with the archeologists teaching the historians about archeology. Further, these historians-as-archeology-students were mixed in with some younger archeology students. People's statuses then became ambiguous and tension occurred. But social tension is not uncommon in field camps and it is usually broken by some social event, as described in section three. But during Program B in 1984 no social event broke the tension. People merely endured the situation, fulfilled their obligations, and went home with an experience to talk about.

Community

Americans are said to be concerned with the idea of community. They are often idealistic about what a community is, meaning, of course, that it should be a certain way. However, prescriptions aside, "The real beginning of a community is when its members have a common relation to the center overriding all other relations: the circle is described by the radii, not by the points along its circumference" (Buber 1949:135). For the archeological community studied here the center was an obligation, a commitment, to the project that became established in one of three ways (the radii): one obligated himself to be a staff member, an A participant, or a B participant. In this section, I discuss the background of the project and how people got involved in it. In doing this, I define the community as persons bound by this common denominator of obligation.

The farm is located on a generally north to south lying peninsula formed by a curl of a large river. It is bounded on the north and east by this river and on the south by a creek of the same name as the farm. A slight ridge runs from the northwest towards the southeast, dividing the farm almost in half. This ridge is, besides the river, the most commanding geographical feature on the farm. In total area, the farm covers about 1500 acres divided into forest, pasture, crops, swamp and shoreline. The principal crops are corn, peanuts and soybeans while livestock include cattle, sheep and horses. The farm is relatively isolated as the nearest country store is two miles away and the nearest town is ten miles away.

The landowner, a retired lawyer, chartered a nonprofit educational foundation, referred to here as the Institution, to preserve and study the cultural history of the local area and to interpret the past to the general public. The farm is designated a state historic landmark and is listed on the National Register of Historic Places. The Institution partially funds the archeology done on the farm and operates a small museum there.

Several other buildings are on the farm. The landowner and his wife live there as do the families of the farm manager and a farmhand. The owner's son lived there in a trailer during the early 1980's, but in 1983 and 1984 he used this place on only weekends. Also, as one would expect, there are numerous sheds, barns and a granary on the farm. In 1982 one of the storage sheds was converted into an office, archeological laboratory, library and work area for the Institution. In 1984, this area was expanded into adjoining sheds for the growing Institution. Prior to all this, these facilities had been housed in the museum. This museum is located in an old school house, which also served as a residence prior to its being used as a museum. It stands just off the ridge overlooking some pasture lands. The archeological field camp has been located on this ridge 75 to 100 yards southeast of the museum every field season.

In 1983 and 1984 the camp consisted of twenty to twenty-five field tents, a tent kitchen, a storage tent, a shower house, and port-o-johns. Crew members usually shared tents, with two people in each, while staff had their own. People slept on cots or air mattresses. In 1983 wooden platforms were made for staff tents; in 1984, most tents had platforms. The kitchen was a large platform with three framed supports covered with a tarp that was held in place with rope. In 1984, the kitchen included a butane stove/oven, a refrigerator, sink, and cupboards. Electricity was taken from a power line near the museum. Only the kitchen had electricity. Water for the kitchen and showers was tapped from faucets in the camp area, which used to be a garden. The storage tent was a small version of the kitchen. These facilities were all supplied by the Institution.

I am not aware of all the details about the Institution but believe that it was set up in 1979. At first the landowner administrated it with help from its director, but gradually a Board of Directors was organized and administrative and financial responsibilities were distributed. This changeover occurred, I believe, in 1982. At that time the Old Timer became a member of the Board of Directors also. In 1983 the Institution's staff consisted of its director, one archeologist, one historian, a museum shop manager, a carpenter, and a couple of others who ran the museum shop, gave tours of the archeological and historical exhibits, and did odd jobs. These people were locals, worked year-round, and provided substantial support to the seasonal archeologists.

The field crews for the project have been recruited in two ways. First, for the years 1980 through 1986, the old Timer had been affiliated with a volunteer program and drew most of his crews through this program. Here I refer to this as Program A. In 1984 the Institution received a three-year grant so that a field school could be offered. The second source of labor came from this field school, referred to as Program B. Overall, the project has had seven field seasons during which time both programs were used as such: In 1980, Program A for two weeks in August; in 1981, 1982 and 1983, Program A for six weeks each year in June and July; in 1984, Program A for four weeks in May and June, and Program B for five weeks in June and July; and in 1985, Program A for four weeks in June and Program B for five weeks in July and August. The seventh season had two weeks of Program A in June and again five weeks of Program B in July and August.

Program A has been sponsored by an organization affiliated with a state university system, referred to as the Organization. For the last several years the Organization has offered research projects from various disciplines that interested lay people could participate in as volunteers. Anthropology has been well represented, and this archeological project has been one of the more popular ones. Project directors have come from universities within the state university system. As the Old Timer has been teaching at one of these campuses and has been directing the museum affiliated with that campus, his participation in the Organization is understandable. The term "Program A" refers to a particular project sponsored by the Organization.

To recruit people for projects, the Organization has advertised internationally by sending out pamphlets and a brochure. These publications have included descriptions of all projects, their dates, cost, and other information concerning application procedures. A four page application has been included in the brochure, had to be filled out, and signed. This application was designed such that applicants evaluated themselves. Applicants were first asked to state their preference of projects (ie. first, second and third choices) that they wished to join. Next they were asked how they heard about the Organization. Following this, personal information was requested, such as, one's name, address, telephone number, occupation, and the same information for someone the Organization could contact in case of emergency. Applicants were then asked to state any special medical conditions they might have had because medical treatment may not have been available or close to the project area. After that, applicants were asked to state their interest in the project of their first choice, why they chose it, and what experience they had had that might have been helpful on the project. What was important here was that the applicant express an interest even though they may not have had any experience. After that section, applicants were asked to state their educational background and any foreign travel experience they had had.

The next two sections of the application required people to evaluate themselves on their own adaptability and certain abilities according to the scale "excellent, good, fair, poor." Since some research areas have been remote with variable conditions, the applicants were asked to rate themselves on their adaptability to isolation, limited and/or unusual food, limited water, primitive facilities, wilderness experience, shared living space, living and working with a small group of people, and extreme heat, cold and humidity. Next, since most projects have been self-contained, it was important for project directors to know what practical skills the volunteers had had. Thus, they were asked to rate themselves on interpersonal, outdoor, mechanical and technical skills. These categories included: observational skills, interviewing experience, patience, flexibility, experience with people from other cultures, ability to work as a team member, ability to follow directions, initiative, sense of humor, knowledge of a foreign language, physical stamina, first aid knowledge, camping, backpacking, hiking, camp cooking, swimming, scuba diving, snorkeling, boat handling, vehicle repair, truck or four-wheel drive vehicle experience, still photography, motion picture and videotaping, sketching, illustrating, drafting, technical drawing, map reading, surveying, computer analysis, electronics, mechanics, professional writing, and journalism. Applicants were then asked if they wished to comment on anything not included in the form or if they wished to elaborate on any skills or experiences rated above. The application concluded with a request for a one-line description from the applicant about themselves to be included in the participant list, which was then distributed to all volunteers on a project.

All applications were reviewed by the project leaders. I have no information on the selection process but feel that few if any applicants have been rejected. The Organization has been partially run by the monies contributed by the volunteers and could not afford to forfeit proffered money. Further, a volunteer had the choice to quit a project at any time and a cancellation before a project began allowed the Organization to provide only a partial refund of monies contributed and to keep the rest as a processing fee.

The interesting point about Program A is that volunteers paid to participate in the project. "Participants", as they were called, were considered active members of the field team and each contributed an equal share of money to cover the project costs. The staff of the project did not pay any fees and their expenses were considered part of the project costs. However, the contributions were tax deductible because the volunteers were said to be donating both funds and personal service to research sponsored by the university system. Part of the contribution covered a volunteer's room and board and was considered an out of pocket expense while he rendered service to the university. The rest went for field costs, staff travel expenses, project planning, and administration; and, it was considered a direct contribution to the university. The contribution qualified as a tax deductible contribution under Federal Income Tax Law, Section 501(c)(3) of the Internal Revenue Code. The Organization collected the money for each project, deducted a percentage for its own operating costs, and released the rest to the project directors.

Furthermore, as the contribution covered only one's room and board during the project, ground transportation during the project, camping and field gear, research equipment and supplies, and orientation materials, the participants had to pay for all travel expenses to and from the project area, visas, passports, inoculations, medical treatment or emergency evacuation expenses, and any other personal expenses such as sight-seeing trips and alcoholic beverages. These personal expenses applied to the staff also. However, the travel expenses were tax deductible if they were direct to and from the project area and documented.

Without the incentive of a tax break, the Organization's projects may not have existed because people probably would not have paid to work without some return. But with this detail included people got, as a morning television show host said about the Organization's projects, "a tax deductible vacation."

Many of the projects were held for several weeks or months. Each project was divided into parts, "sessions", based on the time frame for that project. The applicants chose the session or sessions in which they wished to participate. Program A has always had sessions lasting two weeks, as such: one session in 1980; three sessions each for 1981, 1982, and 1983, two sessions each for 1984 and 1985, and one session in 1986.

Contributions were priced per session or sessions. People could sign up for more than one session and this could be expensive. However, as an incentive to get people to sign up for more than one session, the Organization offered a reduction in the total contribution for subsequent sessions signed up for beyond the first. The total amount of the contribution for Program A, in United States dollars, is given by number of sessions signed up for in Table 8-1 for the years 1983 through 1986. These prices were lower than other projects located within in the United States sponsored by the Organization. This was due to the partial funding of the project by the Institution. Program A was, then, funded by two sources, the Organization and the Institution.

Table 8-1: Amount of Program A contribution in US dollars by number of a session signed up for and years. Source: brochures for 1983-1986.

Year	# of sessions 1	2	3
1983	500	650	775
1984	525	650	-
1985	575	685	-
1986	575	-	-

For the volunteer, these prices were high considering that he also had to pay transportation fees. However, students and teachers could have gotten partial scholarships from the Organization by applying for them. Further incentive was given to college students because they could have gotten credit for their work through their own school, usually as "independent credit" courses. Finally, a person who wanted to participate on a project could have gotten a friend or relative to pay the contribution and travel expenses because the paying party got the tax break. Thus, a person who did not have the income to enjoy a tax break did not necessarily have to pay the contribution and could have still participated.

Table 8-2: Cumulative breakdown of Program A applicants by sex, occupation, and numbers of sessions signed up for: 1981-1984.

Sex	Female				Male				
Sessions:	1	2	3	total	1	2	3	total	Total
Student	11	9	10	(30)	4	9	9	(22)	52
Non-	18	0	0	(18)	11	1	0	(12)	30
Total	29	9	10	(48)	15	10	9	(34)	82

The Organization's projects attracted a variety of people but tended towards students, people who were in high school, college, or were recent graduates without "career" type jobs. From the participant lists for Program A for the years 1981 through 1984, I have the names of 82 people who signed up for the project. These lists do not include people who signed up after these lists were made up, neither do they indicate those people who actually participated during those years, as some people cancelled. However, these lists do reflect the kinds of people who were willing to sign up for such projects. Table 8-2 has the cumulative breakdown for those years divided twice vertically into female and male groups, and indicates whether they signed up for one, two, or three sessions. The horizontal division is by occupation, but since the sample is biased towards students I lumped all the others as nonstudents. The nonstudent category includes insignificant numbers of other categories, such as teachers, engineers, lawyers, physicians, housewives, waitresses, and retired.

From data presented in this table I make the following observations. First, students comprised a little more than half of all applicants, 52 of 82 (63 percent). Second, students tended to sign up for more than one session whereas nonstudents signed up for only one. Of the nonstudents only one retired male signed up for two sessions while 37 of 52 students (71 percent) signed up for more than one session. Third, more women tended to apply than men, with here 48 women to 34 men (or 59 percent women). Among the students, two-thirds were women. These figures accurately reflect the personnel makeup of Program A over the first five years and, perhaps for the Organization's projects on the whole. However, during the two field seasons that I observed, a majority of students stayed for more than one session.

The participant lists were mailed out (along with other information) a few weeks prior to the beginning of the project. Thus people were given a chance to familiarize themselves with the names of people they were likely to have met in camp. But, one was more likely to have found any number of people in camp who were not listed. Table 8-3 contains the actual count of people who participated in Program A for the 1983 and 1984 field seasons. This table is divided vertically in three ways: by year, by sex, and by number of sessions participated in; horizontally, it is again divided into students and nonstudents.

Table 8-3: Participants of Program A for 1983 and 1984 by year, sex, and number of sessions participated in, and occupation.

Year	'83									'84						
Sex	F	F	F	F	M	M	M	M		F	F	F	M	M	M	
Session	1	2	3	T	1	2	3	T	T	1	2	T	1	2	T	T
Student	7	4	4	15	2	3	7	12	27	4	6	10	0	5	5	15
Non-	10	0	0	10	0	0	0	0	10	1	0	1	4	0	4	5
Total	17	4	4	25	2	3	7	12	37	5	6	11	4	5	9	20

In 1983 and 1984 Program A had 37 and 20 participants respectively. Students tended to participate in more than one session; in 1983, 18 of 27 students participated in more than one session while in 1984, 11 of 15 did. On the other hand, not one nonstudent participated in more than one session (although in 1984, one female nonstudent attended the entire Program B field school but not as a participant of that field school). Those students who stayed more than one session comprised more than half of the total labor force for each field season. In 1983, 18 students participated in more than one session and in 1984, 11 did. These students were a core group of workers within each field season. But more importantly, for each session the core group was not only a stable body of experienced workers but also the majority of them. Table 8-4 contains the percentages of core group participants to total participants by session for the 1983 and 1984 Program A seasons. The core group comprised at least 60 percent of the participants for the initial session of each season and this percentage increased for the later sessions. This group was, then, a substantial block within the social organization of the field camp and were recognized as such. They were given some status because of their experience.

Table 8-4: Percentage of core group participants to total participants by session and years: core group/total (percentage)

			Session			
Year	1st		2nd		3rd	
1983	14/23	(61)	18/26	(70)	15/17	(88)
1984	11/17	(65)	11/14	(79)	--	--

However, the status of the core individuals was not due to Program A. There was nothing inherent in the organization of the program which gave its participants any kind of special recognition. Just the opposite was the case: participants were nothing more than that, and ideally their status outside of the program was irrelevant during it. The organization of Program A leveled the statuses of its participants. Therefore, the status of the core participants was acquired during the project. In contrast, Program B was designed to recognize one's social status within the overall society. A person could not participate unless he had a certain status (or potential thereof). The status of Program B participants was, therefore, ascribed. This contrast will be discussed in section four.

Program B was a five-week field school financed by the Institution and by a three-year grant from a national granting institution. The 1986 field season was the last year of Program B unless the grant has been renewed for the forthcoming 1987 season. Renewal of the grant is partially dependent on the success of the program, as determined by the granting institution, the program's staff, and the participant's evaluations of the program. The first field season of this program was in 1984 and one would expect problems to exist during an initial year. Thus the conflict described in section four should not be taken too seriously as it was partially resolved in 1985.

Program B offered high school and college level history and social studies teachers an opportunity to incorporate an archeological perspective into their teaching format by giving them firsthand experience at a group of archeological sites. Through a combination of field excavation, laboratory work, research, and formal lectures, these people were introduced to the basics of archeology and the study of cultural materials. Program B participants also worked on individual research projects that related to the overall goals of the field school and to their own teaching programs.

The Program B application process was more formal than that of Program A. Applicants were solicited throughout the United states and were screened on a competitive basis according to the following three criteria: first, applicants had to supply evidence of demonstrated skill and success as a teacher; second, applicants had to supply evidence that the field school would relate to their teaching fields and that it would enrich their teaching skills; and third, applicants had to supply evidence of a commitment to the concentrated study of the field school. Upon completion of the program, participants received a certificate.

To meet the above criteria, an application form with one's name, age, sex, address, telephone number, level of and subjects teaching, and signature had to be submitted along with a one page resume outlining one's educational and teaching experience. Further, a letter of recommendation from the applicant's department chair, academic dean, or principal had to be submitted separately. This letter should have explained how the applicant's participation in the program would have benefited the applicant and his institution. Also, applicants had to submit a statement discussing their professional and personal reasons for wanting to participate in the program. Finally, applicants could have submitted any other evidence of their teaching skills, academic interests and achievements, and, importantly, of their ability to work with others.

The costs of Program B were minimal to the participants in 1984. Each participant was required to obtain a pledge from their own institution to contribute 250 dollars to the program. This pledge was to have been made in the letter of recommendation. Participants also received a stipend from the program of up to a maximum of 400 dollars to cover their documented travel expenses. Further, they received at no cost all texts, course materials, and room and board. Participants were responsible for all other costs, which were, if documented, tax deductible.

Fifteen people participated in Program B in 1984, which was ten below the limit designated by the sponsors. This low turnout was probably due to the late release of the program announcements and did not reflect a lack of interest in it. All fifteen of the participants were considered professionals, as they were all employed at that time in some capacity dealing with history and the social sciences, or, they were striving to become so. Four college and university history professors attended as did three community college history teachers, three high school teachers, one school district administrator, one librarian, one museum administrator, and two graduate students (one in history and one in American studies). This group reflected the flexibility of the program because while the selection criteria emphasized teachers, non-teachers were welcome too as they provided diversity in camp.

The staff personnel constituted the third group of people in camp. The number of staff people to participate in this project increased steadily over the first five years. In 1980 there were three staff people, in 1982 there were eight and in 1984 there were eleven people during Program B. As the project is still ongoing it will probably not get much larger than it has, for two reasons: first, at any given time there are a limited number of the Old Timer's graduate students who are ready and willing to participate in the project and second, a large increase in the staff would require a reorganization of the project, which would involve a different recruitment process of crew members. However, the increase in staff reflects two concerns held by the Old Timer and his staff. First, there was a concern to give graduate students supervisory experience and sites to work on for their dissertations. In 1980 only one site was tested and that work was supervised by the Old Timer himself, with the help of an assistant. In 1982 three graduate students supervised three sites. And during Program A in 1984 four sites were supervised by graduate students. A fifth site was opened during Program A in 1984 because one of the others was closed at the end of Program A. So crews worked on four sites during the 1984 Program B.

The fifth site was important because of who supervised it. Two of the Old Timer's museum colleagues co-supervised that site. These people were mature responsible men who also helped manage camp. Thus, the second concern was with the smooth operation of Program B. The complexity of Program B and its added funding required and allowed for a larger staff. The Old Timer needed responsible people in key positions so that the initial Program B would be a success. He relegated duties that he had often done himself to other people so that he could attend to overseeing the project. Namely, he reintroduced a camp cook, something he had done in 1981 and 1983, and created the camp manager position, a job that he had always filled himself.

The staff can be divided into three groups based on their responsibilities; these are: the director, the primary staff, and secondary staff. The primary staff performed the professional duties, which were supervisory ones dealing with crew management and archeological field practices. In an analogy with the military, those people were the line officers. The secondary staff performed support duties involving transportation, food and lodging, and documentation of the project. The director coordinated the two branches, dealt with the public, the news media, and distinguished guests. He was also responsible for the planning and operation of the project. To meet their academic and personal goals, the staff had to keep the crew members interested, healthy, and working with minimal interpersonal conflict and miss recording of data. And, since the project did not involve an employer/employee relationship between the staff and crew members, supervision was a matter of tact, encouragement, and example.

The primary staff were the crew chiefs and any assistants they might have had. A crew chief was in charge of the excavation of a particular site in accordance with the standard field techniques of archeology. Briefly, this entailed laying out a grid, mapping, bagging artifacts, noting the progress of the digging, and seeing that workers had the necessary tools to work with, such as, trowels, shovels, buckets, wheelbarrows, and screens. In managing the crew, the chiefs had to be aware of people's attitudes, manual abilities, and social relations so that they could determine work assignments for the crew members. In other words, the chiefs managed the pace of the excavation.

The secondary staff were a diverse group. Since 1981 there has been a photographer on the project. This person was also an employee of the museum that the Old Timer has been directing. His main duty was to take in-progress and final photographs of all the sites. Secondly, he photographed the camp, social events, and crews. Also, as part of the orientation given to crews each year, he gave slide shows of the previous years. And, as occasional nightly entertainment, he gave in progress slide shows during a season. During Program A in 1984, there was also an assistant photographer helping out; she had participated as a volunteer in 1981 and wanted to return for another season. In 1980, 1982, and 1984 a camp cook was in charge of planning and preparing meals, and of the supply of food in camp. For Program B in 1984 an assistant cook was hired to help out; this person was one of the 1984 Program A volunteers. A camp manager position was created in 1984; this person was responsible for the daily camp budget, the project vehicles, arranging transportation to town for people, tent assignments, tent maintenance and arrangement, assigning kitchen patrol duties to crew members, keeping the camp area clean, and any other miscellaneous problems that occurred. I have included myself as a secondary staff member for the years 1983 and 1984, during which time I was the "camp ethnographer". Besides note taking, I ran errands, gave people rides in my car, gave slide shows, and was a "myth maker" because I was always "telling lies" about the early years of the project. See the Appendix for a justification for this position.

In the five-year period of 1980 through 1984 there were at least nineteen people involved in the project as staff (Table 8-5). There may have been more, but if so, I have forgotten them. However, it is important to note that it was in the early years of the project that most of the 1983 and 1984 season's staff people got their introduction to the project. That is, four volunteers from 1980 later became staff; two from 1981 did; and one from 1983 did. On the other hand, this is not to say that staff people were recruited from the volunteer ranks. Prospective staff people were probably encouraged to volunteer, and after they had worked out in the field, they became staff. Of the nineteen staff people, nine had been volunteers before becoming staff, but the other ten entered the project as staff members. Thus, becoming a staff person on the project had little to do with whether one had already participated in it in some other capacity. The

Table 8-5: Staff Personnel and their years of attendance.

Personnel	80	81	Year 19' 82	83	84A	84B	Tie to Old Timer	
Director								
Old Timer	+[a]	+	+	+	+	+		
Primary Staff								
PF1 [b]	+						G[c]	Field assistant
PF2	(+)	+	+	+			G	Crew chief
PF3	(+)			+	+		G	Crew chief
PF4			+	+			G	Field assistant; lab chief
PM1	(+)		v	+	+	+	G	Crew chief
PM2		+	+	+	v	+	G	Crew chief
PM3		(+)	+	+	+	+	G	Crew chief
PM4					v	+	C	Crew chief
PM5					v	+	C	Crew chief
Secondary Staff								
SF1		+					O	Assistant manager
SF2		(+)			+		U	Assistant photographer
SM1	+						S	Camp cook
SM2			+				S	Camp cook
SM3					+	+	R	Camp cook
SM4					(+)	+	U	Assistant cook
SM5				(+)	+	+	U	Camp manager
SM6	v	+	+	v		+	C	Photographer
SM7	(+)	(+)	(+)	+	+	+	E	Ethnographer

Notes:
a. + = attended whole field school; v = arrived late in field school; ( ) = attended but not as staff.
b. PF = primary female; PM = primary male; SF secondary female; SM = secondary male.
c. G = graduate student of Old Timer; Undergraduate student of Old Timer; S = friend of Old Timer; R = relative of Old Timer; O =employee of the Organization; E = exception to the rule.

best characterization of a staff person is that they had some external relationship with the Old Timer; that is, the Old Timer surrounded himself with people he knew well. In relation to him, ten staff people had been students of his; three were colleagues from the museum he directs; one was an employee of the Organization; two were friends of his family; and one was his son. The only staff person who did not know the Old Timer before being involved in the project was myself--and this status is self-proclaimed.

In a general sense, primary staff people have been involved in the project for a much longer period than secondary staff. Of the nine primary staff people in the first five years of the project, four attended for four seasons, one for three seasons, one for two seasons, and three for one season. (However, of these last three, two became involved in the project in 1984 and attended the 1985 and 1986 seasons.) Involvement at the primary staff level has been a long-term commitment whereas a secondary staff position has not. Of the nine secondary staff during the years 1980 through 1984, five attended only one season, two attended two seasons, and two attended for four and five years respectively. (These last two, the photographer and myself, could also have been considered as a fourth category of staff because our roles, like the director's, were not restrained by the work routine, as the other staff's were.) The staff of the project consisted, then, of a stable block of people who knew each other well.

The three groups, the A participants, the B participants, and the project's staff constitute the community under study. I am not including the Institution's personnel nor several other people who lived in camp and whose presence did not affect the status relations in camp. These latter people are referred to as auxiliaries. While some of these outsiders might be offended by being placed in this category, I justify it by considering it only as a heuristic one. Moreover, this community does not reflect the "natives'" point of view as they did not have any explicit conception of themselves as a group; but they did, at times, act as an implicit group.

The criterion used to define this category is the presence of a contract; the members of the community formally obligated themselves to participate in the project. This community contrasted, then, with the Institution's staff because those people were obligated to perform duties for the Institution, which has been responsible for the cultural resources of the farm. Also, the community members were not locals as the Institution's staff were. The auxiliaries, too, were not locals but they contrasted with the community members because they were not contractually committed to the project and attended because of some other relationship. So, as stated earlier, the number of people in camp was variable but the three main groups constituted the community. This is not to say that the others were not important, they were merely marginal to my study.

In 1983, 49 people were in camp during Program A: there were 37 participants, 9 staff, and 3 auxiliaries (two of the latter lived in camp but worked at another archeological project nearby while the other was the son of a staff member). Session one had 35 people in camp, 23 of whom were participants. Session two had 38 people with 26 being participants. And session three had 29 people, with 17 participants.

In 1984, 34 people were in camp during Program A: there were 20 participants, 12 staff, and 2 auxiliaries (both of whom lived in camp but worked at another archeological site nearby). Session one had 31 people in camp, with 17 being participants. And session two had 28 people in camp, with 14 participants. During Program B, 37 people were in camp: there were 15 B participants, 6 A participants, 11 staff, and 5 auxiliaries. The auxiliaries included the two above, the daughter of a staff member, a friend of the Old Timer, and a Program A participant from the 1982 season who wanted to return, but not as a participant.

The routine of the project was much the same for each program, although Program A included more time spent excavating than B. There was a weekly and daily routine. At the beginning of each program in 1984 crew assignments were made. As there were generally four sites being excavated, four crews were created. Participants became a member of a particular crew for the period of their contract. Each crew was assigned to dig at a site for one week, and then rotated to another the next week.

During Program A, people worked Tuesday through Sunday with Monday off. Thus, crews rotated to a new site on Tuesday. This gave core people a chance to work on all four sites and one-session people, two sites. During Program B, people worked Monday through Friday with weekends off. Planned sight-seeing trips to local historic and archeological exhibits were usually done on Saturdays. Thus, crews rotated sites on Monday. As Program B was five weeks long, all crews worked one week at three different sites and the first and last weeks at the same site.

The daily routine for Program A had seven and a half hours of work time. Crews were awakened about five in the morning, taken to their sites at six, returned to camp for breakfast at eight, returned to sites at nine, returned to camp at noon for lunch, returned to sites at one, and they quit work at three-thirty. People could also use what was called the "afternoon option", which was a rule that allowed people to work at another site after lunch. Other than this exception, people were expected to work at their assigned sites. Two participants a day were assigned kitchen patrol duty; this duty rotated through the list of participants and each could expect to do it once every two weeks. Kitchen patrol duty consisted of helping the cook prepare food and cleanup after meals. People on KP had the option to excavate or not that day. Dinner was usually served about seven in the evening.

The daily routine for Program B had four hours of excavation time and one to three hours of lecture. People were called to get up about six, had breakfast at seven, were taken to sites at eight, had a break at ten, returned to camp at noon for lunch, and either went to the laboratory or stayed in camp for lectures from one to about three. Lectures lasted usually about one or two hours, but some extended longer. If the lectures ended early, some people went back out to sites for another hour or so, but this was not expected. Program B people had to do KP duty also, but only one person a day did this because an assistant cook had been hired.

During free time people did as they pleased. They had to amuse themselves and did so by playing card games or horseshoes, walking or jogging around the farm, reading, letter writing, doing laundry, and just loafing. B participants had to do their research, so many of them spent part of their nights in the laboratory after dinner. There was much drinking and parties were held with visiting archeological crews. Thus, free time was usually spent socializing. People tended to congregate in small groups of two to five people, regardless of what crew they belonged to. And there were no cliques as the small groups tended to gather spontaneously. But nonetheless, the camp community during Program B in 1984 fractionated along cultural and contractual lines. This fractionation is discussed in the last three sections. The next section is a brief description of unity in the field camp during Program A in 1983.

Cohesion

Victor Turner wrote at length on the concept of communitas, which to him "emerges where social structure is not" because it involves "the whole man in his relation to other men" (1969: 126, 127). So, ideally, the structure of communitas is no social structure; for it is the leveling of all statuses. Further, his discussion is contained in a broader one about the developmental cycle of the social human being. As people mature they pass through social states and the passage from a lower to a higher status is through a period of statelessness. And, such periods are often sacred and ritualistic, putting not only the matriculating people into communitas with each other but also the observers and directors of the situation or ritual. Thus, a feeling of communal unity is created that revitalizes people such that conflicts, frustrations, and ill feelings are temporarily suspended after the social structure is restored. Finally, sometimes romanticism sets in and people desire to perpetuate communitas by trying to make it the normal state of affairs, thus giving rise to modalities, normative and ideological, of communitas based on the prior spontaneous one (c.f. Turner 1969: 94-165).

And thus the implication is that communitas can be found elsewhere, in other situations that do not involve ritual or sacredness. In any gathering where a communal atmosphere is attained a state of communitas exists. And so, at the risk of overextending this concept, I will describe an unusual event, a talent show, that occurred in the archeological field camp during 1983. The community exhibited a general "bad attitude" prior to the show, and the talent show improved morale and relieved tensions such that the archeological crew was revitalized.

The talent show occurred the night of July 13, 1983, which was the Wednesday of the fourth week of the field season. At the end of that week the crew was going to be reduced by eleven people as their two or four week commitments were about up. Thus during that week almost a third of the camp was looking forward to going home. But for those continuing on, the project had another perspective. The Old Timer, who has had twenty-five years of experience with field crews, once generalized to me a pattern that a crew will go through during a project: At the outset, a crew will be fun loving and enthusiastic; next, they will settle down and work hard; and towards the end, they will be exhausted, burnt out. However, this is not to say that the fun and enthusiasm wanes but that their character changes from being a function of the novel situation to that of enduring, tolerating, that situation. And it is in the latter sense that the talent show should be understood.

On Tuesday of the fourth week, a group photo was taken and pranks increased in camp as the camp mascot, a plastic chicken, was stolen and a brief water fight raged through camp right after work. But besides that good humor six people complained that day of being sick or "under the weather." Two of those people had back pain, two had cramps, one had an infected foot, and one hung over person vomited and collapsed at a site. The camp port-o-johns were noticeably foul most of that day until they were pumped in the afternoon. One crew was assigned to do lab work after lunch but did not enjoy the task as their crew chief was considered to be "grumpy." At another site at that time a tense situation occurred. The Institution's staff archeologist had been trying to help out by building an earthen ramp down to the river with a backhoe. The machine went over the cut bank, hung on some branches and debris, and almost rolled. Everyone who was there was relieved that he was not hurt or killed and joked about it only later. After work, people relaxed, napped, and the cook, the Old Timer, complained about making dinner, a task he usually enjoyed.

Wednesday of that week started misty and muggy with the red sunrise watched from the sites. Some of us had to walk the third of a mile to a site because two of the project vehicles did not work. Later, at noon, the third vehicle quit too. In the meantime the crew I was with shoveled and troweled clay and debris down inside an eighteenth-century icehouse which was said to turn into an "oven" during the heat of the day. The crew worked slow and complained of the ticks that characterized that site. Some of us took a couple minutes break and killed them--I killed 16 within an arm's reach. Then, back at work, one of the crew began to expose a wine bottle, and all of us hoped it would still be intact. Exposing this bottle took thirty minutes and all other work stopped because the crew watched. At one point the tent mate of the bottle digger told him to be careful and was promptly told to shut up in response. The bottle was not intact and that night the digger became a star in the talent show.

At noon that day we were back in camp for lunch and one conversation turned to changing the work routine to avoid the heat of the day; some people wanted to start earlier and quit earlier, which would have meant working in the dark as the crews were at that time already out at six in the morning. Simply, people were complaining about the heat. Then, back at the icehouse, people worked in spurts and one crew member got the water Igloo dumped on him to cool him off after shoveling hard. I took the Igloo to camp, filled it, counted ten stragglers there, noted the shade temperature at 92 degrees, heard a good story, and returned to the icehouse. The story was that down at another site the crew had quit working, "mutinied", because they were angry with their site chief. By three in the afternoon everyone was in camp, having quit half an hour early. Mint juleps, a regular Wednesday afternoon drink, were served and several people napped until dinner. Just before dinner one person told me to emphasize the boring side of field work and another added that there was "nothing to write here."

At dinner there were some notable absences. All but two of the staff were not in camp because they had accepted invitations to spend the night elsewhere. Of the two remaining staff, one stayed in the archeology lab most of the night while the other, a popular site chief, started the talent show. After dinner he announced that the first annual dance would be held in fifteen minutes, but he was told to wait until the temperature cooled off for it was than about 86 degrees.

An hour and a half later, about eight-forty-five, the camp kitchen was cleared of its picnic tables and a tape player was set up. Four men, the crew chief, the bottle digger, the one who had been drenched with water, and one other, began to do a chorus line act for a small crowd. Within a few minutes two more men were on stage and the crowd had grown to include almost all those in camp, about twenty people. Some of the women in the crowd yelled at the dancers to strip down because they were "not skimpy enough." And so the dancers stripped down to their shorts in a burlesque fashion, amid much laughter and applause from the crowd.

Then the bottle digger took the lead by imitating the characteristic behavior of the crew chief. This went on for a few minutes and climaxed when he began chanting one of the officer's favorite sayings, "you got that right slick, uh," with appropriate suggestive movements. He exited stage leaving the crowd impressed with his dancing ability. Next came a juggling act with eggs by another dancer; he broke one egg and added an apple. In this act he was highlighted by a member of the crowd, the one who had been bored earlier, who used a flashlight as a spotlight.

After the juggling act, the six men went back to a chorus line, and kicked up their feet to a song on the player. One female from the crowd, who the day before had had an infected foot, got up and danced with the juggler. She got a dollar bill, held it in her mouth, passed it to the juggler's mouth, who passed it to the one who had gotten drenched earlier, then it went back to the juggler, and then to the woman again. She then danced with the chorus line, while someone in the crowd mentioned that that was the only way to "pass the buck."

Another song came on the radio, the Rolling Stones' old hit "Jumping Jack Flash," and immediately the chorus line began to do jumping jacks. After that song, one of the dancers got another woman from the crowd and danced with her. Then the woman with the dollar again took the lead by doing a suggestive dance along with the bottle digger which ended amid applause when she put the dollar in his shorts. For the next song, some flowers were taken from a vase and each male dancer went around the stage with one in his mouth. At the end of the song they threw the flowers to women in the crowd.

Next, the one who earlier professed that there was nothing to write took the lead and imitated playing guitar and singing a song. The crowd cheered him on and asked him to do his favorite song, "Roxanne." So, as he went to get the tape the chorus line continued, this time with cereal bowls on their heads. The crew chief cried out that this was a "Jewish ceremony," a joke aimed at the bottle digger's ethnicity. The dancing stopped as the rock star returned. He took the center of the stage and all lights went off except the flash spotlight. The crowd went quiet in anticipation of the act and were not disappointed. The rock star imitated the stage antics of a real one by using a broom as a guitar and mouthing the lyrics.

After this act the chorus line ran out of ideas. Some found a roll of toilet paper and wrapped up one ill-feeling person from the day before. Then someone joked about setting him on fire but that idea did not go well with anyone else. The imitation rock star and the bottle digger again began separate solo acts to a song on the player while the rest of the dancers thought of something to do. They decided to get cups of water, did so, and ran out on the stage like they were going to douse the crowd. A wave went through the crowd as several people backed off to avoid getting wet. Seeing this, the dancers turned on the digger, who was then imitating the smoking style of the crew chief, and "put his cigarette out" by dousing him. At this everyone laughed and the chorus line began again with three women from the crowd joining in.

After a song all the dancers took a break and shared a few beers. Dancing then resumed with several women joining the men on stage. Those who did not want to dance or watch began to leave for their tents. At ten the dancing stopped as that was the usual quiet hour in camp. But some people wanted more; they talked and laughed a few minutes and then decided they wanted the bottle digger to do another solo act. But he was then in the shower. A small group ran to the showers, got him out, and chased him across camp back onto the stage. The digger had been able to get his pants on so he then dropped them on stage and used his towel to flash his shorts as he danced around. The remaining crowd enjoyed this last act and broke up when it ended. By eleven the camp was quiet with most people in bed or sitting in the dark watching the heat lightning in the distance. And some expressed their hope that it would rain.

On the following day work proceeded as usual. The "dance night," as it came to be known, was talked about for the rest of the season and the following one, 1984. Work continued with its ups and downs; the icehouse was completed but two of its ten-foot high sidewalls slumped. At three other sites, archeologically important features were defined and examined. But the social high point was the dance night which temporarily relieved the tension in camp, made people laugh and enjoy the company of each other. The camp social hierarchy, while partially removed, was also leveled in the imitations of the authority figure and his counter imitation. The camp was revitalized and the productive season finished with some people concluding that archeology was certainly the most fun one could have with their pants on (c.f. Flannery 1982).

Certainly not all of Program A during 1983 was like this. Most of the days were long but people did not go that far to amuse themselves. The talent show served an important function; it perpetuated the esprit de corps of the community. The second annual talent show was performed during Program A in 1984. But it was a planned affair, was not well attended, and did not revitalize the group. Program A in 1984 was not a socially tense period; I am not sure of how to characterize it. It was not as high spirited as the previous season's had been because it seemed as if an unsaid restriction had been placed on the camp. The staff seemed to be anticipating Program B, preoccupied with it, and so the social life of Program A in 1984 was foreshadowed. But these concerns were mainly those of the older staff personnel and the Institution's staff. Everyone else mingled well and enjoyed themselves.

Inequality

The archeological field schools, Programs A and B, were an intense social period for those involved. For the professional and aspiring archeologists, the field seasons helped to perpetuate or enhance their reputations within the discipline. For the volunteer, the field seasons were a vacation from school or work. For all, the seasons were a break in the yearly cycle and were, non-normal periods. Moreover, during these periods the small things in life became salient such that objects, activities, and events became overly important to people. Some of this heightened awareness may have been due to people's feelings of out-of-placeness in a new environment, de-situation, while some may have been due to the slow pace of the work day and its flexible routine.

There were also more tangible factors that added to the stress and strain of the field situation. Living in a tent for two, four, or six weeks could make one appreciate the comforts of home, for there were no air conditioners, hot tubs, or private rooms. Also, the work required was rough on the soft hands, feet, and backs of people used to sitting behind desks most of the year. For some, the environment could seem hostile especially when mosquitoes and ticks demanded attention and repellent. And, of course, the weather was hard to take when summer daytime temperatures reached highs over ninety degrees only to be offset by violent storms that sometimes flooded sites and camp.

In a social sense, the field camp was full of the intrigues that one would expect to find in any group. Many people entered camp not knowing anyone, and thus friendships were established quickly, often seemed shallow, and usually ended when the group disbanded. The situation was also conducive to fast romances, or unfulfilled hopes thereof. On the other extreme, serious relationships also came about. During the first five years of the project two marriages resulted from the interactions that began in camp. But, for the most part, these relative strangers lived in a patient tolerance of each other's behavior, knowing that shortly it would all end. This restraint belied the intensity of the situation. And when given the opportunity, these people did voice their frustrations.

The conflict to be discussed in this section is that of a fractionation process in the camp community during Program B in 1984. This conflict concerned three groups of people: the staff, the participants of Program B, and some Program A people who stayed for Program B. These three groups held differing conceptions of themselves which indicate an ambiguous social structure.

In brief the conflict resulted when in 1984 as Program A was ending its participants were asked if they wanted to stay and continue doing field work during Program B. Six undergraduate students of the Old Timer did stay and paid a nominal fee priced per week. The staff hoped .that these holdovers would help the incoming B participants ease into the camp setting. However, the presence of the A people did not aid in this adjustment, but rather it enhanced the alienation that some of the B people felt. When, at the end of Program B, those participants were allowed to voice comments about the program in an open forum they complained that the younger people in camp, or those with a "swinger" lifestyle, were running the camp. Certainly, no one group was responsible for the fractionation because all were involved. The ambiguity of the situation becomes apparent when we focus on the grouping of the B people. There were two paradoxes in the camp social structure due to the grouping of B people.

The desire to have the A people help the B people adjust to camp life created the first paradox. The staff considered themselves to be in control of the situation; they had authority because they supervised and supported the non-staff, those without authority. The staff merged A and B people as one group and these people were called "participants", "folks", and "everybody". Staff members tried to maintain this position even though they recognized a contrast between the two non-staff groups. In doing this, they were asserting their authority. Further, there was no reason to believe that the two groups would not get along because Program A had been mixing people of different ages and statuses through five seasons without serious conflict. But the difference between the two groups in terms of authority was reflected in the idea of status and not the generation gap. The holdover A people were all, except for one, students while the B people with two exceptions were all successful professionals. Under normal conditions in American society, B people would have been seen as high status people when compared to the A group. Thus merging the two groups elevated the A people up to the level of the B people. And so, the first paradox was that two incompatible groups were seen as one by the staff.

This elevation of the A people can be best understood from their point of view. These individuals recognized their low status in camp. They described B people as "arrogant", "snobby", and "uptight", terms often used to describe people who act as if they are better than those doing the describing, who might consider themselves as equals or know that they are of low status but wish to berate those of higher status. Further, the A people exploited the staff's attempt to merge the non-staff participants by taking advantage of their greater familiarity with the staff. In effect, they allied themselves with the staff by overemphasizing the arrogant attitude of the B people, of which the staff were also aware. They did this by complaining that the B people would not "lighten up" or "relax". Instead of being elevated to the level of the B people, A personnel tried to elevate themselves to a position equal to that of the staff. Otherwise, they would have been at the bottom of a local social hierarchy: staff, B people, and A people.

Moreover, A people could justify their grouping with the staff in two ways. The first is a matter of precedence; the B people were newcomers and the alliances were well established within the camp community. Second, A people understood that their presence in camp was wanted by the staff, who were taking advantage of the A people's field experience. The holdover

A people were all, but one, core people, each having participated in the entire Program A. They had become familiar enough with the local sites to help the novice B people and the staff.

The staff have always favored core participants during the Program A seasons. At the outset of each season the core people had been singled out as "four weekers" or "six weekers" by the staff because they were people who had to be lived with for a longer period. The "two weekers" have always had a temporary position in camp and, even though they may have been liked, rarely acquired any recognition for their efforts. Two weeks has not been long enough for most people to assert themselves and make a lasting impression on the community. Core people usually did make such impressions and were often rewarded for their efforts by being given little responsibilities that demonstrated the confidence that the staff had in them. For example, on the second day of actual digging during Program B a Group A girl was asked at one site to supervise temporarily a crew of B people, all of whom were at least twice her age. Her four previous weeks of experience qualified her for this position. She enjoyed her task and I do not know the reaction of the crew at that time but this example gives validity to their complaint. The favoritism shown by the staff towards the A people was practical; those with experience were given duties commensurate with their competency.

The alliance between Group A and the staff did have its usefulness. During Program B there were 37 people in camp in four groups: 15 B people, 11 staff (including one holdover A person), 6 A people, and 5 auxiliaries (who had no impact on the status relations in camp). Thus, the alliance was the majority group in camp and could have, in good democratic fashion, asserted their will and felt secure in their numbers.

Group B was a threat to the rest of camp because of the high status stigma, antagonistic stereotype, that was given to its members. These people represented respectability, and their favorable evaluations of Program B were important to the staff for its continuation. Thus, the staff's desire to have a successful initial program meant that they had to perform well for these people, who were making their own judgments about the program's success. The stigma of respectable high status given to the B group reflected back on all the rest, who then had to conform to an ideal conception of "goodness" or lose respect themselves. The staff and the holdover A people knew that as a group they all had to, in their words, "clean up their act". Program B was relatively so formal in its organization and intent that it contrasted sharply with the informality of Program A. And surely, the five previous Program A seasons did not prepare any of the staff for dealing with high status participants during Program B. Since the two programs ran contiguously in 1984, the alliance saw themselves as having to give up their comfortable informal atmosphere for a more formal one. Part of the tension was a resistance to change in the face of respectability by members of the alliance.

Coincidence was also involved in the conflict. The stigma of respectability given to the B people could have been de-emphasized if the first B person to arrive had not been exactly what the alliance had expected. This person was a history professor with a doctorate from a prestigious university. On the one hand he made it clear to all exactly what his status was, as he might have thought he needed to, and on the other hand, he offered friendship. In return, people recognized his status and, working from their first impression, were ambivalent about accepting his friendship. His attempts at friendships with members of the alliance seemed clumsy. Unfortunately, it was too late in the project before people acknowledged that he was honest in presenting both his status and friendliness; that is, he was not as "bad" as they first thought. But the precedent had been set and most of the older B people were treated in this way.

The B people had a different conception of the project than those in Group A. The conditions under which they were participating provided a different orientation than did those in Program A. This distinction is best seen in a comparison of the salient characteristics of both programs. I have already described these programs as informal and formal for A and B respectively. The formal character of Program B was based on its particularistic focus; it was designed to isolate a group of people-- professionals in the social studies field. The salient characteristics of this program were: 1) participants were not explicitly considered to be team members; 2) a participant's institution donated funds to the project; 3) a participant's expenses were partially refunded; 4) a third party letter of recommendation was required; 5) research projects were required; 6) formal lectures were emphasized in the daily routine; and 7) participants received a certificate. In contrast to Program B was the informal character of Program A, which had a general focus and did not isolate any group. Noticeable characteristics of this program were: 1) participants were considered as team members; 2) participants funded themselves; 3) a participant's expenses were not refunded; 4) participants evaluated themselves in the application; 5) no research project was required; 6) excavation was emphasized in the routine; and 7) participants did not receive a certificate. In other words, isolating a particular group of people was a statement of status recognition while a general, everyman emphasis was a statement of status leveling.

Group B people were marked as a group while A people were not. The stigma of respectable high status for B people was best expressed in the term "success", which was a key term in the Program B application form. A person had to demonstrate success in his field to be a Program B participant while participants of A did not have to make any such demonstration. By being accepted to the project, B people had been reassured that they were successful and expected to be treated as such. When such expectations were seen as unfulfilled, B people felt slighted. These .B people demanded respect but did not command it because they were not the only successful people in camp.

The demonstrated success of the B people was a formality while the favoritism of the staff to the A people indicated that this latter group had, as workers in the local context, been successful too. The A people had earned their privileges; B people had not, but they also expected that their given status would allow them certain privileges. Also, the staff resented having to attend to the wants of people who were temporarily subordinate to them, as temporary students, but who also felt themselves to be equals with the staff as successful professionals. Therefore, the alliance treated the B people as guests and not as incorporated team members of the project. During the 1984 field season many of the college students were using the slang term "dude" quite liberally, and it became a joke to refer to anyone as such. In a humorous moment during Program B, one staff person elaborated on this term while reflecting on the obvious fractionation in camp--he said it was like an "Archeological dude ranch". And so it seemed to the alliance.

The second paradox was that B people became members of the community but were treated as guests by the rest of the community. And they had every right to feel some resentment for they were as much "core" people as the A group. But the difference was again one of status. During Program A, core people always had been students and the staff were familiar with the teacher/student relationship. They were not familiar with the teacher/professional-as-student relationship. Much of the tension came from the B group being treated as guests because it placed those people in a "tight" position. Since they were treated as guests they had to respond as such and could not relax and loosen up without losing status.

I think that B people did not see themselves as guests but rather as members of the community, and their complaint was a statement to that effect. I recorded only one complaint concerning the setting a part of the B people and it came from one of the B group's graduate students who did assimilate well into the community. She complained that she felt as if her forehead had been stamped with her group label, something like "B-er". She resented being set apart because she was a member of the community. However, I did note some complaints about the opposition "swingers" and "conservatives" made by members of the B group, which was also the group that used these terms. These complaints were made by people who would have liked to relax but could not because to do so would have meant being considered a swinger. Thus, before B people could relax they would have had to be in control of the camp, running it themselves. Otherwise, they had to remain on their best behavior to keep their status. The B people's complaint was, then, a resentment of the two factors, having been set apart and not having been able to relax.

Obviously, the tension was not simply one of status differences or of who had authority and who did not, as described so far. I believe that the three groups verbalized the problem in the way I have described, but a slightly different picture emerges if one looks at the problem in terms of status and power, not authority. I stated earlier that the conflict did not involve the age factor in terms of authority, but in terms of power it did. In terms of authority, age was less important because several of the staff were in their mid-twenties and were supervising people much older than themselves. And since that relationship was based on agreement and did not exist beyond the duties of the staff, cooperation was a matter of tact, not power. The powerful people were not necessarily those with authority.

The distinction between swingers and conservatives allows me to focus on the problem in terms of power. The swinger group included all those under the age of 35. This group includes the younger B people (the graduate students and museum worker), all the A people but one, and the staff except for four individuals. The conservatives included the four oldest staff (the Old Timer and his three museum colleagues), the 12 B people over 35, and one A person (the non-core person). The term "swinger" was descriptive of the group because that group mingled well, spent much of its free time pursuing enjoyable activities in a seemingly carefree manner, and included some public romances. The conservatives were more reserved and careful to avoid such public behavior.

The conservatives were the powerful people in camp. And this category is split into two groups. The four oldest staff members comprised one group and the rest the other. This staff power bloc included mature men who were successful in their profession. Each had worked over twenty years in their field and held important positions in a museum. In contrast, the rest of the staff were still developing their reputations. The Old Timer's three colleagues essentially ran the camp by taking charge of those duties that required constant or daily attention. Their vigilance in these matters earned them a nickname, the "dodads". The Old Timer knew these men well and knew that they would take charge of the important responsibilities in camp, as apparently they had done at the museum. These men knew this, and one mentioned to me his regret that the project was not a vacation for him but rather a job in itself. In other words, the staff power bloc maintained its position through constant attention to events and problems in camp and not by slacking off at hours defined in the work routine.

The Old Timer, as director, was, of course, responsible for the management of the project and its success or failure. The rest of the staff knew this and respected his wishes during the project because most of them were subordinate to him in some way outside of the project. They knew that their performance on the project would affect their relationship with him at home. In return, he considered their needs and wishes without being too authoritarian. Further, while he could be commanding in private conferences with his staff, he was, as he has jokingly described himself, a "benign dictator". Most notably, during Program B, he did not sleep in camp but at the home of the Organization's director, thereby letting his three lieutenants control the camp. During Program A, even in 1984, he always slept in camp. In other words, he downplayed his position while interacting with his staff and relied on tact and persuasion to manipulate them.

The Old Timer's downplaying of his position was more obvious in public. Geoffrey Gorer's statement of how a powerful American male should behave accurately describes the Old Timer in camp:

> It is imperative for those in positions of great power to manifest .in their persons the absence of authority, or the desire for authority. They must be conspicuously plain citizens, with the interests and mannerisms of their fellows; whatever their private temperament they must act as "one of the boys", glad-handed, extravert, mindful of first names, seeing their subordinates in their shirt sleeves and with their feet on the desk, democratically obscene in their language, with private interests, if any, simple and within the reach of all (Gorer 1964: 40).

This behavior does not contradict his reserved attitude but complements it. He knew that he should not stand out while so many were dependent upon him, for to do so would have labeled him authoritative and perhaps oppressive. His three lieutenants behaved this way too, but to a lesser extent.

The difference between the staff and B power blocs now becomes apparent. The power of the older B people lay in their respectability and the threat of their making unfavorable evaluations of Program B. They were reserved and could not relax, for to do so would have meant that they would have lost not only respectability, as they themselves partly defined it, but also power. That is, for them to have joined the swinger group would have let the staff question any unfavorable evaluation they might have made. Many of them avoided camp in the evenings and night by studying in the laboratory. Further, since they had no authority and that their respectable behavior was not seen as a model to be emulated by others, they resorted to social criticism. That is, by stating that the swingers were running the camp they were: 1) pointing out to all that the younger people were setting the standard lifestyle in camp, 2) stating that this lifestyle was not respectable, and 3) insulting their near peers, the staff power bloc, by implying that they were not really in charge.

In contrast, the staff power bloc was reserved and relaxed. For them to have tightened their hold on camp would have made them appear to be too authoritative. This would not have been appropriate because they were dealing with people who had paid to participate and those who did not. Therefore, as the swinger group contained several staff, the staff power bloc used persuasion and tact to make sure that events did not go beyond the limits of appropriateness. And for the Old Timer this limit involved human dignity; as long as people did not infringe upon the rights of others and bystanders did not get hurt, people could do as they please. And no American could disagree with this position, even though he might have condemned the behavior of others.

There is one final point to be made concerning this conflict and it is a sensitive one in these days of equal rights campaigns. The conflict described was not a violent event but rather a tension in camp between the groups. The only absolutely public expression of the conflict was the open forum, which was a heated discussion where people expressed their opinions of Program B in a ritualistic-like setting. Other than this, the tension in camp was manifested in brief insults between individuals of the different groups. The statements that I recorded about the tension were observations made by men, but it was the women who I observed actively participating in the conflict. Two examples of this are described below: the first event occurred between an A swinger and a B conservative; the second was between a B swinger and a B conservative. While both these confrontations seem trivial in retrospect they did not go unnoticed in camp.

During Programs A and B a couple of the camp rules were that people stay out of the food in the kitchen at night and stay out of the museum after it closed in the evening. However, the museum could be used on occasion when the need arose. At the end of the first week of Program B, two conservative B women moved into the museum for a couple of nights because their tent had been taken down and sent off to be repaired. This was an inconvenience to them because they had to move their possessions each day when the museum opened. One of the swinger A females, who had just returned to camp after spending a few days away and was celebrating her return, confronted the two older women with the fact that they should not be in the museum after dark. The two women were offended by this, especially since it came from someone who was ignorant of their situation. The next day the younger woman found herself assigned to a crew with one of the above conservatives. Each avoided the other as much as possible during the work hours. A week later, these two got into a brief argument in the kitchen. When the younger one was fixing herself a snack after hours, the older woman reminded her of the kitchen rule. And so, the insult was returned.

The second example is best told in the words of one of my informants. When I asked her to write me something about her weekend, she included the following story, which describes events that I had noted too. Where she used names I have substituted others. My editorial remarks are in brackets and she did not use quotation marks. Also, swingers are S, conservatives are C, staff are X, and participants are A or B.

"Now for the juiciest gossip of the day: Everyone was in a good mood trying to get all of the coolers of food and all of us into the van. The back seat was Trudy [CA] and Jeff [CB]; the second to back seat was Steve [CB] and Diane [CB], the third to back seat was Mike [CB], [herself], and Helen [SA]; and in the beginning John [CB], Patty [SB], and Valerie [SB] were in the front [bench] seat but Valerie moved into the front single seat. Fred [CX] drove. Anyway...no one noticed that Liz [CB] had put her jacket and purse on the front seat since we had cups and plates and that sort of stuff right on top of the area where her stuff was. Everyone was in the van about ready to leave when Liz walks up and bitchily asks Patty to hand her her purse and stuff. Patty gave it to her and she stomped over and sat down on a picnic bench under the blue tent [kitchen]. Patty starts apologizing: Is this your seat? I'm sorry--I didn't know! (She starts to get up and move). Liz: Don't bother. I'm not going. Someone else (Steve? or Diane?): There's plenty of room!

"Martha [CB] also was taking her car to [the place they were visiting] so she consoled Liz and just said Liz'll ride with me. (Note: It was really weird -- Martha talked just like Liz was a recalcitrant child and Liz liked it enough to be talked into going!) Strange."

The conflict described in this section centers around other's evaluations of how some individuals behave during their free time. These evaluations have been expressed in terms connoting morality, with the term "swingers" having been a derogatory term. Of course, those who used these terms, the B conservatives, did not impute any immorality to themselves. In doing so, they implied that they are "better" in some sense than the rest. However, while their evaluations were important in a literal sense, they also reflected unstated social relations. This point will be discussed in the next section.

Americana

During Program B several of the lectures were about the concept of culture. People were told that archeologists study culture through the analysis of cultural materials, that is, artifacts and features found in the ground. And if one observes archeologists in the field, they will find that archeologists make a distinction between soils that are the product of human behavior and those that are not. The former soils are called "cultural" and the latter "natural" even though excavation makes all soils exposed "cultural." What this suggests to me is that archeologists, like everyone else, are using their terms to guide their behavior. In this section, the described conflict will be interpreted within its cultural context, American, and in terms of culture change.

The concept of culture is a key symbol in American world view. At the core of this concept is the belief that man is unique in the natural world, which is, of course, defined by humans. This uniqueness is based on the perception that man is self-aware, is sapient, uses symbols, and has technology. Other animals are said to not be like this and have no culture. Moreover, many Christians might argue that man is not even an animal because he has morality, which animals lack. It is morality that makes man human and a man without morals is said to act like an animal.

This anthropocentrism has religious connotations. The American adoration of humanity and things human is linked to their key religious symbol, God, which is an abstraction anthropomorphized as a man controlling the universe. As they worship God, they worship themselves in word and deed because they believe that they control nature. The first responsibility of any human is to control his own natural drives through refinement of behavior and values. It is no wonder, then, that the words culture, cult, and cultus are all cognates of the Latin *colo*, to take care of, attend to, as in the land, self, and the gods.

Further, it is no wonder that "no other nation has given such space to social character explanation of itself" as has the united states (Wilkinson 1983: 167). The American fascination with "self and society" is a distinctive part of their world view. According to Wilkinson, there are five historical and modern reasons for this fascination. First, the Puritan errand requires people to reassess constantly their spiritual and social progress. Second, the idea of republicanism contains the belief that democracy depends on the virtue of the people.

Thirdly, the ideas of nationalism and egalitarianism establish the tension between an individual's achievement and the belief that all Americans are alike. Fourth, there is American intellectualism, which emphasizes asking who we are, what holds us together, and what are we becoming. And fifth, there is American pride and boastfulness, which stress that because of its size, America produces more of everything and that this is not enough (Wilkinson 1983: 184-187). All these themes are indirectly relevant to the conflict in camp.

The tension between self-fulfillment and the idea of social equality is a paradox of American social structure. To say that all men are created equal says nothing about the product of that creation. As being an American is an act of will (Gorer 1963: 188), social equality is an act of will. Betterment, self fulfillment, is a social obligation for Americans because for the individual to expand his horizons, fulfill his potential, "be all that you can be," implies that the nation will be all it can be because individualism implies community (Varenne 1977: 40). And those who do not fulfill this moral obligation are segregated from the majority: Tramps symbolize failure, not only of the individual but of the community (cf. Spradley 1970); the elderly symbolize resignment of fulfilling one's potential, have no future, and do not live in an expanding world but a shrinking one (cf. Jacobs 1974).

This paradox is expressed in the key concept of culture which in contemporary usage has two popular versions, one broad in its semantic range and the other narrow. The broad version is a product of anthropology and is now embedded in the world view of Americans. A contemporary definition is: culture is "the body of learned beliefs, traditions, and guides for behavior that are shared among members of any human society" (Barret 1984: 54). Such a definition is two things at once: it is segregative in that other animals are left out, and, it is universalistic in that all humans are treated the same. This universalism is based on cultural relativism, which is a belief that all ways of life are equally viable. Thus, the universality of mankind is expressed as horizontal segregation. Culture, in this broad sense, is a statement of equality in diversity.

In the narrow sense, culture is a statement of inequality because of diversity. Culture is the act of developing the intellectual and moral faculties, especially by education. Moreover, since people will be variable or perhaps obstinate, in their development of such cultural traits they can be classified according to the degree of development. Or they can be classed as developed and undeveloped, with the developed "better" than the undeveloped. Development is a type of conformity. Further, since the traits used to measure development are not absolute but vary with context, inequality can only be understood in its cultural context (Fallers 1973: 5). Ideas of the individual and equality are not universal but vary with the society and within a society (Beteille 1986).

In this narrow sense then, culture allows for ethnocentrism, the differentiation of cultures, and, within a plural society like America, the formation of classes. "In a true class system, what is ranked are the culture traits. Then one takes one's position by what culture traits one either practices, demonstrates, or stands for. It leads to a system primarily based on education and sophistication" (Bohannan 1963: 172).

The ranking of culture traits includes evaluations of subtle items such as modes of walking, speech, and behavior. Evaluations of behavior are most important. One's position within the class system is achieved, developed, in that one conforms to the traits of a certain class. A class is not an organized social group but is little more than a set of culture traits as marked by the people who practice them (Bohannan 1963: 175, 178).

In America the moral doctrine of equality has allowed for a classification of life styles based on culture. This classification is a horizontal differentiation based not on economics but the respectability of a life style. While capitalism may be the catalyst for the good life, the demarcation of it is guided by moral values. This differentiation is horizontal not vertical because that would imply ranking classes into superior and inferior levels. Also, it would imply a power relationship between levels. But, such ranking is not consistent with the definition of class as given. To suggest that a class is in power implies that it is organized, which classes are not. However, a class can be used as a standard by which other classes are compared: it is a pivotal class. But a class is not a group, although, certainly, class standing can be a criterion for admission to a group (Bohannan 1963: 175). Vertical differentiation in the United State is based on the ranking of roles, situs. Horizontal differentiation is based on ideology. In a democracy where all people are equal through the letter of the law, inequality is a matter of spirit, attitude.

Class in America is based on ideals and expectations of public behavior and appearance. And realities aside, American idealism is very moralistic. This is not to say that Americans are moralistic, rather that they rationalize their world this way. Idealism "is the laying down of rules for the conduct of others which need not apply to oneself" (Gorer 1963: 59-60). Thus, one's public image is important for his class standing because it is evaluated by others.

Those most active and discriminating in evaluating other people are women because they are expected to be the upholders of American morality and virtue. In the "motherland" of the United States, women lay down the rules of conduct for others, and in doing so create and perpetuate class rankings. These rankings are not absolute or nationwide but vary with locality and standards even though the words used may be quite common. There is a general principle that guides the evaluators in making their rankings: it is a statement of respectability, with perhaps an aspect of sophistication, as these are determined by women (cf. Gorer 1963: 50-69, 215-218; Nash 1970: 101-104).

Such a role for women creates a dilemma for some of them. They are forced to balance equality, which denies a difference between men and women, and the biological limitation of motherhood, which does recognize such a difference. For men being a parent and having a career are complimentary roles, whereas for women they are conflicting. Thus, professional women are at a disadvantage in the public sphere in that they have to protect their roles as carriers of morality and their professional standings. Men protect only the later because they are not seen as the upholders of morality. Where a successful man may be applauded for his ability, a successful woman may have to protect her character from suggestions of immorality (cf. Potter 1964). These two conflicting roles for women have been merged because Americans have not yet resolved this dilemma, and to question one is to question the other. Professional women will be quick to protect either one, for each protects the other. In the first conflict described in section four, the conservative B woman returned the insult to defend her moral character and to cast doubt on the other's. And in the second conflict, the conservative B woman feigned submissiveness and made others recognize her position. Throughout the men were passive in the conflict because their social status was not at stake; they were all conservatives or swingers based on their life style, which needed no defense, only acceptance.

In the United State there are two general classes, the respectables and the undesirables. The respectable class is, of course, pivotal. These people consider themselves to be "good", "model citizens", or "middle class", a reference to a life style ideal not a so-called socioeconomic class. The respectables collectively characterize the undesirables as people who drink and are drunk in public, have spontaneous brawls, are unwilling to work, act with sexual license, and have trouble with police. The respectables impute to themselves no such character flaws and ally themselves with American mainstream morality as they define it. Undesirables frequently do not use corresponding labels, probably because they are not concerned with keeping the boundaries (Hannerz 1969: 34-35).

This dichotomy is not a description of what people's lives are like; it is a statement about two opposing poles in a moral continuum. It is easier to label others as respectable or not. These labels reflect only orientation in life style; they are approximations of peoples' ways of life and refer to only the regularities not variances. This continuum can be filled in with other terms, some of which are respectable-oriented and some undesirable-oriented (Hannerz 1969: 36- 37). The two categories, conservative and swinger, are respectable oriented.

The swingers did not fit into the undesirable category because they were only slightly deviant. Undesirables are those who make the "bad" life a way of life: these are the tramps, street-corner people, and hardened criminals in American society. The presence of undesirables shames and offends respectables because they represent the failure of not only the idea of a utopian society but also that of the cultured individual. Prejudice in America is not a matter of the close-minded obstinately defending their rights but of the open minded cultured persons who are prejudiced against those who do not broaden or expand their horizons, that is, conform. Undesirables would not be welcome in an archeological field camp.

In the same sense, shopping malls in the United states are designed to attract the respectables of the society and segregate the undesirables. Malls are characterized by their lack of such stigmatized people. There is a homogeneity of "normal people" (respectable-looking and properly behaved persons) within the mall situation. However, even in malls people make distinctions; they make "deviant mountains out of deviant molehills". Or, stated another way "...anybody who doesn't do things like we do, we think those are weird" (Jacobs 1984: 15, 111). The difference between conservatives and swingers is one of weirdness. Swingers were undesirable-like because of the circumscribed field school situation.

Unlike the undesirables who are relatively unconcerned with keeping social boundaries, the swingers did have labels for the conservatives and vice versa. These labels centered around the loose/tight metaphor, with swingers being loose and conservatives being tight. And this metaphor reflects a general distinction and ambivalence within the respectable class because Americans have no absolute idea of what the good life is--they are ambivalent about the meaning of it (Shi 1985: 277). Thus, those pursuing the good life in one way will consider as weird those going about it another way. And again, there are two ways to go about attaining the good life--that is, there are two definable poles of a continuum. On the one hand, the good life is lived through conspicuous frugality and aestheticism and on the other, conspicuous material consumption. Living the good life is an attitude and people can portray whatever attitude is deemed appropriate for a situation.

Both ways of life may appear arrogant if taken to the extreme: the frugal, in their reserve, can appear prudish and the conspicuously consumptive, in their boastfulness, decadent. Both extremes were present in the field camp. The fact that the project was during summer vacation and Program A was relatively informal, allowed people to relax, even in an intense way. The behavior of the swingers was not inappropriate. What was inappropriate was not relaxing to some extent. During Program B, which was relatively formal and a vacation, people were not sure of how they should act, so most B people maintained their normal life style, and in doing this, appeared prudish to the decadent vacationers.

The conflict was one group's not letting another relax in their propriety by stigmatizing them as respectable, before they, in turn, could be stigmatized. Ambiguity existed because both classes in camp were pivotal, with the swingers having had the advantage because the bulk of them, as staff and A participants, had precedence in camp. The alliance, in protecting its own established life style, rejected the incoming group as team members, and instead, treated them as respected guests. Few people straddled the two groups. In general, the alliance forfeited the friendships that the B people could have given to acknowledge their status. The B people, in receiving ambivalent responses to their offers of friendship were not able to reject the alliance without losing the status given to them. In the United States, friendship requires a suspension of status and role between people; and to be rejected in friendship is to be put in one's place. Thus, the B people responded by labeling the others as swingers for surely they would not have labeled themselves in such a derogatory way.

The conflict in camp occurred in the initial year of Program B and everyone recognized this. As much as people were frustrated and resentful they enjoyed the work, food, and setting. Two B conservative women even expressed a desire to return the next year. I do not know if they did but one of the conservative B men returned in 1985 as camp manager. Reportedly, he did his job quite well. Another man mentioned to me that the "problems" of the field school were insignificant and could be resolved. These people recognized that change was not easy and that it was worthy of pursuit if it were seen as progress and the fulfillment of goals.

The ambiguous social structure within the camp during Program B was the result of a structural change in the archeological project. This change can be looked at in two ways, one localized and one more abstract. In a local sense, the change from Program A to Program B changed the status and role relations within camp: Program A was characterized as a relation between staff and non stigmatized people (who were primarily students) whereas Program B was a relation between staff and stigmatized people (professionals in the social studies field). When some of these non stigmatized people, students, stayed in camp for Program B they were merged with the stigmatized people, the professionals. This merger conflicted with the ideal conceptions of status in American society. The professionals would have been normally considered to be culturally more developed, that is better educated than the students. The students had acquired some status in the local setting. Thus both were developed, and were considered successfully equal. As the staff and A participants had precedence in camp they allied against the stigmatized newcomers and manifested this alliance by characterizing the others as respectable. This characterization reinforced the alliance because they were resisting a change in their life style which they expected to come about. The B people, feeling that they had been slighted by being merged together with A people and having received ambivalent responses to their offers of friendship, expressed their frustration in terms of class labels. These moral taxonomies, swingers and conservatives, were multi-vocalic, expressing simultaneously the conflict between acquired and ascribed status, the contrast between the two programs, and the difference in behavior between the older and younger people in camp.

On a more abstract level, the structural change in the project was a directional one not recurrent. Recurrent changes are those consistent with the continuity of the existing order; they are not changes in form but substance. Directional changes reflect alterations in the formal structure of a preexisting order. These two kinds of change are also referred to as reproduction and transformation (cf. Leach 1954, Vogt 1960, and Sahlins 1981). The directional change was the addition of Program B to the project. From 1980 to 1983 the project consisted only of Program A. For the years 1984, 1985, and 1986, the project consisted of Programs A and B. But, it appears that Program A is being phased out. The years 1981 through 1983 were the highpoint of Program A as they consisted of three sessions each. Only two sessions were offered in 1984 and 1985, and in 1986, only one. Such a change is, of course, dependent on whether the grant for Program B is renewed. If it is, Program A will probably not be continued.

This structural change was the result of a paradigm shift (cf. Wallace 1972), not in a theoretical or methodological sense but in intent, concern. On the whole, the project has had three concerns: the first has been to do archeology; the second has been to give people field experience; and the third has been to make the public more aware of archeology. While both programs have addressed these concerns, Program A has emphasized the first two in that it has utilized labor more effectively in getting work done. Program B has emphasized the first and third concerns in that it has minimized excavation in favor of teaching teachers about archeology. These people were then expected to incorporate an archeological perspective into their lectures. If archeology in the United states is ultimately dependent on the public for financing, then field schools such as Program A, which are the norm in Archeology and cater mostly to students, are less effective in making the public aware of what archeology is all about. Program B is more effective in doing this and is, then, innovative.

Program B was aimed at a third concern which A did not address. This concern was an elaboration on the third, creating public awareness of Archeology. The explicit invitation to history and social studies people for them to become involved in an archeological project was one attempt to resolve a long-standing problem within anthropology; that is, what is the relationship between anthropology and history? Anthropologists and historians have rarely worked well together even though much of their subject matter is the same. This lack of close cooperation is even more evident in areas where the two disciplines overlap, ethnohistory and historical archeology.

In a recent article aimed at historical archeologists, Deagan and Scardaville (1985) discussed three problems that have hindered archeologists and historians from working well together. The first is that archeologists have been criticized by historians for misusing the documentary data base. The second is that historians have not been aware of the anthropological concerns and needs of archeologists. And the third problem is that the integration of archeological and historical data has been hindered by the compartmentalized working structure, which is not designed to promote interdisciplinary harmony. These problems are practicalities due to the mutual ignorance of the other discipline by practitioners of both. The main intent of Program B has been to resolve some of these problems.

But there is a fourth problem that is not a practicality but rather is a paradigmatic conflict due to how each of these disciplines functions in American society. Although both anthropology and history have the description of the human condition as one of their functions, they contrast in their other important function, that of interpretation. Anthropology is a cultural critique for ourselves; its interpretive function is to use knowledge of other cultures to examine the assumptions of our own (Marcus and Fischer 1986). The interpretive function of history is to perpetuate the assumptions of our society; it is a cultural validation not critique. In fulfilling these functions, anthropologists use the concept of culture in the broad sense and historians use it in the narrow sense.

For example, to anthropologists sacred shrines are to be studied when possible. But for historians, such shrines symbolize the greatness of a society. And whereas anthropologists have a romantic, adventurous, image within the general public, historians do not. When archeologists excavate national shrines and create much publicity in doing so, these shrines become profaned, made undignified. And historians become resentful that monuments of the human condition are cheapened. Such has been the case with the Custer National Battlefield in Montana, where archeologists have excavated and much sensationalizing of the battle was done by news journalists (c.f. Utley 1986).

The goal of Program B was to help historians and anthropologists overcome such possible resentments. The open forum where the complaint was made that the swingers were running the camp, ended on a point that should have been made explicit throughout the program, but was not: that is, what is the relationship between historical archeology and History. Historical archeology is a relatively new subfield of anthropology; its main American society was only chartered in the 1960's whereas history has been around for a very long time. And so, the swingers were running the camp in only one sense: that is, members of a new, developing subfield were training members of an old, well established discipline about the new subfield. And this unique training situation was beneficial more to the archeologists than to the participants of Program B, who were primarily historians. If historians would validate the critical function of anthropology, they would be helping to change the romantic image of anthropology within the general public to one of seriousness. When the general public recognizes the seriousness of anthropology, especially archeology, then this discipline will have become developed. Program B might be best characterized, then, as "archeology is good to think."

Moral Fiber

The conflict in camp was the result of an ambiguous social structure and this was expressed in class terms. These moral taxonomies indicated that the boundaries were not clearly defined between those who were in charge of the camp and those who were not. While some staff were clearly in charge, others appeared not to be so; while some participants were clearly only that, others could easily have taken charge if the need arose. This was a continuum of groups in camp based on obligation: the staff power bloc, the non powerful staff, the A participants, the younger B people, and the older B people. The ambiguity was that the staff power bloc and the older B people had more in common in terms of age and culturedness than they had with the groups they were contractually associated. with. The two poles did not merge because people were fulfilling their contracts; the middle groups merged because they did not let their contracts restrain them from making friends. And people endured this situation because by doing so they were bettering themselves by developing their moral fiber, the strength of character by which people fulfill their obligations.

The search for culture may be a recent fad in American world view, and, the experimentation with alternative life styles may lead-people to readjust their traditional values of respectability. But some basic values have not changed and may be the basis of such current fads. The egalitarian belief has always been offset by another, progress. A society of equals is a stagnant, boring one, and progress implies that some members will be left behind. For Americans equality is a legal right; it is something people have, not are, as they better themselves by being open minded, expanding their horizons, and transcending trivia; it is something to be bypassed when possible and confronted when it is a means to betterment. And so, the camp was not one of saints, for that would have been boring.

People attend archeological field schools for various personal reasons but we can generalize their reasons into one: it is an escape from the normal routine of the year. If these people learn something about life or archeology then their time has not been wasted. The Old Timer recognized this, for he did not require field reports from his undergraduates who earned independent credits from him; they got their credits because they showed up and stuck it out, endured. And, of course, enduring means "killing time". When I was note taking in 1983 I was told to emphasize the boring aspect of field work. What I have done is describe some things which happen when people get bored. If the project allowed people to escape from their normal lives then socializing, evaluating, and gossiping were ways to pass the time when they were free of the obligations of the project.

The tension between the community's subgroups occurred within an unusual situation. The organization and intent of Program B brought people of specific statuses together and rearranged those statuses such that expectations of some American norms were not met. These expectations were not met because there were various interpretations by all the people in camp of how successful people should behave and be treated. The situation was a special training one. Professionals from one field were training professionals from another about the former. The main trainees were, then, temporary students with high status. To confuse the situation, students, people of lower status, participated as trainees too. The situation was analogous to a military special training situation where a sergeant or an officer trains a group composed of privates and officers about some specialty. However, in the military situation the officer-trainees assume some form of command during the off-hours of the training period. In this archeological field camp B participants had no such responsibilities during their free time. So, even though their participation in Program B was a verification of their status, it was not verified during their free time.

Group B was, then, hard to identify with because those people were in limbo, simple anomie, which "refers to the state of confusion in a group or society which is subject to conflict [within its] value-system resulting in some degree of uneasiness and a sense of separation from the group" (Merton 1957: 163). No one was sure how the B group fit in and so its members had little sense of in-group solidarity. In contrast, the A group members were in a state much like liminality. They were threshold people, upwardly mobile, and ideally without status (c.f. Turner 1969). They knew that they fit in and had much in-group solidarity.

In terms of class, the staff power bloc identified with the swingers because those younger people were threshold people developing themselves. Liminality is a state that most Americans experience and the older people in camp had already done so. The swinger life style was not emulated by the conservatives because liminality is ideally a state of freedom from obligation, social position. The conservatives had their social positions to consider whereas the swingers could forget their own temporarily. The problem was that the swingers could not forget the statuses of the conservatives and vice versa. That is, the swingers met the obligations of the project because it was an excuse for them to forget the obligations of their normal lives. For the conservatives, the project was an extension of their normal lives and by meeting the obligations of the project they were meeting the obligations of their profession; the irony for them was that they were on vacation.

Appendix

Robert Murphy has discussed the ethnographic dilemma, which he calls a classic double bind:

> It is the dialectics of reducing people to objects while trying to achieve understanding of them and of converting ourselves into instruments while struggling to maintain our identities (Murphy 1980: 11).

In other words, one must deal with the conflict between ascriptions about oneself and the change in these, if any, due to acquired knowledge of others. However, as the ethnographer of this archeological project, I did not confront this problem.

There are two reasons for this: the first is a matter of ideology, and the second, a matter of categorization. It would be convenient to state that I was ignorant of the problem, but I could not have gotten away with it. While doing the field work in 1983 I was asked twice about how I was going to be objective. I replied that I do not believe in it. I reject the objective/subjective concept that is so fundamental to Western ideology not because the ideal of objectivity cannot be practiced but because of the animistic aspect that is inherent in it. My concern has been in trying to understand why people believe such mental, essence-related topics not perpetrating them. And so, I did not to not turn myself into an instrument or my subjects into objects.

Secondly, I did not undergo an identity crisis while in the field; culture shock was not a problem either. I never questioned who I was or what I was doing. Moreover, it was comforting to listen to the Old Timer explain to some A participants in 1983 who I was and what I was doing. The staff, as anthropologists, did not question the validity of my project. At worst, they could have said it would cause tension and ask me not to do it. And now that it is done, they can question my observations and interpretations to alleviate any tension I may have caused.

The problem that confronted me was determining whom to observe. I had to define who the natives were. However, in doing this I had to realize that, while I was a novice ethnographer, I was no "greenhorn" native. I decided that, as I had committed myself to the project, then the natives would be those who had done likewise. As I had once participated in Program A then those participants would, too, be natives. In 1983 the A participants treated me as a staff member; to them my position in camp was ascribed. To the staff I had earned my position by having invested much time, money, and effort to the archeological project. Also, my standing as a graduate student in anthropology allied me with most of them. Moreover, to understand Program A one could not ignore the people who ran it in the field. At the end of Program A in 1984 I debated whether or not I should stay for Program B because my initial plan was to write only about the A program. But by then it was obvious that the two programs contrasted in their organization and intent, so I decided to stay and take notes for comparison. Thus the B participants became natives too.

Obviously, my project held second place to that of the ongoing archeology. And the least obnoxious position for me to take was that of a participant observer. Working from a small personal budget, my field techniques were simple, consisting of observation, casual conversation, and still photography. For the most part I followed people around and noted some of what they did, said, and when and under what circumstances these events occurred. As a standard procedure, I focused on what people said they were going to do and then waited to see if they followed through. I knew that the project had a schedule, so I waited and let things happen, and noted it when they did. Note pads, pens, a watch, and a camera were all that I used. I did not conduct formal interviews or a survey. In 1983 I handed out a questionnaire that people filled out but I did not urge people to do so. I felt that the project was too short for me to be bothering people with time consuming tasks during their free time, so I mostly watched and listened. Thus, like a salvage archeologist, I collected as much information as possible and, then everyone went home.

Surely I could have presented the material differently. The defined community has been presented as having both unity and internal diversity. Further, I could have presented each subgroup in the same way. Therefore, by focusing on the community and the fractionation within it I have had to emphasize each subgroup's unity. This method is the same principle that Americans follow when making their social differentiations. Ultimately, I could have reduced the social structure into as many people as were there. By taking this question of scale into account I have avoided the interpersonal relationships that characterize the camp setting and American society in general. This report is, then, a poor substitute for the great-American-novel.

Thus I did not confront any ethnographic dilemma because I was the disinterested insider. My contact with these people has been limited to the field season. While I consider some of these people to be my friends, all involved were relative strangers to me and I to them. This point has been impressed on me on the few occasions when I have met some of them outside of the field context. If my position as the disinterested insider has led to bias, there are, at least, arguments for and against such a perspective (cf. Augilar 1981). I agree with Hennigh (1981), who believes that the insider can use his bias to make further insights and, perhaps, a more interesting study. Barret (1984: 30) has argued that the problem with being an insider is that one will have to assume a particular role and act according to the obligations and limitations of that role. I agree with this position too.

Since the people under study were familiar with the role of the ethnographer and I had expressed my intention to be one, I had to meet this obligation.

Finally, there is always Nash's point of view (1963), that anthropologists, due to their training, are always strangers in their own land.

from: Patterns Without Rhythm: Social Structure Ambiguity in an Archaeological Field Camp. Master's Thesis, Department of Anthropology, University of Montana, Missoula, 1986.

9 THE IRONIES OF SELF REFLECTION IN ARCHAEOLOGY

Several years ago Robert Murphy wrote that the professional student of society is in a classic type of double bind:

> If liberation has remained an issue to educated Americans, it has become transformed into the liberation of the individual from society and a quixotic search for an ephemeral inner and indivisible self....It [the bind] is the dialectics of reducing people to objects while trying to achieve understanding of them and of converting ourselves into instruments while struggling to maintain our identities. The yield of the agonizing process of ethnography is always incomplete; we skim off the top and come away, if we have done our jobs properly, with a sense of loss and unfulfillment (Murphy 1980: v, 11).

The title of his book, *The Dialectics of Social Life: Alarms and Excursions in Anthropological Theory*, portrayed his belief that there are serious problems in American anthropological theory. This book is useful for archaeologists because it exemplifies the angst that seems to be present within the discipline.

Today, American archaeology is undergoing a re-evaluation of its conceptual foundations, and, there is much personal reassessment going on among archaeologists as well. Murphy stated that this is due to a general all American reawakening of moral consciousness and an attack on the social order (1980: v). This may be so but there are other factors involved in this situation. American archaeology is a double edged sword: it is an end in of itself, and, it is a means to several other ends, the most obvious of which is historic preservation, in its broadest sense.

These two approaches are often conflicting, especially at a personal level. Typically, an American archaeologist is trained in an academic context and then finds a job in the consultant or bureaucratic sectors, both of which serve historic preservation. Academics, however, are still the role models of the discipline. Those that pursue the consultant service industry often have to compromise thorough scholarship for business. Those that find work within local, state, or federal agencies learn that archaeology is driven by legislation, economics, and politics. For many, archaeology has lost its luster--it is no longer a pleasant profession but is just another job and possibly a step towards something else in ones career path. Periodic soul searching appears to be common among modern American archaeologists.

Concurrent with the above issues has been the ongoing conceptual debate between processual and post-processual archaeologists. The New Archaeology of the 1960s and 1970s was spurred on by American historic preservation legislation during those years. Hundreds of jobs were created, millions of dollars were spent on projects, and all archaeologists had plenty of opportunities to investigate their ideas. This economic boom began to break in the early 1980s, as did the debate, and the contexts of archaeology (academic, consultant, and bureaucratic) became entrenched (Patterson 1986). A question and answer period then began in earnest with the sources of funding, the public, and archaeologists all asking about the character of archaeology: When, where, how, and why is it to be done. These questions have not been adequately answered, and now, a decade later, justification is still the name of the game.

One of the issues that have arisen to the forefront of the conceptual debate is the possible need for self-reflection as an aspect of the archaeological record. The strongest advocates of this position are the critical theorists (Leone 1986; Potter 1991a, b) although other post-processualists feel that it is necessary also (Hodder 1991a). Self-reflection is defined as having two parts: first, "reflection into the self, reflection by any individual into his or her own history, motivations, or biases", and second, "reflection on a particular situation or set of relationships with the reflective self at the center" (Potter 1991b:226). It is also clear that they identify it with being socially responsible, which "means having a full awareness of the contexts and consequences of the work one does, the conclusions one reaches, and the modes of expression one chooses" (Potter 1991a:95). Self-reflection in archaeology is, then, an attempt at dissolving the distinctions between professional and personal opinion and public and private knowledge.

Murphy's dilemma seems to be present within American archaeology. The senses of loss and unfulfillment that he expects to occur, if the job is done right, are strange, unexpected, feelings for most archaeologists because when their work is good they expect feelings of gain and fulfillment. They may be well aware that there is more to be done. But they also desire a sense of closure--a project is done, good or poor, and it is time to move on to something else. However, Murphy's expectations are correct from his dialectical perspective. And not all critical theorists or post-processualists in general seem to understand this point. They desire to broaden the context of the discipline, place it in time, and to situate the archaeologist in a social context. They want to make archaeology meaningful for themselves and some undefined set of others. This is to be done by expanding the realm of archaeological discourse, by blurring semantic boundaries, and transforming conceptual opposites into continuums. The end result of this perspective, if pursued, will be a discipline without a subject and de-situated archaeologists. These are the ironies of self-reflection in archaeology.

Reflexivity

The concept of self-reflection is not new. The Greek myth of Narcissus is about a youth who was caused to pine away for love of his own reflection and was turned into a daffodil (the narcissus). Narcissism, our modern concept of egocentrism, takes its name from the old tale. However, the tale is not as negative as its modern counterpart would indicate. Narcissus eventually learned to love others and the world around him by learning to love himself. But he had to retreat from society to do this. And it is this retreat, the self-centeredness and the lack of sociability that is the focus of the modern concept. Narcissus passed through several stages of progressively negative retreat and eventually was transformed into the positive flower (Moore 1992). The point is, to be effective as a way of knowledge and social acceptance, narcissism has to be done thoroughly, without restraint. Are archaeologists ready to isolate themselves to enter into the journey of narcissus? Not likely sense the trend has been the other way--public relations and education are the means by which American archaeologists are trying to make their position in society much more solid.

Reflection, as used by the post-processualists, is actually the concept of reflexivity. These two terms are used interchangeably by some (Potter 1991a; Preucel 1991). But reflexivity is different: at its most abstract, it is being conscious about being conscious; thinking about thinking. Reflexivity describes the capacity of any system of signification to turn back upon itself, to make itself its own object by referring to itself. Subject and object are thought of as distinct and merged. Reflexive knowledge not only contains messages but also information about how it all came into being, the process by which it was obtained. And, this kind of knowledge carries with it the explicit awareness of the implications of one's behavior. For any communicative situation the producer, the process, and the product are interconnected (Myerhoff and Ruby 1982:1-3). Reflection is a related term but does not carry with it awareness of the implications of one's activities. As post-processualists feel that it is socially responsible to be aware of the implications of one's own work, they are really arguing for reflexivity.

The difference is not trivial. Thomas Moore's interpretation of the Narcissus tale given above is not the usual one because he believes that the transformation was completed; it is a success story for him. Typically, however, the story is thought of as a tragedy because the youth did not reflect long enough to effect the transformation; he was reflective but not reflexive (Babcock 1980). Whether the transformation of Narcissus was completed or not both these interpretations stress the need for reflexive, not reflective, knowledge. Self-reflection in archaeology will lead to the tragedy of narcissism. Self-reflexivity can lead an archaeologist into the ethnographic situation of participant-observer of archaeology. The knowledge gained from such studies, such as Moore's (1986) ethnography of archaeologists, may be useful to archaeologists and others but it is not part of the archaeological record. Self-reflexivity may also lead one to choose another occupation.

There are different kinds of and uses for reflexivity. It can be individual or collective, public or private, displayed openly or pondered introspectively (Myerhoff and Ruby 1982). As a cultural phenomenon it can be seen in all aspects of life: sometimes it is a role one assumes or acquires; sometimes reflexivity is institutionalized as ritual or within occupational areas. Scholarship, scientific or humanistic, in itself has a collective reflexive aspect to it because there is the continual evaluation of ideas by the various practitioners of each area. In science reflexivity can be seen in several ways: hypothesis testing, written histories of a subject, peer review, and published critique and commentary. Objective knowledge has withstood this process and has gained value and usefulness for many people because of it. Knowledge gained from self-reflexive thought is useful only to the particular person doing it and on a personal basis. To be useful socially, as in socially responsible, self-reflexive knowledge has to be made collective; it has to be made objective.

For reflexive thought the concepts of opposition and continuum have important roles. Ideas can be turned upside down simply by shifting ones perspective. For example, a coin can be seen as a continuum with the heads and tails being the extremes; it can also be seen as an opposition of heads and tails. Also, any continuum can have its ends opposed, individually or combined, to the middle. This word play can be seen in the uses of the pair nature:culture. For some people all of culture (behavior, cognition, and concepts) is natural because it is the symbolic product of the biochemistry of the body and the environment in which the body exists. Other people feel that nature is a cultural construct because it is people who define what is natural. Continuums of this pair could take the forms: within the natural world there are beliefs of unnaturalness, and, within the realm of culture there are ideas about the observable world that connect and engage the bearers of these ideas to it. Reflexive thought considers all positions at once. It is no wonder that Myerhoff and Ruby (1982:1) introduce the reflexive experience as being exhilarating, frightening, or both.

The Debate

As mentioned earlier, American archaeology is undergoing a period of re-evaluation of its basic assumptions and concepts. This trend is part of a larger movement known in academia as post-modernism. Key conceptual elements of this movement are: 1) individuals are active and creative; 2) Cultural relativity--all ways of life are equally valid; 3) pluralism--ethnocentrism is morally wrong; 4) one-down-man ship--subject's opinion should be presented before one's own and, if possible, they should be allowed to express it themselves in their own words; 5) Knowledge is relative and used for social ends; and 6) objectivity is not possible, so the hidden assumptions and biases of any given knowledge claim need to be exposed, unmasked. Postmodernists have a very democratic and culturalistic demeanor.

Post-modernism is not a wave of new ideas but is the reassertion of several old ones as a reaction to the modernism of the 1950s-1970s. During that period there was a tremendous push for scientific rigor in the social sciences and humanities; there was, for example, the New Ethnography, New Archaeology, and New History. Key concepts of this movement are evolutionary theory, ecology, economics, quantification, systems theory, technology--especially computerization, and objective knowledge as generated by science. Modernism de-emphasized the individual as a participant in social life in favor of analyzing abstract variables. Progress, development, and naturalism characterize modernism.

Processual archaeology developed out of the New Archaeology of the 1960s and 1970s. Dissatisfied with the culture history approach and its focus on chronology building and ethnic identification American archaeologists, basically following Binford (1962; Binford and Binford 1968), focused their attention on culture process, hence the name. Primary processual topics include sociopolitical organization, economics, environment, adaptation, and regional analysis. The philosophical approach of the New Archaeology has been thoroughly reviewed by Kelley and Hanen (1988).

David Clarke once characterized archaeology as having lost its innocence (1973) because it had turned its attention to itself. In the terms being used here he was describing the era of the New Archaeology as a period of collective reflexivity. Unfortunately, reflexive knowledge is not guaranteed to be perfect, and so, the introduction of positivism into archaeology by the New Archaeologists was done too narrowly. Their program was a closed system that discounted those areas not easily studied through neo-evolutionary concepts (Trigger 1991: 553). By the early 1980s its limitations had become apparent and many people began to look for alternatives. For most, positivism was dropped in favor of a broader idea of science which included substantive and contextual features into its discussions (Kelly and Hanen 1988). Contemporary processual archaeology can, then, be distinguished from the New Archaeology by its diversity of approaches to doing science and its acceptance of topics which twenty years earlier would have been taboo--for example, cognition in lithic studies. One of the interesting aspects of the debate is that post-processualists continue to critique positivism even though most processualists gave it up long ago.

Today, American archaeology is typically done in the processual mode. The "grey" literature of historic preservation, which is making up more and more of the archaeological record, is almost exclusively processual because the federal guidelines under which most of this work is being done were first written during the late 1960s and early 1970s, the main period of the New Archaeology. These guidelines stress problem oriented scientific research. Alternative approaches are discouraged. Post-processualists often work within this context, even if they do not find it satisfying. Academic studies and historic preservation studies rewritten for scholarly publication, although, do show the diversity of interests within the discipline.

During the period of the New Archaeology some people were not pleased with the scientism of that approach and so joined the small ranks of humanistic, Marxist, and/or culture history positions which were also being used. Throughout the 1980s these other ways of doing archaeology gained many more adherents, and, they were eventually lumped into the category of "post-processual" because they were seen to be other than mainstream archaeological thought (Patterson 1989; Leone 1986; Leone and Potter 1988; Hodder 1986; Shackel and Little 1992). Post-processualists are not a unified group; they are often just as critical of each other as they are of the processualists. However, these approaches emphasize the struggle of individuals against society. People are described as active participants in their own cultural context and are even sometimes thought of as being "proactive" versus reactive.

Post-processualists also desire to study meaning in the archaeological record. This meaning can be understood in several ways. Structuralists look for cognitive underlying principles which generate superficial patterns; the work of Glassie (1975) and Deetz (1983; 1988a) typify this approach, although both are loaded with culture history concepts as well. Marxist archaeology is very diversified (Spriggs 1984) but these people tend to focus on class relations and ideology; meaning is created by them via the unmasking of contradictions in the social order. Contextual or interpretive archaeology is best identified with Hodder (1986). To him the archaeological record is seen as a text to be deciphered, and, the particular meanings of artifacts and features are to be understood in their "thickly" described context. Post-processualists do two things in their search for meaning. First, they reify all non-material aspects of culture. World view, symbolism, and thought are acted upon as if they were material objects. Second, material culture is anthropomorphized; objects are treated like they were active, animated. Material culture is said to be recursive in that it "recycles culture, returning it [culture] to the concrete and empirical world where it may be experienced, learned, and changed" (Little and Shackel 1992:1).

The concept of data has been a special topic of this debate. Are archaeologists discovering "real" aspects of the world or are they "creating" it? This issue is nothing new as the debate between Spaulding (1953) and Ford (1954) covered it all very well. Much of the New Archaeology followed the idea that real aspects of the world could be discovered. Binford (1987) recognizes that the archaeological record is part of the present and that all data are generated by archaeologists in their terms. This is still an objective scientific perspective because he stresses the public nature of observable facts. This point does raise, however, the issue of all data being theory bound, a standard critique against science. But the critique is weak because the absoluteness of the statement contradicts the relativism upon which it is based. Also, it is trivial for archaeologists, while talking among themselves, to debate the theory laden-ness of flakes, potsherds, and nails. There is a separation between theory and data at this level because if there was not archaeologists would be throwing away their collections every time a theory did not hold up. The issue is not trivial when archaeologists are confronted by outsiders who need to be convinced that a rock is a flake. The importance of the theory embed-ness of data depends on the context in which it is being discussed.

Self-reflection inters the debate at the level of data. Over the years the archaeological record has expanded to include new kinds of data-- radiocarbon dating, phytoliths, micromorphology, etc. The post-processualists are trying to include in this record types of data which are not necessarily observable, such as world view, meaning, and individuality. The question is, do archaeologists, whose task is to study the archaeological record (Binford 1987), want to conceive of this type of information as being part of that record? There is no good answer to this question at this time but obviously if everything in the world becomes data then the discipline has no well defined subject matter and a structural breakdown is likely. A line has to be drawn somewhere and it seems that currently people are still thinking of the record as being primarily material culture. Self-reflection is unique in this instance because the use of it would allow for the introduction of an informant--the archaeologist--directly into the archaeological record. This would greatly change the character of the discipline.

Currently, archaeology has no informants in that it studies the remains of dead people. To avoid a transformation of the discipline into something else must these new found informants be killed? Not really. The data self-reflection generates need not be considered part of the record; it can remain something else, non-archaeological. Producer, process, and product are a unified set but objective, socially useful knowledge is generated from it by separating the producer from the chain. Self-reflection and the producer can be reviewed in their own context. Self and individuality are cultural constructs (Dumont 1986). Americans are very much concerned with issues of psychology and individualism (Wilkinson 1983). It is not surprising, then, to find that more American archaeologists focus on this issue than do others. Thus, this issue of self-reflection provides good data for American popular culture studies.

Relevance and Credibility

One of the ironies of the current debate is that people look to historical archaeology to be the spearhead of the movement towards a more socially relevant, responsive, or responsible archaeology. American prehistoric archaeology is of use to the majority of the American public in the sense that it provides a contrast to their modern lives. Historical archaeology can provide immediate historical depth for their lives. Unfortunately, the general public is not aware that the Society for Historical Archaeology, the main American group, spent the first ten years of its existence debating what its subject matter was; this was a self-proclaimed identity crisis. Then, having chosen the world wide spread of European culture and capitalism -- beginning in the 15th century--as a subject, the 20-year anniversary, in 1987, of the society was marked with "soul-searching" because people were unsure if "questions that count", in a wider social sense, could be addressed archaeologically (Shackel and Little 1992: 5). Apparently the debate focuses on this question in general.

Hodder (1991b) recently defined the goal of archaeology as being socially relevant. The critical theorists take a more active view. The goal of critical theory is to examine the aims of science, which will lead to an understanding of the political uses of science and of the sources of the questions, methods, and results which science produces (Leone 1986:427). Critical theorists intend to produce critiques of oppression and domination, both historically and in the present, and to help create a more humane social order (Epperson 1990:35). The message here is that people can either "know [their] social context, which is the context of advanced industrial capitalism, or be prisoners of it" (Leone and Potter 1988:19). But does knowledge of one's context give one control of it? No--knowledge is not power. It can be used by the powerful and the weak. Also, can archaeologists create a more humane social order? That is not their job. Humane? From whose perspective? Marxist's? Are not the liberated obligated to the liberators? Unmasking the contradictions of the social order is one way the critical theorists hide their agenda for social reform. Reform and relevance are not the same.

So, has archaeology lost its soul? Archaeology is and always has been socially relevant. It seems that all the soul searching indicates that some archaeologists have forgotten this point. The question is, how relevant is archaeology to contemporary life? It is very important in that it provides people with the idea of an origin; it gives people the information upon which to create and reinforce us/them distinctions. Additionally, archaeologists from all approaches ask questions that count—post-processualists do not have a monopoly on that point. For example, why study the collapse of the Maya civilization? Answer: no civilization has withstood the test of time and having an understanding of the reasons for a collapse can help identify the clues to future ones. One real threat to the discipline and its relevance to society is continuing the image that it lacks meaning.

Another threat to the relevance of archaeology is the non-objective perspective of post-processualism. American and European societies value the idea of objective knowledge. Scholars may think of the debate as being just that but the public typically views scholarship as being objective, professional. Self-reflection undermines this image when it dissolves the distinction between professional and personal opinion. Self-reflexive thought allows one to know that a personal opinion can be received as a professional one. This point is the reason that the distinction needs to be maintained. Archaeological information is meaningful and credible to the public only when it is objective and professionally presented. The worst thing for the credibility of archaeology is people charading personal opinions as professional ones.

Dehumanization

Science is a humanistic endeavor. One of its traits is that the concepts used are abstract and distanced from real people. Words like "economy" and "environment" do not conjure up images of people with faces and names; they are sterile, neutral. They were created to be that way by people, and, they are used by people. Scientific knowledge is a double edged sword. It can be pursued as an end in of itself and it can be a means to other ends, good or bad. Humans do this for their own multitude of reasons. Ironically, then, science is often characterized as being a dehumanizing endeavor, or, that its products are dehumanized. This is a myth. What is real is the image of dehumanization; that people do believe that human-ness can be lost. This image is a cultural construct as much as is scientific knowledge.

One of the main critiques of processual archaeology is that it is said to be dehumanized; it is almost devoid of cultural content (Leone 1986:432). Post-processualists argue that they can humanize archaeology by reintroducing cultural content into the literature. In this way archaeology will be meaningful to many people outside of the discipline. This is an interesting juxtaposition because the main topics of processual studies are of interest to most societies: the economy, exploitation of natural resources, and the analysis of social structure. For the processualists the problem is that these topics are too sterile and they do not touch upon all interests of all people. Much of this is due to the material culture that remains in the ground--very little survives to enable archaeologists to talk about the details of the intangible aspects of culture. Post-processualists feel that they can examine these other aspects of culture simply by reifying all of it. The irony here is that this is another way of dehumanizing the archaeological record.

If science dehumanizes life because it abstracts it all into vague concepts, the anti-science approach is to make material everything that is intangible. Reification and abstraction are opposites in this sense. Reification produces the image of dehumanization because the concepts of humanity are, then, no longer unique. A belief is equated with a rock, a flake, a pot shard. This metaphor on life is more difficult to understand than the vague concepts of science as those are at least defined in some sense. The metaphor is a poem, meaningful to society only on the personal level. In that way it is not socially responsive and relevant. The post-processualists search for meaning and social relevance will lead to neither.

This search can lead to personal satisfaction, fulfillment, and gain. But, only if it is done completely, without restraint. And the search itself needs to be temporary; it cannot be made a way of life. Self-reflexivity is a pause in one's life; it is Victor Turner's (1969) state of liminality, that threshold of betwixt and between. It is the purposeful marking of transitions, change. These can be social, ritual, or mundane: births, marriage, diary writing, and saying good-bye and hello. The usefulness of reflexive thought is that distinctions that make a difference are created and recreated, there are closures and beginnings. Not everything is blurred, merged, open ended.

But the post-processualists will be de-situated because they believe in the image of dehumanization. This image is made by breaking conceptual boundaries, blurring the distinctions between things and events. Thinking of abstractions and inanimate objects as being not only animate but also anthropomorphized is one of the best ways to deprive humanity of its uniqueness. By trying to be humanistically connected to everything at once, there are no connections because there are no boundaries. But the Individual does not represent Everyman. And one cannot be self-absorbed and produce meaningful, relevant, studies of society at the same time. By being unable to define what is human they have no subject matter, not even themselves.

Conclusion

One of the strange metaphors within American world view is the idea that reality is deep, not shallow. One supposedly finds reality by looking into something or revealing it. But by revealing something there is just another mask behind it; take away all the masks and there is nothing left. The act of unmasking is very unfulfilling. Murphy was right: if the post-processualists do their jobs correctly, deconstruct everything, they will be dissatisfied with their results. Self-reflection helps this process by taking the individual out of context. Self-reflexivity also creates this non-entity when it is applied too much. It puts one into the realm of liminality. But people do not spend their lives in thresholds, they pass through them.

Post-processualists desire to liberate the individual from society. Metaphorically, they intend to liberate archaeology from same. This is to be done by denying the scientific foundation of social studies and by replacing it with a relativistic humanism informed by animism. Liberation in this sense means blending the discipline into the social fabric of everyday life such that it loses all distinction. And, also ironically, the individual becomes a metonym for society. The reason this endeavor will not be successful is that the myth of the dehumanized person is perpetuated.

Hodder recently (1991b) suggested that the debate end simply by rethinking the opposing camps into a continuum. What relevance will this have for archaeology or society? It can only do harm. In Western societies, where objective knowledge is excepted, useful, relevant, and responsible, the best way to conduct archaeology is through the scientific process. Obscuring the debate will only damage the credibility of the discipline with the public. And if that happens there will be a lot more soul searching and career changing than currently exists.

from: The Ironies of Self-Reflection in Archaeology. In *Archaeological Theory: Progress or Posture?* Edited by Ian Mackenzie, pp. 43-56. Worldwide Archaeology Series #11, Avebury/Ashgate Publishing Co., Brookfield, VT, 1994.

10 GETTING BACK TO WORK

I appreciate McKenzie's comments as he touches on some important issues that need to be discussed further. Let me preface this reply with a position statement. I am not a post-processual archaeologist as he indicates; I have even been known to encourage my local colleagues towards more rigor in applying processual models (Moore 1992). Archaeology should maintain its broad scientific character. However, if this postmodern movement achieves anything, it will be a redefinition of science. In this light, archaeologists might want to initiate a science of context by developing models that link the realms of causality and reciprocity. Second, with regard to the post-processualists, it is not the radicalness that I object to--it is the negative tone. In their denial of positivism they seem to have little positive to say about the good things we enjoy in this life. They could learn a great deal from their more tactful cousins in other fields (c.f. Gould 1987; Lave and Wenger 1991).

However, to continue on, I agree with all three of MacKenzie's main points so let me clarify some of these in the order they were presented. First, MacKenzie has pointed out that my use of the term "the public" was a bit lax. Admittedly so. It is habitual among archaeologists like me who work in public programs. It is a less awkward way of referring to the population of non-archaeologists; it is a we:they pair, to use structural terminology. "They" is always a heterogeneous domain. I could have said "the many publics" (McManamon 1991) but that connotes separateness as if the public can be cut up into many non-overlapping boxes. What McManamon really identified are different audiences and constituencies that crisscross within the public and that need to be assessed. Additionally, archaeologists are part of "the public" from the reference point of any other group.

There is some utility in using this term because it connotes images of

American popular culture, the ideas, values, and expectations which connect most residents of this country to each other. Important to this self-reflexive discussion is that Americans value science and technology very much. Two other concepts are important also, democracy and professionalism. There may be contested and/or negotiated meanings for all these terms but most people in the United States, "the public," will have an idea of what is being referred to when they are used.

These terms are partially connected through the concept of objectivity. For example, the motto of our democratic legal system is "Justice is Blind." The intent of this statement is that politicians and members of the legal professions are to be impartial, fair, and treat everyone as if they were equal. This requires an objective approach to each case and person involved. Likewise, professional behavior and productivity requires this impartiality. Journalists would be seen as unprofessional if they prefaced their reports with personal comments about why they were giving them; surgeons would also not be seen as professional if they discussed personal motivations for doing an operation while taking a patient into the operating room. Archaeologists work under these limitations as well. Adult Americans have, then, a dualistic concept which guides much of their weekly lives, "at work" and "free time." When one is at work "objectivity" is an expected behavior and attitude; free time is when these restraints are relaxed. For people who have jobs which are considered to be scientific, such as archaeologists, the appearance of objectivity is far more emphasized.

Of course there is a difference between theory and practice. During working hours it is not uncommon to find people engaged in personal conversations. These periods are marked by terminology such as "taking a break", "killing time" or "off the clock." These periods are accepted and sometimes encouraged as part of the normal workday because they can create good working relations. When these periods are over they are often marked by some reference to "getting back to work."

In a much broader sense American society is "becoming more private than public in orientation, more gossip-like in public domains" (Tannen 1990:105). While this new "openness" can be seen as both positive and negative, the post-modernists have high aspirations of its positive impact towards a more humane world. Ironically, this openness has led to many embarrassing situations and an active interest in the private lives of public officials and celebrities, often to their detriment. Openness is not always for the best.

Objectivity is more important to the lives of Americans than is generally recognized. It is a state of mind that one strives to master for it lends credibility to ones professional and public images. Subjectivity is always present and it can be diminished through one's style and acknowledgment of biases, as recognized by one's self or others. Some occupations, such as artists, are expected to embellish the subjective aspect of one's self. But the professional actor is also a master of the objective attitude, hiding behind the mask of the role played. Objectivity and subjectivity are always present, like two sides of the same coin.

Post-processualists who deny objectivity are not even good actors because their perspective is anti-objective. They try to delete it from their work. Self-Reflection is their substitute for objectivity. In so doing, they undermine the image of professionalism for the discipline of archaeology. They also undermine their social reform agenda: they claim they want a more democratic world but they try to eliminate a key aspect of it.

MacKenzie's second comment relates to two issues: that of understanding the past in today's terms, and human agents relating to more than one past. I had no intention of implying that archaeologists are the only ones who provide understandings of the past or the many pasts. The work that archaeologists produce supplements and competes with other past-making endeavors such as history, mythology, relic hunting, fiction, and so on. Some of these approaches have more prestige than the others, and, archaeology's competitive edge is its characterization as a science and a profession instead of a hobby or recreation. Life will go on without archaeology.

Further, I have apparently undermined myself by arguing that people require a sense of the past and by not recognizing that that past must be understood in today's terms. I thought I had addressed this issue by citing Binford's (1987) comments that archaeologists do construct their data in their own contemporary terms and by arguing that all brands of archaeology are relevant to the present. But there is another paradox here that needs to be explored in more detail, which is not possible at this time. Basically, sometimes members of the public are not aware that the past(s) is relevant to the present, or, they may not understand how this is so. Also, sometimes members of the public do not want to be asked to make their own judgments about a site or artifact--they want to be told what it is and means. Sometimes Archaeologists have to create their own relevance.

This brings us to the issue of one past or many. Like the concept of the public I see it as a game of semantics. To me the past is a heterogeneous concept but there is some unity to it because it is all behind us. For example, the history of the United States is becoming more multicultural; it no longer starts with Jamestown in Virginia but with the Indians entering North America. All the various ethnic groups and nationalities that have contributed to the whole have received attention in the last two decades. According to federal guidelines for historic preservation all pasts are considered equally important and archaeologists are aware of this, occasionally turning dull sites into potentially significant ones by suggesting an ethnic connection. Some pasts are more equal than others.

The issue of there being one past or many is a product of our linear time mode of thought. Archaeologists, geologists, and historians have been influential in creating this image of deep time and of separating the past, or the many pasts, from the present, or the many presents. We gave created an illusion of linear time from a data base that really suggests multi-linear and multi-cyclical patterns. Having done this, the issue is how to reunite them in some way. I see it all as a question of scale and ones perspective, broad or narrow. We can lump or split as needed.

McKenzie's third comment pointed out that my first paper was inherently self-reflexive; this paper follows that style as well. Only time and further critique will bear out whether I have provided unnecessary diversions or not. My intent in writing these papers has been to open the discussion on self-reflection in archaeology, but also, to take it in a completely different direction, towards American Studies and its equivalents in Europe. I had a couple of choices on how to present this topic. First, knowing that it lends itself easily to self-reflexive jargon, I used it. Also, "fighting fire with fire" can be effective.

The second perspective was to have seen the whole processual\post-processual debate as an aspect of American culture (or its European equivalents). This is the perspective that I believe will be most productive later on regarding the issue of self-reflection. One of the most down played topics in today's American society is the rise of New Age Thought. Apparently there are a lot of Americans who are disillusioned, unhappy, looking for meaning in life, or who are simply seeking a change, rebirth. The literary genre of Self-Help\New Age\Spiritualism which supports this movement is growing faster than bookstores can handle. The basic question addressed in all these books considers the relation between the individual and society. This issue is one of the perennial paradoxes in American culture and history (see Bender 1978 for a modern view and Madsen et. al. 1985 for a postmodern one). The post-processual trend in the United States is one aspect of this larger movement. Only time will tell if it is all a fad or a true revival.

Self-reflection\reflexivity is very relevant to American society. If any country has spent a great deal of time and energy in pursuing the dictum "know thy self" it is the United States. But this pursuit is a "free time" activity. People may derive a lot of meaning in life from their work but few people get paid to be self-reflexive. I have had people tell me that it is silly for a grown man to get paid to look for arrow heads and rusty nails. And sometimes I half agree with them. Asking the public to support self-reflection in archaeology is going a little too far; they may actually agree, but only to let the rumor mills grind us into obscurity.

I wrote these two papers (Moore 194a, b) on my own free time. At work I jotted down some notes but I could not allow myself to spend much time on it there. Potter (1991b:225) starts his self-reflection paper by telling us that it was "composed between 3:00 P.M. on April 26 and 2:00 A.M. on April 27, 1989..." It seems that he too borrowed a little time at work for that paper but basically it was done on his own free time. I have other things to do with my free time.

from: Getting Back to Work: Reply to Mackenzie. In *Archaeological Theory: Progress or Posture?* Edited by Ian Mackenzie, pp. 61-65. Worldwide Archaeology Series #11, Avebury/Ashgate Publishing Co., Brookfield, VT, 1994.

11 STUDYING THE MODERN PERIOD

In a recent review of American historical archaeology Barbara Little (1994) identified two crises within the field. First, during the late 1960s and early 1970s, historical archaeologists were undecided whether their discipline was a subfield of history or anthropology. This issue has been resolved with the latter generally taking the prize. The second crisis stems from a symposium titled "Questions that Count" held during the annual meeting of the Society for Historical Archaeology in 1987 (Honerkamp 1988). At that time the relevance of historical archaeology to contemporary society was discussed. No good answers to this issue were forthcoming, however, mainly because the discipline lacks a clear definition of itself.

Little is correct in identifying the lack of a unifying definition within the discipline. The most common one in use--the archaeology of the spread of European cultures around the world--does not appropriately subsume much of the work currently being done within the field. Little offered another concept, the archaeological study of capitalism, which encompasses more. But it too is not enough. What is needed is a definition that will encompass all the research areas within the field commonly known as historical archaeology; and, one that guides us into new ones. To accommodate such research the main topic of the field can be defined as the archaeology of the Modern Period, which began in the fifteenth century and continues today.

The term "period" is used in the standard archaeological fashion as in Paleoindian, Archaic, and Woodland. This period is of short duration, similar to Mississippian or Late Plains Village. One important difference is that it is very wide spread; it is the first period that is truly global. Modernity is discussed below.

The Modern Period

The Modern Period is characterized by rapid cultural change. In evolutionary terms the last five hundred years can be described as a period of "cultural takeoff." No other period in the human time line has the pace, scale and intensity of cultural development than does the Modern Period. The world changed from consisting of fragmented local and regional economic, political, and social networks to being interconnected via international ones. During this change, many new ideas and ways of life were created, to include: progress, science, specialization, industrialization, humanism, professionalism, capitalism, communism, development, underdevelopment, advanced technology, the nation state, individualism, democracy, rationality, and modern medicine; just to name a few. The European expansions that began in the fifteenth century initiated this trend. Historical archaeologists study the processes and substances of these ongoing cultural changes--the creation of our modern world.

Other scholars have come close to defining the field in this way but their statements are more descriptive than definitive (Handsman 1983; Mrozowski 1993; Little 1994; Orser 1994). Only Schuyler (1970, 1988, 1995) has consistently envisioned the field in such broad terms.

This definition is timely in that historical archaeologists have finally begun to extensively explore regions other than just the New World. Much research is now being done in Africa and the Pacific (DeCorse 1987, 1992; Smith 1990), for example. There is also a renewed interest in more recent sites within Old World archaeology; the "Current Research" section of the *Society for Historical Archaeology Newsletter* now regularly contains descriptions of several ongoing projects. Thus, historical archaeology has taken an international or "global" perspective (Falk 1991; Orser 1994). This is not to mean that historical archaeologists are abandoning their interests in localized interpretations; rather, they are now beginning to study the various levels of cultural integration within any community (Schuyler 1995). This mixing of local and international influences within communities and regions is another hallmark of the Modern Period and it will be a major research topic.

In addition, this definition is not intended to create the idea that modernity is inevitable. There are other choices available and some societies and communities have rejected, resisted and/or followed other paths in their histories. Japan, for example, closed its doors to modern European influences for many years. It would be important to investigate archaeologically the involution of that society during its closure and the changes that occurred there since its doors were opened to these influences. Likewise, here in the United States some groups, like the Amish, have resisted certain aspects of modernity. Their history may begin within the Modern Period but they have rejected many of the changes that others quickly pursue. Understanding the relative nature of the concepts "modern" and "traditional" is crucial when analyzing the Modern Period.

Other Definitions

Over the years historical archaeology has been defined in at least three ways, all of which have shortcomings. The first and earliest definition of historical archaeology is based on the idea that the presence or absence of historical records is meaningful. Prehistoric archaeology is supposedly about those time periods prior to the use of writing; historical archaeology deals with those periods in which there are written records available. This characterization is not really true as it is now known that some Native American societies, such as the Maya, did have forms of writing prior to the European migrations. But Mayan archaeology is not generally thought of as historical archaeology.

This emphasis upon the presence or absence of written records causes conceptual, and probably ethical, problems because it tends to leave Native Americans without a sense of more recent history. It perpetuates the ethnocentric concepts of "people with history" and "people without history." It also opens the prospect that they could be seen by others as being only "prehistoric" or "primitive" and not contemporary in their lifestyles, which is not the case (Fabian 1983). Prehistory versus history is a poor distinction; it is one that needs to be ignored.

The second definition of historical archaeology arose from Robert Schuyler's (1970) attempt at resolving several inconsistencies with the above simplistic view. Focusing on two elements involved, the use of written records to aid archaeological interpretation and the interest in New World European-American history, he defined "Historical archaeology" as any archaeology that used written records. "Historic Sites archaeology" was considered to be the study of the expansion of European cultures into the non-European world, starting in the fifteenth century and ending with industrialization. These two definitions were not generally accepted by most practitioners. In contrast with Schuyler's original terminology, "historical archaeology" became the term used by American archaeologists for studying European-American sites. And, based on an expanded conception of the use of written information, "text-aided archaeology" has recently been used to describe the use of written information in archaeological interpretation (Little 1992).

Therefore, the ability to use historical records does not distinguish historical archaeology from any other type of archaeology. This is best seen in the many cases where historical archaeologists prefer to investigate sites that are not well documented: the remains of unknown settlers, slaves, or laborers. In such cases archaeologists are able to use historical information only as regional context in which to present site specific information. This is little different from prehistoric archaeology, which is often based on regional models.

Historical archaeologists have gone on to develop a subject matter all their own by broadening Schuyler's definition of historic sites archaeology. One recent definition states that they study "...the spread of European societies worldwide, beginning in the fifteenth century, and their subsequent development and impact on native peoples in all parts of the world" (Deetz 1991:1). This takes the subject matter beyond industrialization, as Schuyler defined it, into contemporary times.

There are three problems with this definition. First, understanding the Modern Period cannot be done by ignoring the archaeology of Europe during the past five hundred years. Many people are recognizing this and are now comparing their data with sites in Europe (Horn 1988). The second problem is that the field has outgrown its earlier preoccupation with European colonial settings and is now beginning to address topics far beyond these earlier ones, including twentieth century sites. Rathje's (Rathje and Murphy 1993) garbage projects, for example, must be considered as part of the field. The third problem is the ethnocentric perspective of this definition, which opens it up to much criticism from multicultural perspectives within the American public. The "archaeology of ourselves" attitude of historical archaeology has to be understood as having a diversified ethnic and racial referent. One way to get beyond this European ethnocentrism is to redefine the field in terms that do not overstate the influence of European expansionism. The Modern Period should be neutral enough for this task.

The third definition is the one offered by Little and several others, the study of capitalism (Leone and Potter 1988; Orser 1988; Paynter 1988; Little 1994). While this definition allows scholars to continue studying topics which are popular, such as colonialism, frontier expansions, and the fur trade, it is still too restrictive. Capitalism does not define the Modern Period; rapid cultural change does. In addition, focusing on capitalism does not suggest the study of other forms of political-economic systems, such as dictatorships and communism. Researchers have already begun looking at sites within these kinds of systems in Europe (Calabrese 1994; Meyer 1992). And this too is historical archaeology or, if you will, Modern Period archaeology.

Conclusions
To address questions that count and be relevant to society historical archaeology needs a good definition. The "archaeology of the Modern Period" fulfills this mission. Archaeology's contribution to our society is in providing data, explanations, and interpretations about the past that people use to compare and contrast their lives with other peoples' lives.

Archaeology also explores the linkages between the past and the present; it teaches people how they are connected. Archaeologists, of course, are not the only ones that do this: practitioners of history, natural history, mythology, folklore, and the media all reconstruct the past as well (Moore 1994c). But it is the anthropological aspect of archaeology that turns this information about the past into knowledge about human nature and culture, and allows people to compare themselves with others. By understanding the Modern Period we will understand much about ourselves and many others.

from: Studying the Modern Period: Expanding the Perspective of Historical Archaeology. *Journal of Middle Atlantic Archaeology* 11:119-124, 1995.

12 THE MISPLACED TROWEL

You've been digging a test unit all morning. Then you have to talk to a land developer. An hour later you come back, distracted, and can't find your trowel. Where'd you put it? The rest of the crew breaks for lunch and so do you. Afterwards, you get a cell phone call and your boss wants you to look at some blueprints of a road development. You give some last instructions to the crew, get in the truck, and go back to the office. On the way you remember your trowel and hope that someone finds it. You spend the rest of the week in meetings while the test project is finished. The tools are collected and your trowel is missing. Something is wrong here, out of place. The soul of American archaeology has been misplaced.

Recently, Moeller (2000:352) stated that archaeology, as he once knew it, is dead. I tend to agree with him and believe that many others, particularly those that have left the profession, do as well. Of course 'dead' is a metaphor, meaning that some essence is missing, lost, or misplaced. Archaeology has no meaning or purpose in American society, mostly because non-archaeological issues have distracted it, primarily historic preservation ones. So, it has failed to establish a core message and deliver it to society at large and within its own ranks.

For some, it may seem inappropriate to discuss the topic of soul in a professional archaeology journal. On the contrary, it is necessary. For a community of professionals and avocationals soul is the groups' shared values, character, purpose, goals and intentions combined with *esprit de corps*, passion, and some zealotry. Other professions treat this topic openly. The *Journal of Financial Planning*, the main publication for personal financial planners, has a regular section called "Money and Soul" where authors state their opinions about the meaning of their profession, why one would work in it, and how clients need to be serviced and treated. Archaeologists need to talk about it too. Otherwise they will flounder in their long range planning and not accomplish any goals that are set.

My perspective on this topic comes from a diverse background. I have been both insider and outsider to the profession. I worked for twelve years as an archaeologist, roughly 1984 through 1996. Currently it is an avocation. In the recent past there were even a couple of years that I viewed archaeology as entertainment as I learned another industry. In 1999 I decided to re-engage and now lead small volunteer projects (Moore 2002; Moore and Busch 2003). The view from the outside is interesting; some of this will be related later. Another element to this perspective is that my college training focused more on ethnology and linguistics than on archaeology. I was trained as an ethnographer and did archaeology as seasonal work while in school. After classes were over finding a job in archaeology was easy and that was where I went. Thus, the core of this essay emphasizes semantics and social structure. Years ago I studied archaeologists (Moore 1986). I analyzed the social structure of a field camp and discussed ambiguity within that ad hoc social group. This essay takes a similar approach.

Ambiguity is rampant in archaeology--as it is within American culture. It keeps things interesting and it obscures issues such that defining a problem is itself problematic. Above I said that I 'tend' to agree with Moeller. His essay was bleak and direful. Misplacing one's soul is serious business. At the same time I see it as opportunity for change. From outside archaeology, it is also comical. So irony is present, as it has been for years (Moore 1994a). And finally, from a management perspective, when dealing with problematic behavior, it is best to focus on the behavior to correct rather than the individuals doing it. Therefore I cite some references as examples of broader behavioral patterns. No names are given; I have no desire to single anyone out. No one is doing anything wrong. The archaeological community simply is not focusing on the right things.

The rest of this essay has four parts. All issues are presented as high-level overviews; each could expand into an essay or book--they are that complicated. The problems of historical archaeology are presented first because they lead to a discussion of other problems. As a sub-field comprising half the American profession, historical archaeology is adrift, sitting undefined and purposeless. Part of this is its own ambivalence about the problem and another part is that prehistorians have claimed the dominant archaeological status within American society. These issues are further blurred by historic preservation ones that consume so much attention. In fact, the Society for American Archaeology (SAA) adopted ethics statements in 1996 that were a capitulation to historic preservation. Archaeology became a means to another's end. And there it remains today, apathetic and even blasé. Redemption is possible so some ideas for corrective action are given. Archaeologists must redefine themselves, develop a core message, and demonstrate to society that they are skilled at elucidating the truism 'the past is important to the present'.

The Entrenchment of American Historical Archaeology

A recent issue of the journal *Historical Archaeology* contained a forum of papers around the question Is Historical Archaeology Adrift? Charles Cleland had the lead essay and stated that the field is "drifting to its intellectual boundaries" (2001:7). He also argued that the field was too particularistic, not focusing on larger problems. None of the commentators liked the 'adrift' term but there were some agreements with Cleland. What motivated this symposium? Has there been, in the last several years, some discomfort about the field? There must have or the forum would never have taken place. And now that it has been done and some people have recommitted to doing better research, what will change?

Very little, if anything, will change. The *status quo* of historical archaeology is being adrift. This sub-field has never been defined nor its subject matter identified. Practitioners pursue whatever position they want due to professional courtesy and a belief that pluralism is good (Deetz 1983). This leads to pluralism of purpose, as well as method and theory. Schuyler's (1978) important reader did not emphasize any position but left it open. Is it anthropology or history or just archaeology? Is archaeology a science or a technique? Are we doing local history or social science? Is it about the integration of historical and archaeological records or is it about overseas Europeans? In that book, one can see the debates that went on in the 1960s and 1970s. There was an 'identity crisis' in those days and two major essays used those very words (Cleland and Fitting 1968; Walker 1970). By the mid-1970s the scientific view temporarily became dominant surrounding the release of South's processual study (1977). By the early 1980s much of that perspective was under critique as the postmodern versus processual debate began. Later, another forum was held about Questions that Count in Historical Archaeology (Honerkamp 1988). Once again there was a recommitment to social science, along with a toleration of diversity of opinions. At this point historical archaeology was generally considered social science, and 'science' was open to interpretation as to what it was.

The 1990s brought these issues full circle. Archaeologists revived the 1960s debate of whether the emphasis of historical archaeology is methodological or substantive. To some, historical archaeology is the study of the material remains from any historic period and its unity is due to its methodology of investigation rather than the historical subject under study. For others, it deals with a specific subject that has temporal, spatial, and cultural boundaries, more specifically European impact on the New World (Schuyler 1970). These versions were called 'historical archaeology' and 'historic sites archaeology' respectively. Although both terms date to the 1950s and earlier, the second term was obsolete by the 1980s and everything was called 'historical archaeology.'

The interest in studying European expansionism and its outcome, however, was anything but obsolete. It was gaining popularity and was already fragmented into different strains of thought. The groups are: the humanists (Kelso 1984); the culture history group (Deetz 1977; Schuyler 1988); the archaeology of capitalism group (Paynter 1988; Little 1994; Leone and Potter 1999); and the modern sites archaeology group (Moore 1995; Orser 1996; Hardesty 1999). Recently most people realize that all these groups are accommodated within the overall concept of studying the modern world, taking their lead from Schuyler (1991). Method and theory may vary; the central theme is galvanizing. The major debate has been between these groups and those who adhere to the methodological view of the field (Funari, Hall and Jones 1999). Orser (1996) recently reviewed the above issues in his modern world archaeology book and titled that chapter "A Crisis in Historical Archaeology." As is evident, the identity crisis is still present. And so the sub-field spins, void of focus.

It may seem odd to suggest that historical archaeology has misplaced some essence when the field has spun its wheels for decades and appears to not have anything to lose. But practitioners have had much enthusiasm in the past and revivals towards social science do take place on a regular cycle. It is this enthusiasm that has been lost. The frustrations recently expressed by Cleland and others are quite real. That he would focus on particularism as a problem is understandable given the ambiguous nature of the field. But particularism is only a symptom. The problem is the pluralism of purpose. Archaeologists need to decide if they are studying the rise of the modern world or are they going to develop a historiography that integrates with archaeological research. Both need to be done. Only one, however, is critical. A few people can have good careers doing the historiography. Within the next decade there should be a textbook on how historical methods integrate with archaeological research. More importantly, the whole discipline of American Archaeology will benefit if the rise of the modern world becomes a central focus.

The Old Handmaiden Tales

While modern sites archaeologists—and that term is used going forward for all varieties mentioned above—perpetuate their identity crisis, their prehistoric oriented colleagues go about their business of dominating the image of archaeology within American society. After all, prehistorians, within their own ranks, do not have such a crisis. In the lexicon of American archaeology 'archaeology' means the study of prehistory. And this, of course, makes modern sites archaeology anomalous. It also makes all archaeology ambiguous because American society does not distinguish between human prehistory and all of prehistory.

The anomalous social status of modern sites archaeology is a gaping wound. Only among its practitioners are there discussions about inferiority complexes, upstarts, underdogs and the junior varsity in relation to prehistorians (Orser 1996:14; Armstrong 2001:9; Little 1994:30). Years ago the image of the sub-field was tarnished by the remark 'archaeology: the handmaiden of history' (Noel Hume 1964). This statement was made in the early days of the identity crisis. It was used to re-enforce the idea that modern sites archaeology was a tool of history and historic conservation. Later, this concept was re-used by Deagan (1988) to express her frustration that the sub-field was unable to develop its own set of theories and that they continued to borrow from prehistorians--therefore it became 'handmaiden to prehistoric archaeology.' This comment points to a class conflict within American archaeology. Prehistorians control the image of archaeology in American society and the modern sites side is a self-proclaimed second-class citizen.

Both sides continue to perpetuate this issue, in different ways. Modern sites archaeologists complain about it, as shown above, and they fulfill it by not commanding parity for their good work. Prehistorians need only sustain the *status quo* and make no effort to change. The *status quo* includes both professional's and the American layperson's understandings of archaeology. In his classic textbook David H. Thomas (1989) tried to correct two myths, first that all archaeology is academic and, second, that archaeology is only about prehistory. The second (1989:134) is dealt with first.

To Americans 'archaeology' and 'prehistory' are nearly synonymous terms. Except in the towns of Williamsburg, Virginia, and St. Augustine, Florida, places where excavations of colonial features are popular attractions, the title 'archaeologist' is equated with studying prehistoric Indians, Egypt, or dinosaurs. The title 'historical archaeologist' is not understood and attempts at defining it during social gatherings (cocktail parties, for example) are ludicrous.

Another way to understand this class problem is through the concepts of marked and unmarked words. In America the category 'archaeologist' is unmarked meaning that the word can refer to both a generic role and a specific one. The category is unmodified, neither prefixed nor suffixed. The generic role is someone who studies the ancient past. Typically this person works on another continent and is familiar with Stonehenge, Egypt, or Mayan pyramids. The specific role is a North American prehistorian. The category 'historical archaeologist' is marked as the word 'archaeologist' is prefixed by the word 'historical'. This category is always a specialist (even when the specialty is undefined) and is used only within the community of archaeologists, historians, and preservationists.

One outcome of this is that prehistorians, as unmarked generalists, are able to expand their career opportunities by crossing over to modern sites projects or any time period on other continents. Modern sites archaeologists, as a marked class, are blocked from going the other way. If they change continents they stay within the modern stage as a subject of study. Several well known prehistorians have done modern sites archaeology (e.g. Harrington, Cotter, Schiffer, Binford, and Thomas). Are there any prominent scholars today who started out as modern sites archaeologists and who have also made significant contributions to prehistory? The late James Deetz is the only one who might qualify for that rare distinction.

The generalist versus specialist distinction is seen in other ways as well. Lightfoot (1995) discussed how projects at Fort Ross in California were planned based on a division of labor. The prehistorians did Native American studies and the modern sites staff did Russian-American studies. Post-contact Native American data was divided based on proximity to modern deposits not prehistoric ones. The prehistorians who worked on post-contact data did not identify their work as 'historical archaeology.' Therefore, it was just 'archaeology' to them, in the general sense. As both labor groups used different methods and techniques Lightfoot argued for a more unified research program. Some progress may have been made towards that goal but given the professional divisions his expectations were unrealized. Current (circa 2000) job postings on the SAA web site, for example, continue to reflect these divisions of labor.

This generalist versus specialist distinction is also seen in publications. Sometimes it has little effect on the reader and in other cases it leads to serious miss-communications. An example of the former is the edited volume *Archaeology on the Great Plains* (University Press of Kansas, Lawrence, KS, 1998). The book has fourteen chapters. After the introduction and an environmental review there are eleven essays on prehistory. The fourteenth chapter is a review of modern sites archaeology, or Euro-American archaeology. The Introduction reviewed prehistoric and post-contact Native American issues of interest to prehistorians. The archaeology of Euro-Americans is never mentioned in the introduction. The final chapter appears as an afterthought in the book and could have been left out without affecting the wholeness of the publication.

Another observation about this book is that the terms 'archaeology' and 'prehistory' are never formally defined. The introduction has an indirect definition of archaeology in the first paragraph but otherwise it is assumed that readers understand these two terms. All authors do define within their essays the chronological period and the region they discuss. In the modern sites chapter a definition of the specialty is also given. Therefore, only the modern sites author is compelled to define his profession. The generalists do not have any such compulsions. The marked category always has to be defined and the unmarked one does not.

On a more serious note, an essay titled "Archaeology and the First Americans" (*American Anthropologist* 94:816-836, 1992) denies the identity and existence of modern sites archaeologists. The author's intent was to demonstrate that in America archaeologists and anthropologists had co-opted the value of Native American histories, oral histories, and identity. The essay provides an historical review of Indian and White relations in America and of prehistoric archaeology in the Southwest region. The term 'archaeology' is used throughout. One sentence from the Conclusion on page 828 reflects the view that archaeology is both prehistory and generalized: "The time has come for archeologists to reunite their object of study, the Indian past, with its descendants, and to ask about the needs of Indian people and address those needs." What about modern sites archaeology and the study of Euro-American culture change? There is no mention of modern sites work in this essay. Therefore one could conclude that it did not exist—when a large body of work did exist for the Southwest. This author, in trying to assist Native American's with their identity issue, denied the existence of half the archaeological profession. A balanced view would have been more appropriate. Ironically, this author is also a prehistorian who has done much modern sites work. Would this essay have had a different meaning and impact if the word 'archaeology' meant both modern and prehistoric sites archaeology? I believe that it would. And, possibly, it would never have been written.

There is another subtle issue here. On the Plains, at Fort Ross, and in the Southwest, Native American Studies is the purview of prehistorians; therefore post-contact studies can be viewed as both prehistory and general archaeology. This is one source of the idea that contemporary Native Americans live in the past--that prehistory is still present. While it is insulting to Native Americans it is also insulting to American culture, if one views it as inclusive and heterogeneous.

What has this class conflict got to do with misplacing soul? Half the profession is demeaned by it. And, doing it or allowing it to be done corrupts the other half. There is no *esprit de corps*. No parity among peers. There is, unfortunately, a pattern of dominance behavior being played out. The prehistorians take the role of passive aggressors and the modern sites scholars are the dependants. Now, this is not a malicious rivalry. Sometimes it is good natured and fun. But from outside the profession this behavior appears as unprofessional, and it is not helpful to the image of archaeology.

Moreover, Americans generally do not distinguish between human prehistory and dinosaurs (Ramos and Duganne 2000:31), so they do not distinguish archaeologists from paleontologists. If they have trouble at that level are they going to know the different brands of archaeologists? At this time, there is no reason for them to do this. I believe, however, they should have reason to understand archaeologists, without witnessing the profession's internal strife. Therefore, there is reason for archaeologists to redefine themselves to the public in a way that is exclusive of paleontology, is inclusive of both modern and prehistoric sites archaeology, and maintains the character of various research topics and time periods within the profession.

The New Handmaiden's Tale

The handmaiden expressions above are, of course, powerful images. No one wants to be a handmaiden, servant, to anything (Waselkov 2001:20). But were the uses of these phrases accurate? The first usage (Noel Hume's) would have been correct if one agreed that archaeology serves history. If not, then that statement was probably inflammatory. Deagan's version was not directly accurate. The issue of borrowing theory is not about servitude. The statement plays off the servant image and is a metaphor about class conflict. In the social sciences, those with theory have prestige and those without it do not. And, it is even more insulting when borrowing it. One saving grace is that these status ills are confined to the professional leagues and academic institutions. The American public (including avocationalists) does not care about theory and any presentation to them about it will be viewed as 'academic'. So let's look at Thomas' other myth.

Thomas (1989:131) tried to correct the idea that archaeology was 'academic', that is, the work was only located in universities, colleges, museums, and think tanks. He described how archaeologists are also found in government and private sector consultant jobs, what is known as Cultural Resource Management (CRM) or compliance archaeology. The task of correcting the myth is huge. The American public views the profession as academic, and so do professionals. The problem is one of cognitive dissonance. Every year hundreds of students are lured into graduate programs with the idea of doing interesting archaeological research and the prospect of having an academic job (Zeder 1997:61). By the end of their training most are spun out to government and consultant positions. Did these students join archaeology so that they can become historic preservationists? Do they go into their mentor's office and say: "help me find a CRM job because I want to save sites?" I doubt it.

Veteran professionals suffer from this dissonance as well. Many carry their academic values with them into their CRM jobs. They are interested in theory, methodology, and making serious contributions to regional studies. And yet they find themselves sitting in planning meetings, worrying about the alignment of a road. Or, they get to do a few days of site survey and recommend that a couple of interesting sites be tested. Months later they ponder over a testing report that claims that these same sites are not significant and that no further work is needed. Likewise, the consultant who wrote the report spent hours trying to justify a mitigation study but quit to spend the rest of their day responding to a new Request-For-Proposal. Archaeology has become a 'bait and switch' game. Most go in wanting to do archaeological research, and yet, end up doing compliance or small business management indirectly about archaeology. The passion for archaeology is stifled and often transferred to something else.

Archaeology is no longer an academic profession. Academic positions, teaching and museum work, constitute a smaller percentage of available archaeology jobs in the United States than ever before. And, every year that goes by this academic portion gets smaller relative to the compliance side, government work and consulting. Across the nation academia had a growth spurt in the 1950s and 1960s. With the passage of the National Historic Preservation Act of 1966 compliance archaeology boomed. By the mid-1980s SAA membership was evenly divided between the two, compliance and academic. Today the academic group is a minority. The numbers are probably growing wider as many compliance workers are not members of SAA, especially the numerous low paid technicians (Zeder 1997:47). The bottom line is that the vast majority of American archaeology done each year is done in the compliance environment. It is the only area of growth within the profession. Archaeology is an applied profession.

Tensions between the values of academic research and CRM preservation were high during the 1970s and 1980s. By the 1990s the values of CRM gained control of the discipline. In the early 1990s a new slogan permeated the field: "Save the Past for the Future." A prominent academic (*Archaeology* 1993,46[6]:14-16) even berated the profession for living in a "hierarchical value system that considers research, excavation, new discoveries, and publication the pinnacle of achievement." He went on to advocate for a conservation ethic in archaeology. Historic preservation was needed in archaeology graduate programs; students need to be exposed to it. He also went so far as to suggest that archaeologists try to understand the psychology of looting. Admittedly, his essay was written in a fit of anger after seeing a shell mound that had been looted. A few years later, the preservation ethic had become the majority and was codified in 1996 by the passage of a set of SAA ethical statements (Lynot and Wylie 1995; 2000) and a Mission Statement. People's passion for archaeology was formally transferred to preservation.

The primary ethic statement is called Stewardship and it is viewed as the central principle of archaeological ethics. The other seven statements are written with this core concept in mind. Archaeologists are supposed to be stewards of the past, regardless of where they work. This value represents a pragmatic shift away from research-oriented archaeology to the preservation of archaeological resources. Even education of the public is sublimated to this goal. Archaeology is no longer a goal unto itself. Public education about archaeology is not a goal. Both are now handmaidens to historic preservation. Lipe (1996) touched on this goals-versus-means issue but did not stress it hard enough. Archaeologists have given up any purpose, goal, that they had for their own profession and have adopted another profession's purpose. Years from now, when scholars rewrite the history of archaeology they will refer to the decade of the 1990s as the "Big Oops."

In the 1990s ambiguity truly set in for the profession. Many maintained the ideals of academia and accepted the pragmatic values of CRM. There is some good irony here in that the word 'academic' is also unmarked. The Ivory Tower version referencing research and teaching is the specific form. The generic form is a referent to something that is theoretical without having practical or useful significance. The specific version of 'academic' is a positive term, for those who enjoy research. The general version is negative within American usage. When archaeologists adopted the preservation ethic they also expanded their view of academic from the specific sense to the generic sense. In doing so, they misplaced their original purpose and lost their trowel.

Linking the Past with Contemporary Life

A recent report from the Society for American Archaeology titled "Exploring Public Perceptions and Attitudes about Archaeology" (Ramos and Duganne 2000) is useful to understanding what archaeologists need to focus on. The report has research findings on the public's awareness of, interest in, and valuation of archaeology. Additionally, there is a section on the public's attitudes about conservation of sites and objects. One valuable statement in the summary is that Americans "believe that archaeology is important because we improve the future by learning about the past and because archaeology helps us understand the modern world" (2000:31). This is a wonderful statement. It is a core message for archaeologists. The past is important for living in the present and for looking into the future. What do archaeologists need to do next?

First, the field needs to redefine itself to the American public. The above report made explicit that Americans have "both a misconception and lack a clear knowledge of what the study of archaeology encompasses" (Ramos and Duganne 2000:31). The distinction between archaeology and paleontology needs to be made clear. Taking tacit credit for the work of paleontology is a professional discourtesy. The class conflict between modern and prehistoric sites archaeologists needs to cease. Parity between the two groups will lead to better research opportunities and method and theory. Editors of journals need to support this inclusive definition of archaeology as well.

In addition, the above report did not indicate that Americans viewed archaeologists as conservationists. They viewed archaeology as important, and, conserving sites and objects was seen as somewhat important. The concept 'archaeologists are conservationists' was not in the report because the question was never asked. However, open-ended questions about what came to mind after hearing the word 'archaeology' generated a high percentage of responses about 'digging' (2000:12), a destructive behavior. Trying to sell the idea that archaeology is conservation will be like pushing a boulder uphill.

Another aspect to better defining the discipline is to adjust job titles to reflect what people really do. An archaeologist is someone who spends a great deal of time doing archaeology. Historic preservation duties that involve archaeology and archaeological research need not be confused. A person who does mostly compliance-about-archaeology is more appropriately titled 'Heritage Resource Specialist' or 'Cultural Resource Specialist.' The title 'State Archaeologist' is the pinnacle of cognitive dissonance; these people are Heritage Resource Managers or Directors. The federal GS-0193 series needs to be revamped. Positions at GS grade 11 or above need to be evaluated for their percentages of archaeological, administrative, and compliance duties. Those jobs that rank low on archaeology need to be reclassified.

Changing job titles will cause some people identity crises. People want to be known as archaeologists and they take pride in it. But one can also take pride in being a Heritage Resource Specialist and keep their archaeology memberships. It seems, though, that some people are already suffering from identity crisis. The merging, blending, of archaeology into historic preservation is taking it away from them. Many archaeologists have lost focus of what archaeology is because they do consider compliance tasks to be archaeology. It is necessary to define clearly what duties are archaeological and those that are not. Job titles need to reflect the duties.

CRM has changed archaeology forever. Pure archaeology, if it ever really existed, is a thing of the past. And now, the preservation ethic needs to be put back into a secondary role. The priorities of the profession need to be re-centered on archaeological research. Promote the doing of archaeology through education and preservation. As it stands now the profession promotes preservation via research and education. An analogy is useful. Think of thesis, antithesis, and synthesis. Archaeology used to be a means and goal unto itself. Archaeology is now a means to do historic preservation. Transform that into--preservation and education are the means to doing archaeology. Real archaeology will be done in an applied context.

Lightfoot (1995) is right that archaeology needs to be done within a unified research program. The profession needs a coherent set of research topics and questions. A forum on Questions That Count in North American Archaeology needs to be held jointly by the major professional societies from Canada and the United States. Compile a master list of important questions: When was the first peopling of the Americas? Is the Archaic better described as a mobile lifestyle or semi-sedentary? How does the rise of the modern world get reflected in sites? The master list can be updated as needed. The important part is to have one. Next, recognize that these questions will be addressed mostly through CRM projects. Therefore, each state and province needs to have its own set of questions that link to the master set. Likewise each local area or land management unit can have its own set of questions linking upward as well. Encouragement and enforcement of the master research agenda can be done via compliance channels. After all, the guidelines set forth by the Federal government are wide open. They allow discretion as to what is important and professionals are the ones that make these determinations. Saying that a site is potentially significant because it may yield information useful to understanding prehistory or history is common but what set of questions is it going to be linked to? Having a master plan is where it all comes together.

One important element in this master plan is to merge modern and prehistoric sites archaeology. Don't separate the recent past from the distant past. Make it one continuous chronology based on the theories of evolution and culture change, and end it with 'the present.' Across the continent prehistorians use some version of the sequence Paleo-Indian, Archaic, and Late Prehistoric. Add to this the Modern Stage. Currently, the sequence used by prehistorians is a model of evolutionary culture change. If they mention the modern stage it is done vaguely. On the other hand, modern sites archaeologists have never used such a model and have divided the Stage arbitrarily into centuries, following historians. But the Modern Stage is part of evolution and can be studied that way (O'Brien and Lyman 2000). Table 12-1 is an example of how it can look. The prehistoric portion comes directly from a recent overview of the South Platte River in Colorado (Gilmore et. al. 1999). I added the Modern Stage to it and included the Protohistoric period as part of it. For an earlier version with Virginia data see Moore (1994a). What this model accomplishes is that it shows the continuity of human life. Archaeologists can fill in the substantive details and narratives from any theoretical perspective they choose. Likewise, the model begins to meet the public's need to understand their modern life in relation to the past. It sets the stage for presentation of the core message.

Table 12-1: Chronological Outline of the Denver, Colorado, Metropolitan Area.

Stage	Period	Date Range
Paleoindian		12040-5740 BC
	Clovis	12040-9750 BC
	Folsom	11340-8720 BC
	Plano	10,850-5740 BC
Archaic		5500 BC – AD 150
	Early Archaic	5500-3000 BC
	Middle Archaic	3000-1000 BC
	Late Archaic	1000 BC – AD 150
Late Prehistoric		AD 150 – 1540
	Early Ceramic	AD 150-1150
	Middle Ceramic	AD 1150- 1540
Modern		AD 1540- present
	Protohistoric	AD 1540-1860
	Capitalism	AD 1860-1921
	Post-Capitalism	AD 1921 - present

The last change for archaeologists is that they need to become more effective with their communications to the public. Americans like archaeology and feel that there is value in it. Is this enough? No. As a profession and industry archaeology competes with several other professions and beliefs about the past. The archaeological story is one among many. To be heard and given preference the conclusions of archaeology need to be delivered in ways that are more powerful and meaningful than competing stories. The traditional academic writing style is not appropriate and will never deliver the powerful meaning that the public needs to hear. The style to be used is a business, journalistic or fiction based one. Further, presenters need to define archaeology in the inclusive way and have the core message up front at all times. They need to be better than anyone else in the ability to elucidate the idea that the past is relevant to the present and to the future. To be somewhat crass, archaeologists need to sell themselves to the public. Archaeology has to be made "good to think," to twist a structuralist's phrase.

It Matters What You Focus On

One of the more interesting aspects of doing ethnography is that one can observe what people say they are doing and take note of what they are doing. The difference between words and deeds is often great. Sometimes this disconnect is unimportant while other times it is unproductive and needs to be resolved. Resolution is often a matter of recognizing that there is disconnection and understanding it. The next step is to have a plan of action and implement the change. So:

- Define and give direction to historical archaeology as modern sites archaeology
- Redefine archaeology as inclusive of both modern and prehistoric sites
- Focus on archaeological research being done in the CRM context
- Deliver a unified message to the public that the past is relevant to the present

The disconnect is that archaeology, which was once a worthy goal unto itself, is currently a means to another goal, the implementation of historic preservation policy. Ironically and fortunately, professionals and the public still recognize the worthiness of the old goal. Change is necessary but going back to the good old days of research purity is not possible. In today's context the old goal can best be achieved through a synthesis of many goals. Attain the goals that are legally required, but focus on the one that has the most meaning to the profession. Acknowledge that archaeology is an applied profession and do interesting research through that context. It does matter what you focus on. Stop focusing on preservation, develop a new slogan about doing archaeology, find your trowel, and use it.

from: The Misplaced Trowel. *North American Archaeologist* 22(4): 387-402, 2001.

13 ARCHAEOLOGY'S HIGH SOCIETY BLUES

Recently, I suggested changes to American archaeology that could make our work more interesting to the public (Moore 2006b). McGimsey (2006) replied. My suggestions were based on the observation that since archaeology is embedded within and supported by American society the former mirrors trends in the latter. Over the last forty years an ideological transformation has changed America with a new dominant ideology emerging (Table 13-1). This change has been a typical Awakening, the concept that describes ideological transformations (McLaughlin 1978). Many archaeologists are already immersed in this new ideology; many more will follow. As there is no simple answer to McGimsey I can only describe in broad terms this transformation and its impact on archaeology.

Romanticism alternates with Enlightenment

I had argued that more fieldwork is needed and that projects should be designed and marketed such that they attract the public (Moore 2006). To this, McGimsey (2006:4) replied:

> [I]f this increased involvement by the public were to follow along the lines that Moore seems to envision, it would be a travesty. The public's attraction to archaeology must not be pandered to, but rather must be channeled so they can contribute to the ongoing effort to gain greater understanding of the human past…[T]he only legitimate justification for digging is the need to recover, interpret, and preserve valuable scientific data.

His statement assumes that archaeologists unilaterally control archaeology, and that they can influence the public into serving archaeological goals. Such assumptions are nostalgic for the scientific high of American archaeology, years 1945-1980, when archaeologists did have more control over when, where, and why archaeology got done. In those Good Old Days archaeology served its internal needs and was part of the dominant national ideological consensus known as Liberal Protestantism that held sway in America circa 1890-1990 (McLoughlin 1978; Pyle and Koch 2001). This rationalistic ideology privileges higher education, science, and evolutionary theory through an open minded theology. It is liberal in that it contrasts with (Protestant) Christian fundamentalism. Liberal Protestantism is allied with secular humanism, the ideology of nonreligious Western scientists, because it does not support the inerrancy of the Bible as fundamentalism does. Liberal Protestantism is the ideology of the now dethroned Protestant Establishment (Presbyterians, Episcopalians, and Congregationalists), which was the centerpiece of the broader hegemony known as White Anglo Saxon Protestant (WASP) America.

Table 13-1: The alternation between rational and intuitive eras in American history.

Era	Rational	Awakening	Intuitive	Circa
Puritan Awakening		X		1610-1640
Puritan Age of Faith			X	
First Awakening		X		1730-1760
Enlightenment Age of Reason	X			
Second Awakening		X		1800-1830
National Romanticism			X	
Third Awakening		X		1890-1920
Liberal Protestant Age of Scientism	X			
Fourth Awakening		X		1960-1990
Romantic Egalitarianism			X	present

Sources: Adapted from Alsen 1996, Fogel 2002, and McLoughlin 1978.

Based upon rationality, the Liberal Protestant era was similar to the eighteenth century American Enlightenment with its climax in Federalism and Jeffersonian democracy wherein learned social elites controlled society. Forming early in the Third Awakening and gaining power throughout that era, Liberal Protestantism then became the driving force that created the twentieth century political-military-industrial complex and the welfare state. Some of its core beliefs have been social progress, modernism, and the scientific management of society. This ideology was successful for about 70 years; it developed nuclear energy and put men on the moon. Beginning about 1960 and intensifying through the Vietnam War debacle, the Protestant Establishment and its ideological consensus broke down into a minority status (Kaufman 2004; Pyle and Koch 2001) because Americans became disillusioned with its leadership and distrustful of scientists managing society, especially after the Challenger disaster of 1986. Simply, the Protestant Establishment had lost its moral authority.

Post-modernism refers to the diversity of romantic egalitarian values and ideas that have vied for control due to Liberal Protestant disestablishment. The culture wars of the 1980s and 1990s ended the Liberal Protestant Establishment and fragmented the entire WASP hold on America as Catholics, Jews, and many other non-Protestants gained social and political power. America is now a Post-Protestant society (Porterfield 2001) that does not have an organized core.

The new dominant ideology that has emerged since the rights conscientiousness of the 1960s is based in another old American concept, egalitarianism (Fogel 2000). This new egalitarianism is tolerant towards religion, atheism, science, mysticism, politics, and apolitical behaviors; it privileges none and concedes value to all. It is also a new form of laissez faire individualism, which gives it the unorganized character. The old WASP myth of Anglo Saxon mono-culturalism has been replaced with numerous myths about a multicultural (meaning Post-Protestant) society. This new ideology is also romantic, motivated by intuition, imagery, emotion, and participatory behaviors. Literary critics and marketing professionals first recognized romanticism's broad based re-emergence in American society (Alsen 1996; Campbell 1987). Romanticism is the usual reaction to excessive rationality. Right brain and left brain cultural processes alternate in dominance. Once again in America, John Locke has been replaced by Ralph Waldo Emerson, Jeffersonian democracy by Jacksonian. Comparisons between this new romantic egalitarianism and the American Romantic Nationalism era with its Manifest Destiny and Gilded Age are appropriate.

With the return of romantic egalitarianism archaeologists have been losing control of a large portion of their profession, and, the reasons for doing archaeology have expanded beyond the pursuit of science into romanticism (Wallace 2004). In CRM archaeologists do not control when, where or why archaeology gets done. They have input about these issues but non-archaeologist-senior-managers are the ones who actually control funding and choose the development projects that get implemented, thereby controlling the amount of archaeological work. Likewise, since the passage of NAGPRA in 1990, Native Americans are participating more in the management of archaeology; their motivations for doing fieldwork likely support tribal concerns not scientific ones. Additionally, studies about archaeology as popular culture (Holtorf 2005, 2007; Lovata 2006) highlight that archaeologists do not seriously influence the public's engagement with archaeology; they do, however, describe the romanticism of popular archaeology. Archaeologists now share their profession with many non-archaeologists and these others are becoming more aggressive with their claims to interpret the past. As there are several interest groups appropriating archaeology, this is multilateral archaeology not unilateral.

Romantic egalitarianism is a form of American democracy that professional archaeologists have never experienced because the last time it held sway in America there was no profession of archaeology. Rationalists tend to believe in ascribed authority and orderly rule driven systematic society; they give exclusive moral authority to specialists, such as scientists. Under egalitarianism (equality of opportunity) exclusive privileges are not necessarily given to any group; moral authority is viewed as inclusive, offered to everyman. Egalitarianism creates an eclectic nonsystematic free-for-all type of society in which most everything, including archaeology, is up for grabs. Social equality is not an outcome of egalitarianism because success is idiosyncratic. Likewise, romanticism indicates that mainstream society is moved more by the heart than the mind, that storytelling is more effective than lecturing. Romanticism does not privilege rationality but considers it as just another emotion. For those who prefer being rational intellectuals this is a conflicted environment.

Egalitarian social structures

Like the above issue, the next one also has deep roots in American history and culture. McGimsey (2006:4) made the following comment (the schism he refers to occurred between traditionalists defending Salvage Archaeology and progressives pursuing CRM during the 1970s and 1980s):

> Should all aspects of Moore's vision of the practice of archaeology attract a following, I can foresee schism developing again. This time it would be Moore's populists vs. the scientists.

Here McGimsey is casting the discussion in terms of moral taxonomies, social categories derived from diverging values. He contrasts scientists versus populists with the insinuation that science is more worthy than populism. This is another version of so-called "high class" intellectualism versus commoner anti-intellectualism. Holtorf (2007:113) also identified this distinction.

American society currently has four moral classes (intellectuals, middle class, anti-intellectuals, and unacceptable). The first contrast is harsh, acceptable/unacceptable. Acceptable people are about 90 percent of the population; the other 10 percent are the unacceptable ones who are separated from mainstream society for some reason (criminals, mentally ill, etc.). Modern morals compel the belief that unacceptables can be re-integrated into society. The three acceptable classes still retain some of their eighteenth century stereotypes about social stratification based on wealth, birthright, and education. During the Enlightenment rank in America was identified through those qualities and the upper class had them. The commoners were unsophisticated and uncouth. It was high class versus low class with an emerging middle class in between. Over time this switched from being a vertical ranking into a horizontal spectrum. That change occurred during the Second Awakening as the romantic egalitarian values of Jacksonian democracy emerged in America (Wilentz 2005). Later, during the Third Awakening, the high class/low class (this time referred to as high culture/low culture) conception was stair-stepped again (Lavine 1988) as Liberal Protestant elites began placing "experts" in selected positions of authority. But, they could not recreate an aristocracy because many anti-intellectuals and middle class members retained some power. In the Third Awakening the high arts and science became revered, sacralized, while popular culture was demoted. During the Fourth Awakening rising egalitarianism once again leveled highbrow society, raised popular culture, and demoted science. Television shows such as *Marcus Welby, Md* (1969-1976) used to portray infallible scientists living model family lives. Today, *ER* (1994-present) depicts the messy lives of fallible doctors. Scientists are now just average people because science has been desacralized. Highly educated professionals are no longer the role models of society; instead, college drop-outs such as Bill Gates are.

The two ends of this new egalitarian spectrum are well defined. On one end are those who view America as a meritocracy with education and intellectual prowess as markers of status. Intellectuals are about 10 percent of the population. These folks tend to view themselves as better than everyone else because they have impressive credentials or artistic talent. Most everyone else views them as snobs. When not promoting themselves they promote social agendas to make the world a better place, as they define it. On the other end are the anti-intellectuals, comprising about 30 percent of society. This group includes most of the super rich, and, it includes the numerous populists who challenge the intellectual authority of the other end (hence the term anti-intellectual). Many populists are self ascribed rednecks seeking power and material accumulation, or, they are perfecting the art of "just getting by." Populists are always reminding others that no one is better than them. While they openly demand equality they are always seeking an unequal advantage on life. In between the ends is the lump-all middle class, comprising the remainder of society. Here, people with all levels of education and wealth rub elbows. This heterogeneous group is generally unconcerned or ambivalent about intellectualism or sophistication. They recognize the values of education, talent, and equality; when asked to prioritize these values its members usually become conflicted because they also don't want to be seen as unfair to anyone. Fairness is a great concern of the middle class; members of the other two acceptable classes don't worry about it unless it affects them personally.

Under Liberal Protestantism archaeologists enjoyed an elevated status in society. Having a PhD was the key to a privileged career path. Inversions of meritocracy were rare. Today, there are many paths to success and prestige in archaeology. Only universities maintain archaeological meritocracies and even there PhDs can be abused. In today's CRM, inversions of meritocracy occur frequently. MAs with much experience often have higher pay and more responsibility than PhDs with less experience. Similarly, there are often situations were a BA with much experience might supervise someone with a graduate degree. CRM certainly started out as a highbrow endeavor aimed at protecting the most select of resources, as defined by experts. Today, egalitarian CRMers vacillate between everything is significant, nothing is significant, and avoiding significance determinations as much as possible. The egalitarian transformation made archaeology a conflicted middle class profession.

As the egalitarian transformation has not yet been recognized everywhere, many Americans, including archeologists, continue to stereotype "academic" endeavors as "high status" ones, instead of identifying them as middle class ones. This is an unnecessary holdover from the Liberal Protestant decades. The culture wars that continue are predictable. When archaeologists argue among themselves (e.g. the old schism) the dispute polarizes within pro-intellectual values, such as one side accusing the other of not being scientific enough, or it divides into science versus humanism. When archaeologists get into conflict with non-archaeologists the dispute usually polarizes across the intellectualism spectrum, just as McGimsey warns. The oldest dispute that archaeologists have is with relic hunters (a blend of middle class and populist folks). Archaeologists and relic hunters don't mix because they polarize quickly, the intellectuals versus everyman, the cultured versus the uncouth. When the dispute gets heated it rises to the next moral level. Archaeologists claim that relic hunters are unacceptable, like criminals; in response, the other side holds the center and claims that the snobs are being unfair.

During the era of Liberal Protestantism rational argument was often the winning technique for dispute resolution. Science usually trumped populism because of status differences. Today, rationalism is no longer a successful strategy because intuitive thought processes dominate society. Populism now generally trumps science. To survive in an egalitarian society, and to avoid future schism within the profession, archaeologists need to learn how to argue and debate from within the center of the middle class. During conflict archaeologists must seek fairness not rationality. Holtorf (2007:119-123) provides a Democratic Model that is an excellent approach.

Archaeology as the affirmation of Democracy

I realize these ideas may bother some archaeologists. Balancing scientific ideals with fairness may seem like the "dumbing down" of archaeology; likewise, enabling the "unwashed" more access to the domain of archaeology will certainly be seen by some as a "travesty." However, archaeologists no longer have a privileged domain protected by a dominant rational ideology. Egalitarianism has once again leveled the playing field, and, romanticism has shifted dominant ideological perspectives from intellectualism to anti-intellectualism, from rationality to intuition. These changes are subtle and well advanced in American society; Al Gore's (2007) complaints about it are 30 years too late. Archaeologists are actually adapting. They have been calling themselves "storytellers" for more than a decade (Praetzellis and Praetzellis 1998) and the phrase "democratic archaeology" is gaining currency (McDavid 2004; Wood 2002). These are signs that romantic egalitarian values are waxing within the profession and that values supporting "elitist archaeology" are waning.

Archaeologists have shifted moral categories, from stereotypical high status experts to middle class "diplomats" (Latour 2004) negotiating the when, where, why, and who of archaeology. We are not alone. All of science has fallen off the Liberal Protestant pedestal. The respect and reverence that was once readily ascribed to scientists must now be hard fought as public skepticism of scientific moral authority remains high. Recognizing that something had gone awry, Horgan (1996) declared that science was dead, that there is nothing new to discover about life. We know he is wrong; there will be new truths discovered. Science will continue as a recessive subordinate trait in society until the next Awakening, maybe 40 years hence, when rationality will have a chance to rebound into dominance. Meanwhile, scientists will continue to provide what non-scientists really want--their lives enhanced, to live longer, their gasoline to be cheaper, and to be entertained in new ways. To be successful in this new Gilded Age the products of science need to be marketed and packaged in ways that satisfies the middle class. For archaeologists, that packaging should be multilateral conflicted public archaeology.

from: Archaeology's High Society Blues: Reply to McGimsey. *The SAA Archaeological Record* 7(4): 11-14, 32, 2007

14 The La Jolla Skeletons and Kennewick Man

A recent essay at Wired.com (Dalton 2011) highlights the current character of American Archaeology--it is a profession that has lost control of its purpose and its database. Archaeology has been appropriated by non-archaeologists for purposes far beyond the pursuit of science or knowledge; it has become a commodity for sale to the highest bidder with its *authority* trampled in the dust. Welcome to Post Modern Romanticism where populist and egalitarian impulses drive the process.

The story in Wired is about the La Jolla skeletons that are in the midst of controversy. University administrators want to repatriate the bones under the Native American Graves and Repatriation Act to a local tribe that has made a claim while scientists want to do further studies on a database first excavated in the 1970s. The tribe has lots of money and has become a local power player. The bones are between 9000 and 9600 years old and they are good candidates for interesting DNA studies. This is a good example of how advances in technology can be used to re-analyze old data, and potentially discover important new insights. To date, the request to do additional studies has been blocked.

The scientists are said to hope for collaborative discussions and efforts. What I didn't get out of the story was any sense that the scientists had seriously approached the tribe or administrators for such collaboration. I hope they have because, otherwise, they appear to be on the defensive side of the issue. They wrote letters to science magazines and stated their position in that venue, which comes across as whining and pandering to the scientific community.

In the Wired essay there is a comment that this La Jolla case is 'Kennewick Man II', a reference to an earlier case were scientists and Native Americans fought bitterly over the ability to analyze ancient remains. In that case, scientists eventually were successful at doing the research. The

Kennewick Man case was hard fought, taking about eight years (1996-2004) in the courts. It also divided scientists with some defending their scientism and others the rights of Native Americans.

The ultimate outcome of the Kennewick case is that modernist scientists lost power and authority and the tribes gained both. Those scientists defending old modernist ideals of scientism and meritocracy are now the marginal ones playing defense; the tribes have taken a mainstream stance and represent the values of Dionysian America—express yourself and respect the values of others. Many post-modern scientists will support them. In the Kennewick Man case, scientists won the battle but lost the public relations campaign. They came across as pompous arrogant intellectuals pursuing "irrelevant" goals and questions.

In recent years, public archaeology has been redefined. It is now archaeology "by the people for the people". This contrasts with the old public archaeology that basically stated that archaeology was done by archaeologists for the good of the people; if the public wanted to be involved then they would have to follow the lead of scientists. Both versions are still out there in use today, but the latter is fading. Today, 'relevance' is defined by many factions, not just the scientists, and, the interests of science often are trumped by the interests of nonscientists.

I hope the La Jolla case doesn't escalate into another Kennewick Man issue. It would be more salt poured on open wounds of the tribes and scientists. Collaboration is the answer.

from: The Age of Intuition, May 29, 2011.

15 A FORCAST FOR AMERICAN ARCHAEOLOGY

As archaeologists, we all know that culture change is a continuous process. As we study the past we can also study contemporary events and speculate on what is to come. That is the purpose of this essay. American society is changing in numerous ways and many of these will be extraordinary. Can we use these changes to our advantage? Can we grow and expand our profession, in terms of increased career, business, and research opportunities? I believe we can.

However, there is good news and bad news to discuss. There will be limits on our possibilities, and, it will only be with creativity that growth will be achieved. Of course, I am assuming that growth is good for the profession. Some of you may like things the way they are and others would have archaeology smaller. All these outcomes are theoretically possible. Realistically, our options will be either pursue growth or get very much smaller.

In this essay the big picture of the possible future is presented. In two following essays various cycles within American archaeology and a prospect for growth are discussed. Here, the Baby Boomer generation, people born in the years 1946 through 1964, is discussed, as are thoughts by economic forecasters about the aging of that generation and its impact on American society over the next thirty years. The main forecast is that by the year 2016 American archaeology will have become different in kind, not degree, from what it is today. The new version will last in full form until approximately 2034 when it starts changing again. These two years are seventy years beyond 1946 and 1964, respectively. The details of these changes will come in later essays. The rundown is that the 2016-2034 years will become the high point in American public archaeology, a leisure industry that needs to be aggressively developed.

Like weather forecasting, economic forecasting is better at short-term prediction. Both are also slanted towards identifying poor conditions because Americans generally want to know when the storms are going to arrive. The economic forecast given here includes a storm. As forecasting is quite popular here are some references to the best in the business, from my perspective: Dent 2004; Kotlikoff and Burns 2004; Peterson 2003; and Prechter 2003. All these books vary in analysis and content but they have a general theme: significant economic change is coming. Add politics into the discussion and a major storm is on the horizon. Growth for American archaeology will have to be done within this economic and political transformation.

For your information, I participated in archaeology and cultural resource management (CRM) from 1980 to mid 1996. I switched to financial services for seven years and then returned to CRM work in late 2002. I am a contrarian thinker. In the financial industries, contrarians try to identify where the investing herd is likely to go and then get there first. They are viewed as aggressive investors. This approach is applied in this set of essays. More conventional thinking can be found as the headliner essays of the *Wall Street Journal* or *Barons Magazine*.

Demographics and the Economy

The range of this forecast, from five to thirty years from now, may seem a bit too far out. It is all due to the aging Baby Boomer generation. Their retirement will be one of the main driving forces of this ongoing social transformation. It is ongoing because it has already has begun. The oldest folks of this generation turned sixty this year, which means they have access to their retirement accounts without income tax penalties. Many of these folks are already retiring. Age seventy is another useful threshold. It is at that age that people, on average, tend to significantly reduce their outgoing physical activities. Only a small percentage of Americans actually continue to do work, paid or unpaid, after age seventy. The retired yet active years are thus ages sixty through seventy. The impact of this on archaeology will continue from 2005 through 2034 but it will be difficult to discern it until further into the cycle, about 2010. Those of you doing public outreach archaeology will feel the effects first as there will be increasing demand for your services.

For sixty years the United States (US) economy has had to accommodate this generation because of its size. The US has almost 296 million people and about 78 million are Baby Boomers, roughly twenty-six percent (US Census Bureau, www.census.gov). The US also has approximately 140 million people who are employed. Of these, 78 million, fifty-six percent, are over age forty (US Bureau of Labor Statistics, www.bls.gov). The majority of these are Baby Boomers and the rest are older. The accommodation of this generation will continue until most have passed away. Their parents had to raise and feed them. The labor markets had to expand to let them work. Next, the labor markets will contract as they stop working. The recent political debates about ensuring Social Security and health care entitlements are all tied to analysis that incorporates a forecast that an aging Baby Boomer generation will wreck havoc on the federal budget, and in the financial and health care industries--it probably will. The question here is: Will it wreck havoc on American archaeology? There is a good chance that it will but it does not have to be that way. Our goal is to ride this demographic wave without getting crushed by it.

Bucking the Trend

For many years some forecasters have been calling for the next great economic depression. Such forecasts are not about doom and gloom alarmism. They are thoughtful, realistic assessments of trends and cycles that move through the economy. The US has had several depressions and recessions in the last two hundred-twenty years and it is reasonable to expect them to occur again. Harry S. Dent (1993, 2004) is one such forecaster. In the early 1990s, when others were worried about recession, he was forecasting a boom for the second half of the 1990s and another boom for the years 2005 through 2009. He also forecasts a depression starting about 2010 that will last approximately twelve years. Dent is not alone in making these forecasts. Prechter (2003), for example, argues that the US economy is already in depression with the 2000 to 2002 recession having been the first phase. Sensationalists (Arnold 2002) have also joined the game, so beware. Also be aware that more conventional economists forecast modest growth for the US economy. I prefer the models that use cycles, demographics, and wave theory. Culture change is also fractal because there are cycles within large cycles within larger cycles. At most scales of analysis, culture change through gradualism does not make any sense.

The simplest and shortest way to explain Dent's economic forecast is to emphasize the obvious--the US has a consumer driven economy. Currently, the Baby Boomers are the people who are maximizing their income levels, and, they spend most or all of their income. The demographic peak in this maximization of income will last another four years, through 2009. Dent believes that these years will be the greatest boom period in US history. As more of that generation goes into retirement, consumer spending declines dramatically because Baby Boomers will have less income in retirement. On average, retired people live on sixty or seventy percent of their last level of earned income. This will translate into a thirty to forty percent drop in spending per household. Magnify this across the extremely large number of Baby Boomer households and one can readily forecast a severe drop in national consumer spending along with a contraction in the US economy. The spending levels of the following small generation, the Gen Xers (birth years 1965-1978), are not large enough to offset these changes. Demographically, the decline will start about the year 2010. The next era of economic growth will start about 2022 when the next moderately large generation, the Echo Boomers (birth years 1979-1986), reaches its highest income generating levels. The rising wave of retirements in the Baby Boomer generation triggers the economic depression. Once the depression starts it will have its own internal dynamics driving it until the next large demographic group hits their maximum spending years. Basically, Dent is forecasting economic boom (2005-2009), economic depression (2010-2021), and modest growth starting about 2022 that lasts a couple of decades. Dent's ideas about a proposed boom in 2005-2009 are getting much media attention. However, journalists don't seem to care about phase two of the forecast. The "D" word isn't popular in financial news. It should be extremely interesting to American archaeologists.

What is an economic depression? Few of us have experience with such a severe negative reversal of the economy because the US has been on a long growth trend for over seventy years. A depression is different from a bad recession, such as the one from 2000 through 2002, in that it is much more severe. Both are contractions in economic productivity. Using the storm analogy, a recession is like a category one or two hurricane. A depression is a category four or five. Contractions are also not all alike. For example, they can be deflationary or inflationary. This one will likely be an era of widespread uncontrolled deflation (a contraction in monetary and credit supply), the effect of which will be downward pricing, downward wages, and downward valuations in almost everything. The US has had two deflationary depressions previously, 1835-1842 and 1929-1932. The Great Depression of the early 1930s was maybe a category four storm. What Dent is forecasting is a category five because several economic and social cycles will be coalescing.

During a deflationary depression things that increase include unemployment, bankruptcy, foreclosures, suicide, terrorism, crime, and warfare. People stop buying as much and companies stop making as much. Tax revenues decline dramatically. Governments reprioritize their programs, make swift adjustments, and then raise taxes. Lots of businesses close and people get laid off in huge numbers. The US economy suffers when it's at six or seven percent unemployment. At fifteen percent, envision the re-establishment of numerous Civilian Conservation Corps camps. In terms of culture change a depression is the transition phase when a modern society morphs from old social structures and values into new ones. As US society is still growing it will be like a great snake that sheds an old skin for a new one. A lot of obsolete and nonessential garbage will get shed from the economy.

What social structures might be changing? Dent (2004) argues that this coming depression will fully implement a change that is currently underway, the shift from a Standardized economy to a Customized economy. Since the introduction of the assembly line process in the early twentieth century Americans have been using standardized products and services. For many years customization of products was a luxury of the wealthy. Today, customization is rapidly spreading throughout the US economy and society. Instead of having to buy a pair of standardized shoes off a shelf one can now order a pair online, get a different size for each foot, and a different color for each if desired. This is doable at very little cost. The terms customized, individualized, and localized are now ubiquitous in marketing and advertising. In the sciences, broad based theorizing is being replaced with theories about local contexts and situations. Likewise, within archaeology the recent popular usage of the term 'context' is part of this trend.

Along with the Standardized economy came values of top down management and policy making. These values will become less adequate in the future. The emerging Customized society will have values that place more decision making at the frontlines of business and politics. American democracy already gives people lots of choices. A Customized society will increase the variety and diversity of choices everywhere--note the electronic changes that President Kenneth Ames was promoting in his May 31, 2005 letter to the Society for American Archaeology (SAA). This means that rules, regulations, and laws will change to reflect the need for decision making at the local level. This should make local politics far more exciting than currently. This will be the customization of democracy.

Think of this Customizing trend as the political contextualization of the US. In its early years of polity formation, from the Revolution to the Civil War, the US was a decentralized nation. Political control was more at the state level than the national level. After the Civil War, the US had become a centralized nation with a strong federal government. The next phase will be a contextualized political economy. Decentralized, centralized, and contextualized appears to be the evolving pattern. Another idea to consider is that the US is an empire that has reached a peak in its life cycle (Taagapera 1968, 1978, 1997). It is currently the sole superpower on a global scale. The question is, where to from here? No one knows, of course, but a deflationary depression may generate an answer to it. The political changes that could ramify from an oncoming economic crisis will be far greater than what occurred in the 1930s depression. All of us are likely witnesses to and participants in political evolution.

Given the magnitude of these coming changes how will American archaeology manage through these rough seas? History is a useful guide. In the 1930s depression American archaeology did extraordinarily well. Several archaeological societies, including SAA, were created and several great universities began to build their archaeology departments. The New Deal programs focused on putting people back to work and building out the infrastructure of the new US economy. High unemployment meant that labor-intensive industries that used simple tools and machinery would survive. Archaeology fit this profile very well. It became part of the solution to the crisis because it took hordes of untrained workers and conducted huge surveys and huge block excavations. American archaeology did, for a few years, provide an essential service to society. The reward was incredible. William Haag (1985:278) put it this way: "There has never been a greater revolution in American archaeology than that engendered by the New Deal period."

The cycle may be repeating. Our potential opportunity is the next great revolution in American archaeology. Our goal is to seize it when the time comes. Noting that the coming economic crisis could be a degree larger in magnitude than the previous one then this new revolution could be greater than the previous one. SAA's 2004 membership was 7,024. This number could be tripled over the next ten years if growth is pursued. Alternatively, maintaining current status quo is unlikely given the demographic changes underway. Ignoring this opportunity entirely will likely lead to American archaeology shrinking by sixty to eighty percent over those years.

A To-Do List

The intention here has been to motivate you to think about the future of archaeology. With or without a looming depression we can build a new cycle of growth for archaeology. The alternative is not enticing. The themes of Baby Boomer accommodation, archaeology's integration into the new Customized political economy, and the need to provide an essential service to society in a time of crisis will be discussed in the last essay. The second essay describes how archaeology could quickly melt down due to the demographic changes that are ongoing. It also provides additional background information to support the growth plan given in the third essay.

Enjoy the short economic boom that may come soon. Double your net worth, if possible. Then defend yourself by going liquid (cash, CDs, money markets) with your assets. As you may be reading this in late 2005, place on your calendar a To-Do list to start in January 2006. Enjoy the holidays and then read three books, all of which have been reprinted numerous times, so no need for formal citation. The first is the finest book ever written about personal finance, *The Richest Man in Babylon* by George S. Clason. It is a series of parables that were done in the 1920s. It will also satisfy your interest in the past. The other two books were written during the last great US depression and each won the Pulitzer Prize for fiction. They are, as you might guess, about living in difficult times. You already know them, Margaret Mitchell's *Gone with the Wind* (1936) and John Steinbeck's *The Grapes of Wrath* (1939). There is nothing wrong with reading good books, especially if the forecast is wrong.

from: A Forecast for American Archaeology. *The SAA Archaeological Record* 5(4): 13-16, 2005.

16 CRM: BEYOND ITS PEAK

In the previous essay (Moore 2005a), a mixed forecast was given. In the near future, we can anticipate exciting archaeological opportunities and economic crisis. As we look forward to the opportunities, it is also important to assess where we are today, which is the goal of this essay. American archaeology is in transition after the growth phases of two important cycles have completed. One cycle is cultural resource management (CRM), an aged industry in a vulnerable position. The other cycle is the academic debates that stimulated the profession for over 50 years and can be viewed as a source of strength in the future. These cycles are associated with two value systems operating within American archaeology: historic preservationist and archaeological scholarship. The preservationist ethic is currently dominant, although this will likely change in the near future. Finally, a demographic cycle is maturing that could jeopardize American archaeology. Recognizing these issues facilitates preparation for growth and avoiding an untimely demise.

The Dual Ethics

While several value systems operate within American archaeology, two are widespread. They are often blended but can be identified by the initial concept that is emphasized: research or preservation.

Since the earliest days of the profession, American archaeology has had a value system focused on scholarly research. Within this ethic, archaeological tasks are done to achieve archaeological goals, and honest, disinterested, and competent research is valued. Also included in this ethic is a mild version of cultural relativism. The Society for American Archaeology's (SAA) Ethics Statement of 1961 (*American Antiquity* 27[2]:137–138) was one of four statements characterizing professional scholarship. SAA's Mission Statement of 1996 is a contemporary revision of this ethic, framed as a Public Archaeology statement.

The historic preservationist value system was added into American archaeology in the 1970s, and by the end of the 1980s it was the dominant ethic within the profession. Preservation of cultural resources and cultural traditions is the focus of this ethic. It is an ethic of advocacy, and strong cultural relativism is common. Knowledge of and skill at maneuvering within complicated legislations are valued. SAA's Ethics Statements of 1996 reflect this value system.

At times, these ethics have conflicted, most clearly when preservation work has been accused of lacking in scholarship. In historic preservation venues, archaeology is done to achieve historic preservation goals. Scholarly research can be done through preservation projects, but it is not essential because it is not the main goal of the work.

Cycles in American Archaeology

Two industry cycles can be identified from the last 60 years. The first is CRM, which has become prominent in terms of the number of people working in this industry, the amount of money expended within it, and the preservation ethic associated with it. CRM is part of a broader historic preservation industry generally led by historians, architects, and architectural historians. For archaeologists, this cycle began as a research-driven agenda that morphed into a historic preservation agenda. It started in the late 1960s while the Moss-Bennett Act of 1974, the planned extension of Salvage Archaeology (River Basin Surveys and Highway Salvage), was lobbied and negotiated. Today, the National Historic Preservation Act of 1966 (NHPA), as amended, leads it. Like all industries, CRM is working its way through a predictable industry cycle. The five-phase industry model is presented as a bell-shaped curve, with time as the horizontal axis and change as the vertical axis. The phases are: 1. A developmental phase 2. A rapid growth phase 3. A de-accelerating growth phase that rolls onto a plateau and levels out 4. A phase that leads to a roll-over and rapid decline 5. The final bottoming-out phase.

The first three phases are represented by an S-shaped curve of development, growth, and maturity. CRM's early phases dated roughly (1) 1966–1975, (2) 1976–1988, and (3) 1989–April 2005. It was during Phase 2 that CRM moved from a research agenda into a historic preservation one because federal priorities shifted from sponsorship of scholarly research (via Salvage Archaeology projects) to sponsorship of historic preservation (via NHPA). In the late 1970s, federal agencies needed to streamline their archaeological compliance efforts by either invoking NHPA or Moss-Bennett. Invoking both was viewed as duplication of efforts. The NHPA, with its 1980 amendment, became the centerpiece legislation, which

Table 16-1: Selected SAA membership numbers from 1935 through 2004.

Year		Members	Percent change in Members	Annual Growth rate	Comment
1935		332			SAA's initial membership number
1936		531			
1942		852			End of New Deal programs
1946		673			
1956		980			
1966		1707			NHPA passed
1976		4784			
1979		4789			High mark in individual memberships until1994
1984		4453			
1993		4769			
1994		5300			
2004		7024			All time high number
------	--------	------------	-------------	----------	-------------------------
1935	-1942		157	14.41	New Deal revolution in archaeology
1936	-1946		27	2.40	
1946	-1956		46	3.83	
1956	-1966		74	5.71	
1966	-1976		180	10.86	Phase 1 of CRM cycle
1994	-2004		33	2.86	

Sources: SAA Annual Reports as published in *American Antiquity* and by the SAA.

completed the conversion of CRM from pursuing a research agenda to a preservation agenda.

The value shift that archaeologists made to accompany this policy and funding change took several more years. Conflict between the needs and values of scholarship-focused archaeologists, government agencies, and preservation-focused archaeologists began in the mid 1970s. By 1980, all these folks were at extreme odds, and a bifurcation occurred within American archaeology. This change is seen in SAA membership (Table 16-1 and Figure 16-1), which peaked in 1976 and 1979 before declining through the 1980s as preservation-focused archaeologists avoided SAA, viewing it as a scholastic club. At the beginning of CRM Phase 3, the preservation ethic became prominent within SAA itself, tensions within the profession decreased greatly, and SAA membership rebounded to new highs. The growth in SAA membership between 1990 and 1995 was amplified by veteran preservation-focused practitioners joining SAA, solidifying the preservation ethic within the organization.

The second industry cycle is the academic debates that had American archaeology running for 50 years. The phases of this cycle are (1) 1948–1961, (2) 1962–1982, and (3) 1983–1999. Phase 1 began when Walter Taylor's (1948) critique of American archaeology challenged a profession that was intellectually plodding in the mid-1940s. During Phase 2, the New Archaeology of the 1960s and 1970s stampeded the profession. New Archaeologists debated mostly with Culture Historians, trying to make archaeology a better science. Flannery's (1982) Golden Marshalltown essay likely transitioned the cycle into Phase 3, the Processual-Post-processual debates that questioned almost everything related to science, archaeology, and historic preservation. The polite and synthetic VanPool (1999) essay likely marks the end of the intellectual run as American archaeology moderated its passion for philosophical and theoretical debate.

Figure 16-1: SAA membership numbers from 1935 to 2004. Data for some years was not available or was unreliable.

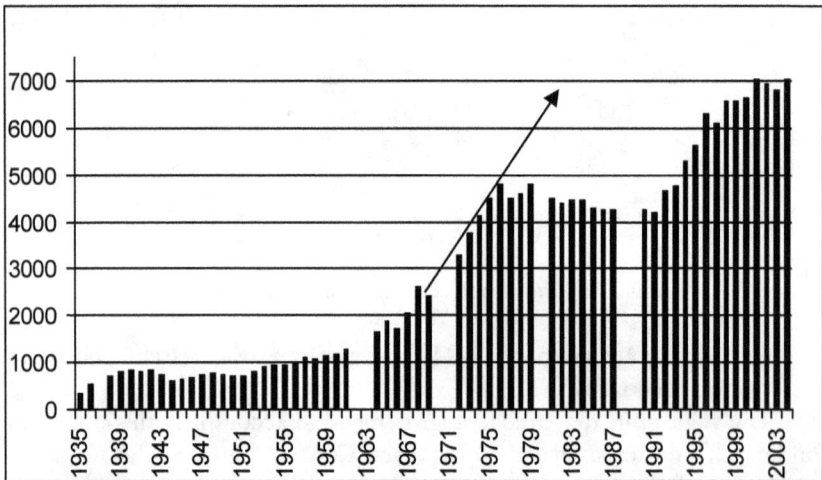

The years 1988 to 1996 may have been the most intense and confusing years in the history of American archaeology. This was the climax of the NHPA-funded Post-processual preservation era. It was the highpoint of the Processual-Postprocessual debates, when hyper-reflexive and culturally relativistic discourse was common. CRM reached peak status as well, readily stopping a political assault against NHPA in the mid-1990s. These were also the years that the preservation ethic fully saturated SAA via the "Save the Past for the Future" campaign. The climax culminated in 1996 with SAA adopting its popular Ethics Statements.

Since this climax, much has changed. The intellectual debates successfully closed and something new is developing. The preservation ethic is now more about ethics than preservation. CRM lingered a few years as its Phase 3 came to a close and is now in a vulnerable position. The most obvious threat is the April 2005 proposed amendments to the NHPA that would weaken its Section 106 process. This active proposal moved CRM into Phase 4, which has two parts: the time leading up to an inflection point--the point of no return--and afterword, the precipitous decline.

CRM Approaching Freefall

Phase 2 and Phase 4 of industry cycles are similar because they are periods of rapid change with inflection points. They also represent positive and negative high-energy phases, respectively. In CRM, the negative energy is rising.

Currently (2005), NHPA is the hub of the CRM industry. Other federal laws feed into it, and state and local compliance programs are often modeled after it. Forty years after NHPA enactment, the CRM compliance process is at maximum capacity with nowhere else to expand federal historic preservation policy. Likewise, the consultant industry created around it is overly competitive, keeping wages low. CRM, the most industrious part of American archaeology, is an aged industry that has worn out its welcome. American society values historic preservation but it is also increasingly resistant to standardized federal compliance. Having entered Phase 4, CRM's decline is accelerating. Figure 16-2 shows a partially developed bell-shaped curve of CRM field projects. From the mid-1980s through 2000, fieldwork nationwide declined nearly 40 percent. The long-term trend is downward, with the slope getting steeper. CRM Phase 3, the maturity phase, was a period of declining fieldwork as planning processes expanded across a generally fixed environment (fixed number of federal agencies, fixed corridors for projects, fixed number of federal lands, etc.) that led to redundancies in project locations, diminishing opportunities for fieldwork, and diminishing returns from fieldwork. As planning successes compound, fieldwork continues to decline, and the industry notches downward even further.

Significant changes to the industry are also underway. Politicians are re-evaluating NHPA. The standardizing aspects of it, the Section 106 process, are targeted for reduction, while customizing aspects of it, Preserve America and Certified Local Government programs, are being enhanced (customizing changes were made as Public Law 109-453 in 2006). Likewise, the office of the Keeper of the National Register of Historic Places was severely reorganized in 2005. The Advisory Council for Historic Preservation (ACHP), the NHPA supporting agency, revised its policy document (36.CFR.800) in 2004, such that its control over the Section 106 process was weakened, and its two offices were consolidated in 2005. Additionally, ACHP is now administering part of the Preserve America program, likely a new direction for the agency.

Figure 16-2: The NADB Wave.

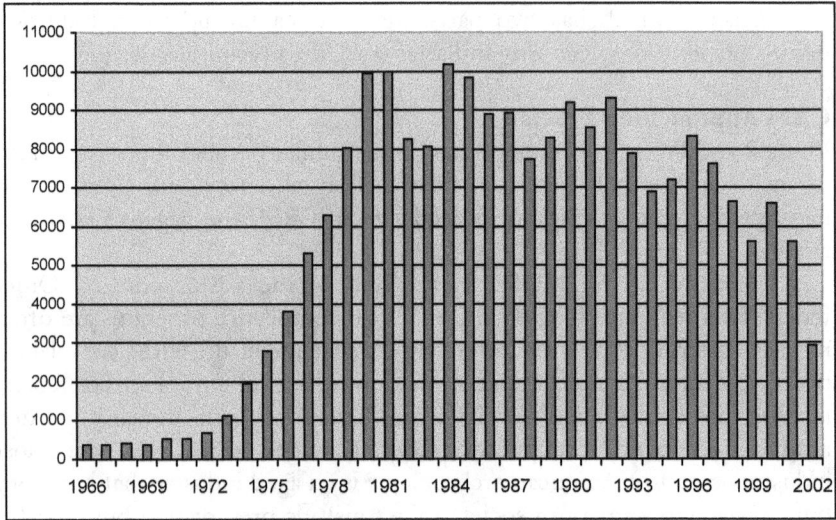

The NADB Wave shows the explosive growth and steady decline of CRM fieldwork in American archaeology. The chart plots the number of reports per year from 1966 to 2001 from 18 states as listed in the National Archaeological Database (NADB), August 2004 update. These states have fairly complete listings for those years: Alabama, Alaska, California, Colorado, Delaware, Hawaii, Iowa, Kansas, Kentucky, Maryland, Minnesota, Montana, Ohio, Oklahoma, Oregon, Texas, Utah, and Vermont. All other states do not fully participate in the database. The NADB is not a comprehensive list of reports and publications, and contains redundancies. This sample uses 212,110 listings from the approximate 354,244 total within NADB.

Stress from these changes is increasing, as expressed in frequent negative commentaries on industry chat boards. Additional stress is coming in the form of another value shift. In CRM Phase 4, the tensions between the ethics of archaeological scholarship and historic preservation will reappear as archaeologists again struggle with reprioritizing their values. A new ethic is emerging that involves Public Archaeology and multi-vocal interpretive discourse. CRM hasn't breached the inflection point of Phase 4 yet. But it will--in one to five years. While the proposed 2005 NHPA amendments put CRM into Phase 4, something else will trigger the inflection point. This larger threat to CRM and all American archaeology is the rising wave of Baby Boomer retirements.

Going Critical

The Baby Boomer wave rolling through American society is bringing great changes. The US economy expanded to accommodate this large generation as they entered the workforce. Most of American archaeology's growth since 1966 is due to this expansion. The American workforce, however, will contract as the Baby Boomers retire, and archaeology will also contract unless it uses the wave to its advantage.

While American archaeology is currently not in decline, as seen by SAA reaching a membership high in 2004, the profession is not expanding either. The profession has a high turnover rate, and staffing has been on a plateau for about 20 years. Zero growth in staffing can be inferred from SAA membership patterns. Table 16-1 and Figure 16-1 show membership patterns going back to 1935. After growing rapidly from 1966 to 1976, membership declined in the 1980s because the profession was bifurcated. On Figure 16-1, a straight line has been drawn to represent the rapid growth slope extended to 1984, when the Baby Boomer expansion ended. This speculative curve indicates what SAA membership could have been if there had not been a bifurcation in the profession. Quantitative projections actually suggest that American archaeology greatly overshot the plateau in the early 1980s and pulled back in the mid-1980s. The number of field reports generated in the 1980s (Figure 16-2) supports the idea that the rapid growth rate continued well into that decade. Growth in the profession ended when the Baby Boomer expansion into the workforce ended.

When the forthcoming labor contraction sets in, two things will happen. First, the number of archaeologists will decline disproportionately. The Baby Boomers are currently about 48 percent of the profession, based on the 1994 SAA census (Zeder 1997) compared to the 2004 total. Baby Boomers entering American archaeology created a growth rate of almost 11 percent during the years 1966–1976 (Table 16-1). Since demographic waves generally have symmetrical characteristics, the decline rate will be equivalent. The retirement of 48 percent of the profession will compound to reduce staffing by nearly 75 percent during the years 2009 through 2016. At the same time, American archaeology will enter into an era of leadership crisis. Baby Boomers are not evenly distributed across their generation. Two-thirds of this group is bunched at the oldest end, the mid-50s to 61 (Association Research Inc. 2005:3). As this generation controls American archaeology, the retirement of the senior management level will break the social networks that keep the industry functional, and there will be fewer people in important positions to advocate for CRM. Academia will decline as well, lagging CRM as enrollments decline. Whole programs, businesses, and departments will be consolidated or terminated.

Initially, the contraction will be considered a labor shortage. Actually, it will be a large imbalance between labor supply and demand that vanishes as managers decide that fewer staff is appropriate. Vacancies will not be refilled unless they are viewed as essential or beneficial; archaeology is not normally essential to society, nor is its benefits widely acknowledged. Archaeology, especially CRM, is in position to be eliminated. Therefore, it has to be repositioned, taking advantage of the demographic trend. The most important task is to create new jobs in new areas for entry-level and mid-career archaeologists. These new positions and work venues must have growth potential, meaning they will not be CRM jobs. The new job market instead is Public Archaeology. Changing the job descriptions of those who are not ready to retire toward different types of work is also important. People currently doing mostly CRM tasks need to do more interpretive projects engaging the public, such as Passport in Time. Finally, retired archaeologists need to stay involved as long as possible, volunteering or working on a temporary basis.

Conclusion

American archaeology is approaching another milestone in its history. On the one hand, its intellectual vigor has successfully completed a growth curve through academic debates. More phases of intellectual growth are to come. On the other hand, the CRM cycle has run into a decline phase. It will likely shrink to a minimum level. Finally, all American archaeology is threatened by the demographic changes ongoing in American society. The best way to take advantage of these changes is to place young people in new jobs in Public Archaeology. We know that the particulars of history do not repeat themselves; but cycles do. Look again at Figure 16-2, renaming it the Public Archaeology Wave of the Future. In 1968, Salvage Archaeology was declining and CRM was on the horizon. Today, CRM is declining and Public Archaeology is on the horizon. We could have that entire wave ahead of us because it represents another Baby Boomer transformation of our society.

from: CRM: Beyond its Peak. *The SAA Archaeological Record* 6(1): 30-33, 2006.

17 GOING PUBLIC

Previously, forecasts for significant socioeconomic change for the United States (US) and for cultural resource management (CRM) were made (Moore 2005a, 2006a). The claim is that a large demographic shift, the retirement of the Baby Boomer generation, threatens the future of American archaeology. As US society and economy will be significantly changing then so too will the conditions for why, when, and where archaeology gets done (Van der Leeuw and Redman 2002:597). The goal here is to identify the new conditions and values that could lead archaeology for many years.

Over the next decade, American archaeologists should take advantage of the coming demographic shift by expanding their applied talents into a growing market place, the leisure industries. Through numerous excavations, archaeologists can provide recreation that is interesting to Americans. This will take the profession further into the public domain, perhaps ending up on Main Street America. This expansion in infrastructure can be achieved through customization, an additional trend that is transforming America.

Customization

One of the more memorable Baby Boomer sayings has been "Think globally, act locally." This phrase expresses a customized value. Most everything in the US is being localized or personalized, and yet it is all tied to macro level current affairs. Localization and personalization are varieties of customization, a process that emphasizes flexibility at the point of action. Customization is a democratic and diversifying process, driven by technological proficiency and favorable values that encourage innovation and open economic markets.

Customization is replacing standardization, the process that saturated

US society with standardized products, services, and values about standards. Standardization emphasized uniformity, consistency, conformity, and congruency--of and between products, of and between social institutions, and behaviors across situations. Standardization is also expressed as normative concepts within the sciences. Standardization developed over most of the nineteenth century and climaxed in the early twentieth century. Sprouting from standardization, customization began in earnest after World War II. Customization inserts multiple standardized products and services, along with values promoting flexibility, into every conceivable situation such that their placement is targeted or appears distinctive.

Customization replaces one-size-fits-all and cookie-cutter standards with values that promote flexibility, diversity, convenience, and fine-tuning. 401k plans are replacing pensions because 401ks are customizable and pensions are not. In warfare, aerial carpet bombing was a standardized tactic; today's smart-bombings are targeted strikes. In education the Standards movement is eroding because customization is penetrating from all directions, from personalized curricula to personalized websites and student accounts with debit cards at colleges. In the workplace, workflow processes are customized to technological changes. Frequent adjustments and upgrades create adaptable quick-learning workers. Knowledge is no longer viewed as static but transitory. Rules and regulations are impermanent. In terms of political and business leadership, people want rules from the top that are flexible at the point of use, the bottom. Customization recognizes that what works well in one context may not work well in other similar contexts, and adjusting "standards" for that knowledge.

Customization also creates possibilities for excessive diversity. Retail stores previously sold few varieties of tennis shoes; now there are athletic shoes for every conceivable function. Socially, some people embrace multiculturalism and moral relativity while others tolerate or resist them.

Local Heritage Management

As an industry, historic preservation is localizing. CRM, led by the National Historic Preservation Act (NHPA), is becoming local heritage management, to be led by state and local policies with commercial ties to economic development, tourism, recreation, and education. Some states, like California and New York, are several years into this transformation; many states have hardly begun.

The outcome of this process is diversity of local preservation implementation. In 2003 the City of Fort Collins acquired the Lindenmeier site as part of its Soapstone Prairie Natural Area, a local conservation area. In 2005, Hamilton County Parks and Recreation, in Indiana, unveiled six miles of recreation trails within its Strawtown Koteewi Park, visiting its numerous archaeological sites. In Cortez, Colorado, the Indian Camp Ranch subdivision has archaeological concerns written into its homeowner association bylaws. Congress is also providing new customizing legislations; 36 bills are currently being considered that relate to National Heritage Areas which integrate economic development, tourism, historic preservation, and local planning.

All the recent NHPA enhancements have been customizing ones. The Preserve America Initiative, its associated Executive Order (EO 13287), and the current amendments before Congress expand preservation initiatives at the local level. In the future the NHPA likely won't be the centerpiece legislation driving historic preservation because there will be numerous federal legislations targeting different issues and thousands at the local level.

The standardized Section 106 process of the NHPA can be customized by replacing its focus on identifying national historic properties with a process that identifies multiple categories of useful resources across multiple jurisdictions. For example, inventories could identify resources that meet the listing criteria for local, state, and national registers of historic properties, and, resources that are suitable as tourist sites or educational ones where training could be conducted.

Local communities are wide-open to archaeologists for infrastructural expansion. From the 2000 census the US has 3,142 counties and 239 large cities. Within these, there are possibly 50 active municipal archaeology programs today. In ten years there could be 1,000 programs. Cressey et al (2003) and Kenny and Murray (2003) offer useful insight on ways to integrate archaeology into community planning.

Recreation Archaeology

The retirement of the Baby Boomers ushers in another era of social change for the US. Leisure industries will benefit greatly from this, even if the economy turns negative. The best way to accommodate this change is by personalizing archaeology to the public. To accomplish this, an infrastructure is needed.

Recreation Archaeology, as a variety of Public Archaeology, includes volunteer programs, paid participant programs, and travel-expedition programs. Two thousand of these programs need to be spread around the county. There is also time to develop this infrastructure. The Baby Boomer wave of retirements begins about 2009 but the heyday of Recreation Archaeology will be 2016 to 2034, the years with maximum retiree participation. A few hundred enterprising archaeologists can make it happen.

Half of the needed recreation programs can develop along with the local heritage management expansion described above. The Community

Archaeology programs in Alexandria and Fairfax Counties in Virginia are two examples that have been operating this way for many years. The other half can come from numerous sources. Every college, university, museum, for-profit, nonprofit, and local archaeological society can run these programs. For example, in Northern Virginia there is the Mount Vernon volunteer program, run by a non-profit organization. The University of West Florida is establishing seven Public Archaeology programs across that state. Likewise, fifty more centers like Crow Canyon need to be spread around the country. There is also room for a few more travel programs like what The Archaeological Conservancy offers. Lastly, almost every large federal land managing agency will be running volunteer programs at full capacity in the near future.

Recreation programs are timely in two important ways. First, they are the essence of customizing archaeology to the public because participation is a personal action. Second, recreation and volunteerism will gain recognition as key ingredients within the US economy. Politicians and high-level managers will be creating these programs instead of trying to cut them. Recreation Archaeology will become a leisure industry that replaces CRM as the dominant career track within the profession.

Marketing Popular Culture

To be successful at Recreation Archaeology significant multimedia exposure and interesting excavation topics are needed. The first is already in hand because archaeology has become a modest theme within popular culture (Holtorf 2005). The Indiana Jones icon generated this popularity. Significant media currently include the Archaeology Channel, the History Channel, the Discovery Channel, and shows like *Stargate SG-1*. There are also video games and mystery-adventure novels that have archaeology as a subject matter. Other important media include information web pages, such as archaeology.about.com and archaeologyfieldwork.com. All these exposures indicate that archaeology will remain as popular culture.

The second item for success is interesting excavation topics. Going forward, archaeologists must focus on topics that are appealing to the general public, topics that draw much media attention and numerous volunteers. The reason for this is that during the coming leisure economy Americans will be overwhelmed with the choices presented to them on how to use their leisure time. To compete in this market, archaeologists have to maintain high visibility with fascinating projects. Overly academic topics will do poorly in a leisure economy.

The way to compete strongly is to identify useful themes within American popular culture and then structure projects around them. This is target marketing. For example, in Oklahoma (Moore 2005b) themes that have local and regional appeal include the relocation of Native Americans to Indian Territory and the Western theme, as in the archaeology of cowboy culture. Another theme is "Firsts" because Americans like knowing the first occurrence of any type of event or process, and the people connected with them. This could include excavating sites like the first school house or the first homestead in a county; and, it also includes Paleo-Indian studies. Genealogy is another theme, it being the most common hobby in the US. For this theme a Firsts homestead project might also be marketed as a genealogy one. A catch-all theme might be Exotic-Spectacular-Rare where anything that is considered exotic, spectacular, or rare is interesting to Americans. For Oklahoma archaeology this includes sites that display well and have a rich collection of artifacts and features, such as Spiro.

It is easy to decide if a theme is popular or not. If it can be presented as an episode on the Archaeology Channel or as an essay in *Archaeology* magazine then it is a popular theme. The main value of a Public Archaeology project will be its public appeal; scholarly contributions and historic preservation are secondary concerns.

This use of popular culture themes is commercial. It is an essential trait of this new Public Archaeology. The profession isn't giving up museum, academic, or preservation concerns; Public Archaeology is another venue expanding beyond them because they currently are diminishing venues. Going-public means taking applied archaeology into new territory and creating new opportunities. It means focusing on external interests deriving from the general public rather than the internal concerns of the profession.

The Civil War

A catalyst is needed to create growth for all areas of archaeology, a topic to focus on that can create pin-action for the profession. In bowling, to get a strike the lead pin must be hit hard, allowing the ricochet effect to knock down the rest, the desired result. Likewise, archaeologists need a popular topic that can spread its rewards throughout the profession. The Civil War is an excellent lead pin because it is the most important heritage related theme in American popular culture.

Conveniently, the sesquicentennial of the war will be the years 2011 through 2015. Archaeologists have to help facilitate the enjoyment of this anniversary for hundreds-of-thousands, maybe millions, of people by having large open-area excavations available for public volunteerism and visitation everywhere possible during those years. This anniversary is a Public Archaeology opportunity that cannot be missed because it is likely the catalyst that drives the next revolution in American archaeology. Timing is important; concentration on the Civil War for its anniversary should guarantee significant growth in all areas of the profession.

The last anniversary of the Civil War, 1961-1965, was surrounded by social unrest. The social unrest attendant with this next anniversary has already begun (e.g. immigration reform; antiwar protests). Thus, the new Public Archaeology will likely have a stronger social reform agenda than the previous Post-processual cycle did.

Incongruity is Valuable

American archaeology is obviously customizing. One legacy of the Processual-Post Processual debates is that they transitioned much of archaeology away from standardized conceptions of culture, science, and archaeology into customizing ones. Few people care about Culture Areas or the Midwestern Taxonomic System anymore because they were standardized, homogeneity-laden concepts from the early twentieth century. Diffusionism as normative carpet bombing style interpretation is unacceptable today; diffusionism as localized targeted interpretation (e.g. Jones and Klar 2005) is acceptable because it doesn't automatically modify interpretations anywhere else. Archaeologists today offer generalizations that express the heterogeneous, multi-dynamic, and multi-vocalic character of culture change, and, the new common denominator of the archaeological record is local variation.

American historical archaeology is already well customized. While numerous definitions of the subfield have been offered none are dominant; its practitioners prefer this unbounded, no rules, landscape. It may be at risk of excessive diversity. If unity is to be found it is that current results can be considered globalized particularism with individual sites interpreted as local negotiations of assorted global processes.

Customization has brought problems into the profession. On one hand, archaeologists now respect local variation. Some CRM permitting procedures now require consultants to have local experience and knowledge. On the other hand, customization doesn't necessarily create local experts. The American workforce is more flexible, mobile, and impermanent today than any time in the last seventy-five years, and this is increasing. Localization is not about maximizing local knowledge but instituting flexibility at the point of use and implementation. Customization creates adaptable quick learners capable of targeted action using portable communications tools. This is necessary in today's world which treats information as transitory, including archaeological information. Local knowledge certainly has merits but mandating it is counterproductive when the workforce is being pulled in another direction.

Customization is diversifying archaeology. It is now acceptable to speak of multiple archaeologies, even if presented by non-archaeologists. Looking ahead, boundaries between professional and non-professional will likely blur, forcing negotiations with other interested parties such as modern material culture specialists, Native Americans, and relic collectors. The Secretary of Interior's definitions for two kinds of archaeologists (prehistoric; historic) are also approaching obsolescence. Several definitions may be needed or one that is exceptionally generic.

Archaeologists today have more roles in society than previously. During the standardized years, archaeologists had few roles with the primary ones being authorities or educators. The new customized archaeologist shifts roles based on context, sometimes being an authority, sometimes a mentor, translator, facilitator, bottleneck, negotiator, mediator, or bystander. In Public Archaeology a competent archaeologist knows their many contexts, such that debunking myths and folklore may be appropriate in some situations while in most others enabling and facilitating them are the appropriate actions.

Going-public means that archaeologists respect values from the public domain and nurture them. This new ethic is based in the wisdom that, more frequently than not, the external interests of the public are more important to the profession's future than are the internal concerns of its practitioners; the metaphors about archaeology held by members of the public are usually more important to them than professional accuracy and correctness. Incongruity is useful, allowing archaeologists to have their own professional opinions while supporting multiple opinions from the general public.

The key metaphor of archaeology that the public seems to care about is the process of discovery (Holtorf 2005), best evoked by the term "digging." What the public seems to want from archaeology is an outlet for digging. The purpose of Public Archaeology is to create situations that allow people to follow the process of discovery, and to self-discover whatever it is they want to discover while experiencing archaeology.

Digging for Prosperity

Customization in America has many years to its climax. Meanwhile, recognize that Americans have the wondrous ability to take trends into the absurd. Standardization climaxed with people referring to their behaviors as machine-like. Today, Americans believe that everyone is unique and special, yet they aren't quite certain how to act on such claims. Excessive diversification can happen to archaeology. How many versions of it will there be? How multi-vocalic can it become? No one knows. But let's try to avoid the absurdities. Out there somewhere is a customized compromise that most of us can live with such that we'll recognize each other as archaeologists when we meet.

Throughout these forecasting essays the years 2009-2016 have been viewed as important. In those years the Baby Boomer retirements will reach critical mass such that economic and political crisis are likely. The rapid decline of CRM is very likely. The leisure industries will grow exponentially.

And, we'll have the anniversary of the Civil War with its attendant social unrest. Understanding these changes, we can position archaeology for prosperity by expanding local heritage management and recreation archaeology. Both are accommodations to a changing society. Both create new jobs in new places. If the economy goes badly, these changes also position us to absorb large numbers of laborers, giving us an essential role in society, a unique opportunity.

Everything recommended means substantial increases in excavations because digging is the best way to keep the public interested in archaeology. Digging is our leverage. If the economy stays strong digging will ensure growth while going public. If the economy becomes adverse, digging safeguards our profession.

from: Going Public: Customization and American Archaeology. *The SAA Archaeological Record* 6(3): 16-19, 2006.

18 A STUDY IN REFLEXIVE ARCHAEOLOGY

Introduction

The works of William Shakespeare are usually good for a quote. A line from *Henry VIII* is offered, as it expresses the end-desire of many restless Baby Boomers working in archaeology: "I know myself now, and I feel within me a peace above all earthly dignities, a still and quiet conscience..." Here, I suggest that the Boomers have many years to wait before finding their inner peace and quiet; they won't get there until they are elders. When they do find it American archaeology will be very different from what it is now.

Since the mid 1980s reflexive perspectives in archaeology have grown to be commonplace. These perspectives will assist us in understanding the human condition via analysis of its material remains, which is the ever elusive goal of archaeology. However, they are not a lasting effort as they are part of a cyclical process that has about ten to fifteen years still to run. In addition, before they phase out, they have one last major task to accomplish, the redefinition of archaeology.

To further this along several questions are addressed: What is reflexive archaeology? Is ethnography of archaeology a viable approach to doing it? And, where is the profession going? While there are many ways to be reflexive about archaeology, the ethnographic approach will be most productive. As background context for these issues a brief social history of recent American archaeology and ethnography is offered, demonstrating that each is embedded in the cycles of American history, generational changes, and current affairs. From this review it becomes evident that archaeology has a serious problem to resolve, the avoidance of getting stuck in identity traps as the profession is redefined.

Self Awareness, Reflexivity, and Individualism

Reflexivity is currently a broad ranging concept. It is a complex version of self awareness which, at its core, is the simple act of thinking about and referencing one's self. Self awareness can be personal, as in using the words *I* and *me*; it can also be inclusively collective, as in words like *we* and *us*. Self awareness and reflexivity don't have to be verbal either since most communication is nonverbal--just point at yourself. The complexity of reflexivity is in the cognitive ability to make many distinctions, with some of them being self-referential, and being able to make judgments and decisions about those distinctions. Reflexivity is also inherently analytical; it is self analysis, individual and collective. Self analysis can also be intense, as in being self-critical (*I screwed up*) or boastful (*We're better than them*); likewise, it can be nearly neutral, as in answering a roll call with *I'm here*, an analysis that recognizes that you are not somewhere else. The degree of reflexive intensity can be expressed as a range from extreme to nearly neutral. The more intense it is, the more likely reflexivity will be formalized (visiting a psychologist; writing a research design) or ritualized (a birthday party; an archaeology conference), and it will be temporary in duration.

It has long been recognized that self awareness is an important variable in defining humanness, and perhaps many mammals. However, academic interest in and expansion of the reflexivity concept is fairly recent (Table 18-1). Before 1930 reflexivity was primarily a mathematical and linguistic concept; activities that today would be called reflexive were then simply called by their common names, such as meditation, confession, and diary writing. During the 1930s the use of reflexivity expanded into philosophy and psychology. In the mid 1960s its broad usage as a generic for critical self awareness became commonplace in academia as American society began a spiritual awakening known as the Consciousness Revolution (discussed later); its use has been exponential since then.

Table 18-1 shows the results of Google Scholar word searches from 1880 to mid 2006. The numbers presented are the number of hits per search, each hit representing a publication in which the word Reflexive appears, it being the most common form for Reflexivity. Its frequency of use in *American Anthropologist* (start date 1888) and for *American Antiquity* (start date 1935) are also presented. In *American Anthropologist* early uses of the word were in linguistic discussions. The first use of the word in its broad contemporary meaning appeared in a paper by Stocking (1966). Anthropological debates about reflexive critique first appear in a paper by Kaplan (1974). The first appearance of its contemporary usage in *American Antiquity* was in a paper by Leone (1982). For Google Scholar, gross numbers may be slightly biased toward recent years as older publications may not be searchable; for *American Anthropologist* and *American Antiquity* the recent interest in reflexivity is clearly evident.

Table 18-1: The frequency of usage for the word Reflexive in scholarly studies.

Years	Google Scholar	American Anthropologist	American Antiquity
1880-1889	48	1	na
1890-1899	84	3	na
1900-1909	120	9	na
1910-1919	132	11	na
1920-1929	162	3	na
1930-1939	287	3	0
1940-1949	416	5	0
1950-1959	742	1	0
1960-1969	1,650	4	0
1970-1979	4,800	6	0
1980-1989	9,020	16	4
1990-1999	24,300	59	14
2000-2006	26,700	32	8

Source: Google Scholar advanced search at http://scholar.google.com/ last accessed on October 5, 2006.

Argued later is that reflexive discussions in academia are events associated with the Baby Boomer and Generation X generations, both of which are strongly individualistic and self centered. Younger following generations are not individualistic or self centered; they are outward directed, socially focused, and will eventually replace individualism with values focused on community connectedness. Thus, Table 18-1 likely reflects the early half of a bell shaped curve of Reflexivity usage with the 2000-2009 decade being the peak.

The Staging of Reflexive Archaeology

All culture and human conduct have reflexive patterns within them. Some individuals and generations are more prone to focus on them than are others. In academia the study of humans by humans is institutionalized reflexive behavior; the very purpose of archaeology is reflexive by definition. What, then, is reflexive archaeology?

Reflexive archaeology is envisioning the profession as being on the great stage of life and studying it as such. Archaeology is conceptualized as social and cultural practice and performance; archaeologists are just people doing the usual things that people do. The digging, cataloging, conferences, ethics, theories and methods, the artifacts, books, journals, and tools of the profession are all cultural manifestations. It's a neat trick to take a knowledge producing profession and turn it sideways, tilt it, and look at it from a different angle. Moreover, archaeologists are the ones who are strong advocates for staging archaeology; it is a new kind of self analysis for them. Reflexive archaeology, as a specific version of reflexive behavior, will be referred to as RA going forward.

Placing archaeology on a stage has been around for several years. Earlier advocates of RA equated archaeology with theater (Pearson and Shanks, 2000; Tilly, 1989) because archaeology is conceptualized as performance. These folks seem to have revived the truism that "All the World's a Stage," a famous line from William Shakespeare's play *As You Like It*. The term *craft* is also used to describe archaeology (Shanks and McGuire, 1996) because this is how actors describe their work, and, it also associates with the concept of craftsmanship and the dashed lines separating the arts and crafts, and art and science.

The conceptualization of archaeology as craftwork and theatrical performance are ways to demystify the aura of professional science and history that typically envelop the profession. It strips away some of the power and authority ascribed to professionals. At the same time, these conceptions are nostalgic, rationalizing and perpetuating the social structures that generate them (Chadwick, 2003). Like the old guild system, one enters craftwork as an apprentice; next, one becomes a journeyman, and then a master. These titles are similar to career paths in academia (undergraduate/graduate/professor; Assistant Professor/Associate Professor/Professor). In higher education, this social structure is one of the few feudalistic structures still residual in American society. Placing archaeology on Shakespeare's stage is appropriate for conducting RA; however, to improve archaeology, and science overall, RA needs to be transformative, a vector of change not continuity.

Ethnographies of Archaeology

In the 1980s and 1990s, in the midst of the Processual-Post Processual debates, the post-processualists made many calls for reflexivity and self-reflection; Potter's (1991b) essay is still cited often. Those early discussions were ethical, moralistic, and activist oriented; archaeology was to be a platform for promoting social reforms and empowering the disempowered. Moore (1994b) cautioned that these issues were ironic and that narcissism, losses of identity, or feelings of dehumanization, were likely outcomes of such behavior. Those generic calls for self analysis eventually transformed into a focused analysis of archaeology via ethnography. Edgeworth (1990), Roveland (2000), Goodwin (1994), Gero (1996) and Castaneda (1991) were early pioneers; this early block of work was phase one of RA. Currently, much ethnography of archaeology is done in Europe, Turkey, and Latin America (Bender et al., 2006; Hodder, 2000, 2003; Sandlin and Bey, 2006) and phase two will eventually encompass North America.

To get a better picture of ethnography of archaeology this section briefly analyzes a recent book, *Ethnographies of Archaeological Practice*

(Edgeworth, 2006). The book will be treated as an artifact with social implications and referred to as *Ethnographies* going forward. In *Ethnographies* Edgeworth collects fifteen essays. The contributors are divided equally between archaeologists-doing-ethnography and professional ethnographers. These insider and outsider perspectives are interesting to compare; for example, chapters by archaeologists tend to minimize formal social theory while several chapters by sociologists and social anthropologists have explicit theoretical perspectives.

Two chapters are useful examples of the genre. Carman (2006) describes how archaeology is part of the social and political economy of its host countries, and yet is able to maintain a sense of autonomy. He argues that in the United Kingdom archaeological projects operate in spaces that are physically separated from other activities occurring around them. Project crews also have social relations that are focused inward, and are focused on the tasks at hand; simply, archaeological crews typically have strong inner directed cohesion. This makes them similar to the way other work crews that live and travel together (oil rig crews, military units) are organized and socialized rather than the outward perspective that other occupations might have (public administrators, retail sales). Moore (1986) also documented cohesion for a crew in the United States.

Rodriguez (2006) discusses a Mayan community in Mexico that stalled an archaeological project and stopped the development of a museum because they cultivate the land upon which archaeology was to be done. These locals argued that their control of the land was based on events dating within fairly recent history. On the other hand, archaeologists, who wanted to foster tourism by developing a museum at the site, tried to emphasize local's associations with much older Mayan culture. The locals were successful in asserting their claim that their more recent history was more important to them than archaeologist's opinions about prehistoric Mayan culture, and a museum was not built. In that essay Archaeologists appear to be amazed that non-archaeologists don't have the same opinions and values about the past that archaeologists do. It demonstrates that an inward focused profession will likely be clumsy as it tries to effect change outside itself, even if the change is well intended.

Ethnography can be very helpful in assisting archaeology toward understanding its place in society and the many roles it can assume; likewise, it can identify social weaknesses that archaeologists themselves are unable to see. All the chapters in *Ethnographies* either describe or demonstrate the inward focus of the profession or its awkward relations with non-professionals. Contemporary archaeology has a strong insider/outsider distinction, partly due to its crew based culture and, as discussed later, partly due to the cycles of history. The inward focus and structure of archaeology, its day to day work environments and socializations that create a community of archaeologists, can be called its microcosm. The macrocosm of archaeology is where archaeologists look outward from their profession and engage with non-professionals, locals, and the general public.

As will be discussed later, American society oscillates between the extremes of individualism and community connectedness or "communitas". Currently, Americans are experiencing extreme individualism. Thus, the momentum will soon swing back toward a community focused perspective. American archaeologists also follow this pattern. They are currently at their peak of social fragmentation, being a community of individualists pursuing individual goals; over the next decade they will transform into a community of team players pursuing team goals. During this recent individualistic era they have also focused on their microcosm, damaging their connections with outsiders, the public. Over time, this focus will shift towards a moderately strong emphasis on the macrocosm, improving relations with the public. Additionally, American archaeologists are concurrently redefining both their microcosm and macrocosm because they have begun a transformation of their identity. To assist understanding these interrelated changes, a review of ethnography's recent history and American social history is needed.

The Landscape of Ethnography

In general, practitioners of RA have not linked the trends in archaeology with trends in ethnography. This is a manifestation of the profession's current fragmentation and individualization. However, American archaeology is tied to American social anthropology, as both are usually subsumed under the academic field of anthropology; currently the tie is weak but their histories are unified. Ethnography is historically associated with two professions, sociology and social anthropology (also known as cultural anthropology). Ethnography is also known as participant observation and as qualitative research.

Ethnographers have also done their own reflexive ethnography as numerous studies about doing and experiencing ethnography have been written. Whyte's (1955) appendix to the enlarged edition of his classic *Street Corner Society* is one of the earliest reflexive discussions about doing ethnographic fieldwork. Berreman (1962) followed with his *Behind Many Masks*, which is another classic. Hymes (1972) edited a volume called *Reinventing Anthropology* that was a major reflexive assessment of Anthropology; it raised the self-conscious level of Anthropology to a new high. Ruby's (1982) edited volume, *A Crack in the Mirror*, placed reflexive perspectives into mainstream social anthropology. Concurrently in Europe, Pierre Bourdieu spent much of his career writing about reflexive sociology (Bourdieu and Wacquant, 1992). Some of this reflexive work also uses the theatrical analogy (Schechner, 1985). By the 1990s essays on realistic experiences in ethnography were common (Lareau and Shultz, 1996), leading Robertson (2002) to suggest that reflexive discussions were a requirement for ethnographic studies to be deemed excellent.

A second trend starting in the 1970s was the establishment of new genres, the ethnographies of science, work, leisure-tourism, and education. The ethnography of science became an overnight sensation with the publication of *Laboratory Life* by Latour and Woolgar (1979). Since then there have been more ethnographies of laboratory life, ethnographies of ethnographic field schools, and of the field experiences of ecologists (Gmelch and Gmelch, 1999; Lynch, 1985; Roth and Bowen, 2001; Wallace, 1999), all activities similar to archaeological research. Moore's (1986) early ethnography of an archaeological field school was part of this trend rather than the later RA discussions.

A recent third trend in Ethnography has been the rebirth of applied social anthropology. This field had a brief era of productivity (roughly 1930 to 1960) and then struggled for several years. During the 1970s and 1980s this field revived becoming a productive consulting industry. American business leaders feared the rise of Japanese economic power and to offset that perceived threat, ethnographers studied Japanese and American business practices so that American businesses could be made more competitive (Doktor, 1983; Hamada, 1985; Redding, 1987). Ethnographers working within businesses are common today (Jordan, 2002) and much of this work is done in conjunction with quantitative surveys. Through Applied Anthropology, ethnography has gained widespread understanding and acceptance within American society, especially in the workplace where it is called Business Anthropology. This applied trend has obvious parallels in archaeology: applied archaeology is found within cultural resource management; and, the work of Alison Wylie (2002) is applied philosophy done upon archaeology.

Applied ethnography, which is about identifying problems and suggesting solutions, is a means for change with ethnographers as change agents. Since RA needs to be a vector of change, phase two of RA should be done as applied ethnography with support from quantitative surveys.

Boomers and Post Modernism
The above trends suggest that the mid 1960s through the 1980s were years of significant change in the social sciences. These were the years that the Baby Boomer generation, folks born between 1943 and 1960 (Strauss and Howe, 1991), entered the American job market. For American archaeology, the profession expanded greatly to accommodate the need to employ so many people from this extra large generation (Moore, 2005a, 2006a); all of academia did too.

The Boomer generation is paradoxical because its archetypical personality is idealistic. Most of it members hold very strong yet diversified opinions about everything; they are an argumentative and polarizing generation, unlike other generational types that are much less argumentative. In the 1960s and 1970s many of these folks danced in the streets as Hippies, challenging the civic authority and social conformity of the 1950s and 1960s; many others went to work, expressing that conformity; many also fought in Vietnam, a controversial war. As Boomers settled in to raise families, some became obsessed with frugality, others with conspicuous consumption, the latter being tagged with the label *Yuppie* (young urban professional).

As a group, the Boomers have been concerned with the meaning of life. In spiritual and ideological terms, many pursued religious fundamentalism while others sought openness through New Age ideology, non-Christian religions, science, atheism, and agnosticism. Whatever choice they made was generally pursued passionately. Throughout the 1980s the generation became inward looking and self absorbed; all versions of self-help (health, mind, body, spirit, motivation, career advice, time management, etc.) became popular commodities. Although not a Boomer, Stephen Covey's (1990) *Seven Habits of Highly Effective People* moved the self help movement to a saturation point. The Boomer "Me Generation" of the 1980s continues to live with self help as a routine concept and behavioral pattern. The opening quote from Shakespeare accurately describes this generation's motivations.

The 1980s was also the decade that Post Modernism became vogue in academic America, as education and scholarly research seems to have attracted a larger percentage of post modern advocates into its ranks than did other occupational areas (accounting, farming). Post Modernism is a heterogeneous movement best described as a rejection of modernism, defined as the period and concepts associated with the rise of the Western World from the late fifteenth century to the present. Some central values in Modernity embrace progress, rationality, science, and conformity to top down hierarchy. Post Modernism rejects those values and promotes values associated with individualism (agency) and ethics; and, reflexive discussions have been the means by which those values are often promoted. Academic Post Modernism of the 1980s and 1990s was a Boomer-led rejection of the most recent modernistic, civic minded, and institutionally focused era that occurred post World War II. The book *Philosophy and the Mirror of Nature* (Rorty, 1979) influenced the academic trend.

In archaeology, many of the oldest Boomers adopted the scientism of the 1960s and 1970s New Archaeology. That version of archaeology would have been appealing to them because it searched for "natural laws" within the archaeological record. Superficially, this quest for the essence of nature seems similar to the works of an earlier idealist generation, the Transcendentalists, typified by Ralph Waldo Emerson (*Nature*, 1936) and David Henry Thoreau (*Walden*, 1854). However, lacking any expression of individualism, the New Archaeology was later abandoned in favor of broader expressions of science, and other perspectives. By the mid 1980s, a critical mass of Boomers seeking individualistic expression and desiring to rationalize those expressions had entered archaeology, and the Processual-Post Processual debate was held with extreme passion.

Post modernism in academia has often been referred to as radical thinking but its 1980s through 1990s phase is best described as rebellious narcissism more akin to the New Age and Self Help ideologies of the Boomer generation than to religious or scientific fundamentalism. The goal of its early practitioners was to replace existing status quos, the received views, with new ones and then sustain those new views from positions of newly attained social power. Its process was Machiavellian because its advocates tore down others to promote themselves, consistent with idealistic inward looking individualism. In archaeology, the post-modernists, that idiosyncratic group collectively known as post-processualists, intellectually shredded processualism, archaeology's version of modern science, and, they waged a dog-eat-dog war among themselves. Today, post modern Boomers control most of archaeology. The current status of post modernism is no longer rebellious; it is status quo and moralistic, seeking a vision and a quiet conscience.

Post modernism and the Boomer generation are inseparable as post modernity is a popular value system within the Boomer generation; phase one of RA was part of that post modern movement. Although post modernism intended to implement social reforms and empower Others, ultimately it became academic self help for archaeology, assisting Boomers in their restructuring of the profession.

However, there is more to the generational connection than might be expected. Post Modernism and its reflexive discussions have been generational events. Take away the fancy words and they are the manifestations of an inner driven generation championing individualism.

Reflexivity and Generational Cycles
American historians have identified cycles that are regular in American history. These cycles have origins in European cycles, and together, they continue nearly in sync. This section follows the concepts of Strauss and Howe (1991, 1997, 2001, and Howe and Strauss, 2000).

The best known cycle consists of the social moments that dramatically shape the social and cultural environment of America. There are two kinds of social moments, spiritual awakenings and secular crises. During spiritual awakenings society focuses on transforming the inner world of personal values and behaviors. There have been six spiritual awakenings that have influenced America (Table 18-2) with the most recent being the Consciousness Revolution (1964-1984). These awakenings have both religious and secular manifestations because they are about self discovery.

During secular crises society focuses on changing the outer world of institutions and public behavior; during these social moments institutions are dramatically changed and society is redirected. There have been six secular crises that have influenced American history, with the last one being the Great Depression-World War II (1929-1946). Previous crises have always climaxed in total warfare; the current Millennial Crisis (2001-present) is in an early phase and hasn't climaxed yet.

The two social moments alternate through time (Table 18-2). The years between the social moments are also described as inner driven and outer driven providing a four part cycle of spiritual awakening, inner driven era, secular crisis, outer driven era, and then the cycle repeats. Strauss and Howe (1991, 1997) describe how this cycle has repeated four times in American history, and a fifth is well underway.

Inner driven eras are when individualism and narcissism pervades society, and topics related to self awareness are popular; these eras follow spiritual awakenings. During outer driven eras society has a strong sense of community (communitas) which suppresses individualism through values of social conformity. Outer driven eras can be described as cultural highs full of artistic and scientific achievement; inner driven eras are when society unravels the social fabric of the preceding high. The dialectical push-pull effect between individualism and community connectedness is well documented in American social history (Bender, 1978; Madsen et al., 1985). Recent inner driven eras were 1908-1929 and 1984-2001; the previous outer driven era was 1946-1964 and was the last time American archaeology focused on its macrocosm.

Strauss and Howe went on to integrate generational attributes into the four part cycle. There have been nineteen generations that have influenced American culture since the beginning of European colonization. These generations are described in four sequential categories or archetypes: idealist, reactive, civic, and adaptive (Table 18-3). The idealist and civic generations are dominant ones, meaning that society is always focused on their needs; the other two are recessive generations that are generally overshadowed by the dominant ones. Similarly, idealistic and reactive generations are individualistic; the other two are outer directed, team oriented, and civic minded.

Important to this reflexive discussion are the idealist and reactive generations (Tables 18-3 & 18-4). Strauss and Howe (1991:74) define an idealist generation as an inner fixated generation who are raised as indulged youths after a secular crisis, they then come of age inspiring a spiritual

Table 18-2: The American pattern of alternating spiritual awakenings and secular crises.

Social Era	Spiritual Awakening	Inner Driven	Secular Crisis	Outer Driven
Tudor Renaissance				x
Protestant Reformation	1517-1542			
Intolerance & Martyrdom		x		
Spanish Armada crisis			1569-1594	
Merrie England				x
Puritan Awakening	1621-1649			
Reaction & Restoration		x		
Glorious Revolution			1675-1704	
Augustan Age of Empire				x
Great Awakening	1727-1746			
French & Indian Wars		x		
American Revolution			1773-1794	
The Era of Good Feelings				x
Transcendental Awakening	1822-1844			
Mexican War & Sectionalism		x		
The American Civil War			1860-1865	
Reconstruction & Gilded Age				x
The Missionary Awakening	1886-1908			
World War I & Prohibition		x		
Great Depression & World War II			1929-1946	
The American High				x
Consciousness Revolution	1964-1984			
Culture Wars		x		
Millennium Crisis			2001-present	

Adapted from Strauss and Howe (1991, 1997, 2001).

awakening, then they fragment into narcissistic young adults, then they become moralistic midlife adults, later they become visionary elders guiding the next secular crisis. The first idealistic generation to influence professional archaeology was the Missionary Generation, birth years 1860-1882. That generation included Americans Alfred Kroeber and Hetty Goldman, and European born Howard Carter. In Table 18-1 the spike in Reflexive usage within *American Anthropologist* during 1910-1919 was due to Missionary linguists pursuing self awareness topics during an inner driven era.

The Boomers were indulged children who went on to have a spiritual awakening (the Consciousness Revolution); they then turned narcissistic during the 1980s and 1990s, giving America it's Me Generation and the Culture Wars; and, currently they are moralistic mid-lifers approaching their elder years having already taken American society into an early arriving secular crisis (because the Boomers ascended to high political office too soon). Given the rapidly expanding use of the reflexive concept since the mid 1960s (Table 18-1), and then the explosive use of it since the mid 1980s, the Boomer generation has probably taken self consciousness to an unprecedented extreme.

Table 18-3: Life cycle changes within the four generational archetypes.

Types/age	Youth 0-21	Young Adults 22-43	Midlife Adults 44-65	Elders 66-87
Idealist	indulged	narcissistic	moralistic	visionary
Reactive	criticized	alienated	pragmatic	reclusive
Civic	protected	heroic	powerful	busy
Adaptive	suffocated	conformist	indecisive	sensitive

Adapted from Strauss and Howe (1991).

Members of reactive generations will also be individualists. Reactionaries spend two thirds of their life queuing off the behavior and values of next-older idealists; the last third is lived in the shadow of the next younger civic generation. Reactionaries grow up as criticized youths, emerge as alienated young adults, mellow into pragmatic midlife adults, and spend their elder years as recluses (Strauss and Howe, 1991:74). The first reactive generation to influence professional archaeology was the Lost Generation, birth years 1883-1900, whose members included Alfred V. Kidder and Ann A. Morris. Reactionaries may also be interested in reflexivity but in a different way. To idealists, reflexivity is a moral or spiritual effort; to reactionaries, reflexivity is a tool to be used, as needed.

Since idealists and reactionaries are both individualists, society reaches its peak of individualism when the idealists are approaching their elder years and when reactionaries are approaching their mature adult years. The

Table 18-4: Recent generations with their types and traits, with archaeologist examples.

Name	Type	Birth years	Traits	Examples
Missionary	idealist	1860-1882	individualistic, dominant, moralistic	A. L. Kroeber H. Goldman H. Carter H. B. Hawes
Lost	reactive	1883-1900	individualistic, recessive, pragmatic	A. V. Kidder A. A. Morris W. Lamb D. A. Garrod
GI "Greatest"	civic	1901-1924	team player, dominant heroic	W. R. Wedel B. J. Meggars J. B. Griffin M. D. Leakey
Silent	adaptive	1925-1942	team player, recessive, classy	J. Deetz C. Irwin-Williams L. Binford A. B. Kehoe
Baby Boomers	idealist	1943-1960	individualistic, dominant, moralistic	I. Hodder D. Pearsall M. Schiffer A. Wylie
Generation X	reactive	1961-1981	individualistic, recessive, pragmatic	J. Kanter L. Wilkie T. de Boer K. J. Dixon
Millennials	civic	1982-2002	team player, dominant heroic	Students in primary school to graduate school
new Progressives	adaptive	2002-	team player, recessive, classy	

Adapted from Strauss and Howe (1991, 1997, 2001) and Howe and Strauss (2000). The Millennials will be heroic and dominant only if they are victorious in the secular crisis climax. Otherwise, the generation fizzles out and merges with adjacent generations; this occurred once previously, after the Civil War, a crisis that arrived early and ended with everyone feeling tragic.

Boomers and Generation Xers are currently in this transition and have recently put American society into its most extreme individualistic status ever recorded. Based on the 2000 census and 2005 household estimates, the US Census Bureau reported in October 2006 that for the first time American married households are no longer the majority household type; they are a "new minority" (StarTribune 2006), estimated at 49.7 percent of households, which was down over fifty percent from the 2000 estimate. All other households are headed by individuals living by themselves, single parent households, or by non-married couples who are cohabitating. This data should be viewed as a peaking of individualism and that the momentum is likely turning the other way, towards strengthening community values. The other two generational types, civics and adaptives, are focused on community values and will eventually suppress individualism as they mature and control society.

The Rhythm of American Modernity

As the cycle has four parts, a spiritual awakening, an era of inward looking individualism, a secular crisis, and an era of outward looking social conformity, it takes four generations to fully rotate. The most recent rotations are reviewed below (Table 18-5).

The last secular crisis was the Great Depression-World War II (1929-1946). During that crisis America solved some of its secular problems, waged total war, and redirected society into superpower status. Before the war, American archaeology was done in crisis mode as New Deal programs sought outlets for putting people to work; archaeology was later suspended for the duration of the war. Afterward was an era of increasing social conformity, a cultural high that took American prosperity to new highs (1946-1964). Institutions were generally effective and efficient. Attempts at excessive conformity can be seen in the McCarthyism of the era; counter trends to the conformity were the Beatnik subculture and the Civil Rights movement. During that cultural high American science reached new levels of development, including a maturing archaeology profession built around Salvage programs; American archaeology was then a community of rising team players pursuing team goals. Next came the Consciousness Revolution (1964-1984), during which a generation of idealists (Boomers) came-of-age and rejected the conformity of the preceding cultural high. Spiritual awakenings are when Americans rediscover youth and individualism, and explore the sacredness of humanity and nature. New Archaeologists of the era may have been ambivalent towards the Sacred but they certainly were passionate in their claims to being scientific while searching for "natural" laws within the archaeological record.

Afterward came an era of increasing individualism (1984-2001) during which American society became inner directed, narcissistic, and argumentative; counter trends are referred to as fundamentalism. During this era institutions thought to be too socially conforming were retooled to accommodate individualism. The Culture Wars, disputes about various acceptable life styles and values, were also fought. The era concluded with society extremely polarized and most of its institutions dysfunctional. The

Table 18-5: Recent rotations of the generational model and American anthropology.

Social Era	Secular Crisis	Outer focus	Awakening	Inner focus	Secular Crisis
Years	1929-1946	1946-1964	1964-1984	1984-2001	2001-present
American events	Depression, WWII	American High	Consciousness Revolution	Culture Wars	Millennial Crisis
Archaeology	Crisis mode archaeology	Salvage Archaeology	New Archaeology debates	Post Modern debates	Identity Crisis
Social Anthropology	Boas & Malinowski schools	Functionalism General systems	Re-definition	Post Modern debates	Reflexive, engaged, & multilateral anthropology

The Millennial secular crisis arrived early by 4 to 12 years because the Silent generation has had no US presidents. The GI generation had seven presidents, from Kennedy to Bush Sr.; next came Boomers Clinton and Bush Jr. The early arriving Boomer presidencies escalated institutional dysfunction and polarization of the nation, and made it appear weak to outside threats, compelling an attack such as 9/11. As of year-end 2006 the aging of generations is reverting to the model, suggesting that this crisis era may be lengthy.

presidential election of 2000 is a good example with the popular vote evenly divided between candidates and the Electoral College process dysfunctional leading to a constitutional crisis. In archaeology, scientism was rejected during the era because it appeared to constrain agency. Throughout the era American archaeology was a community of rising individualists pursuing individual goals; public relations between archaeologists and non-archaeologists became increasingly dysfunctional despite the many calls to improve them.

Secular crises follow inner driven eras; they begin when an event comes along which in other eras would be handled reasonably well but this time it leads to widespread fear, anxiety, and an urgent need to solve secular problems. Since 9/11, 2001, America has been in a secular crisis. The early half of a secular crisis is characterized by extreme individualism, institutional dysfunction, social polarization, fear, anxiety, and urgency. During this half American archaeology entered an identity crisis (discussed later). The second half of the secular crisis begins when another event becomes a catalyst for change; afterward society unites under a new agenda, and moves to solve its urgent problems. In the previous crisis the stock market crash of 1929 started the crisis era; the attack at Peal Harbor in December 1941 was the catalyst for change. All previous secular crises (the Great Depression-World War II, the America Civil War, the American Revolution, and the Glorious Revolution of the late 17th century) climaxed in total war. Unless America has exceptional leadership and avoids such a catastrophe, assume the cycle will repeat. Afterward there will be resolution to the urgent problems and a new cultural high will begin.

Wars can be fought during any era but only during the crisis climax are they fought as total war. American warfare in Afghanistan and Iraq since 2001 have been inconclusive limited war efforts. During total war American society mobilizes most everything for the war effort and the war is fought to a decisive conclusion. During WWII American archaeology was mostly suspended for the duration of the war; if America goes into another total war, expect another suspension of archaeology. After WWII archaeologists picked up what pieces they could and built new programs which then prospered in a new cultural high; increasing social conformity worked in their favor. If America again goes into total war, afterward archaeologists will likely pick up the pieces and restart the profession. The social conformism of the next high will likely not support the interests of traditional archaeologists unless the profession accepts multilateral perspectives (discussed later).

The Millennial crisis will eventually transition America from an inner driven society into an outer driven one dominated by a civic minded generation, the Millennials, birth years 1981-2002. During the crisis the Generation Xers will stop queuing off the narcissisms of the Boomers to meet the needs of the Millennials. Archaeology will shift from an inner driven profession to an outer driven one, assuming it survives the crisis.

Boomer professors have been teaching reflexivity to reactive Generation Xers for about two decades with some success. The Xers are only going to pursue the topic as long as they see utility in it. The Millennial generation, the oldest of whom entered graduate school about 2003, generally will not be interested in reflexivity unless it can be done as a team project because their focus is on communitas. Thus, the reflexive window for archaeology is closing with about ten to fifteen years left before the Millennials overwhelm the profession. However, reflexivity has one more useful task to complete before it goes away for many years, reemerging between 2045 and 2060.

Who's Your Other?

Returning to American anthropology, in the 1970s and 1980s, during the Consciousness Revolution, social anthropology transformed itself into something new. Today, American archaeology is doing it too. The lag time between the two changes is probably due to the crew based culture of archaeology compared to the solitary research done by ethnographers that is akin to commission based sales (very outward looking to begin with). In the 1970s and 1980s, American social anthropology redefined itself, and its microcosm and macrocosm.

The social anthropology of today is much different from its predecessor, the old fashioned Boas and Malinowski inspired version. Before the 1970s Ethnographic Others were perceived to be peoples of the undeveloped world who retained some resemblance of non-modern or pre-modern life-ways. These natives had been treated like living fossils. Today, social anthropology is focused on studying the Modern World and globalization, and everyone is considered modern; to refer to any culture as a living fossil is inappropriate. These changes began with the publication of Malinowski's diary (Malinowski, 1989 [1967]), which demonstrated the contradictions of the old Ethnographic Other; the works of Wolf (1982) and Fabian (1983) put an end to old style social anthropology.

Wolf (1982) and Fabian (1983) explored the contradictions of modern anthropology. Their work summed up the growing awareness that there weren't enough old-fashioned Others in the world to keep Anthropologists employed; that the old anthropological agenda wasn't interesting or relevant anymore. The world had changed such that it was increasingly harder to find suitable Others to study because modernity had saturated too much of the planet. Therefore, social anthropology was re-characterized, away from the study of natives-of-the-Other-world, in the tradition of Boas and Malinowski, into the study of modernity and globalization, in the new tradition of Wolf (1982). And, this new tradition includes a generous portion of all new ethnographic research being conducted on the home ground (Grant et al., 1999; Messerschmidt, 1981; Spradley and Rynkiewich, 1975). By the mid 1980s the study of Ourselves had became mainstream in social anthropology as it had in American society. Along with this change has been a constant re-definition and expansion of what Otherness is (Fabian, 2006). In today's social anthropology there is no distinction between Self and Other because they have blended. The Other is now anyone, including yourself, as reflected in the popularity of auto-ethnography (Reed-Danahay, 1997), the climax of reflexive ethnography.

If archaeology is still a major part of American anthropology, does it also have a new Archaeological Other? The traditional Archaeological Other has always been linked to that Ethnographic Other of Boas and Malinowski. Archaeologists examined the prehistoric portion of it, and they had nearly complete unilateral power and authority over the topic (Kehoe, 1998). In this way, prehistory has been the main core of American archaeology for most of the profession's history, even as historical archaeology developed as a subfield.

But, is this perspective still accurate for American archaeology? Have Self and Other blended in American archaeology?

For American historical archaeology the answer has become fairly clear; it is *yes*. The Society for Historical Archaeology was established in 1967 and spent its first two decades developing its identity and debating its subject matter (Moore, 2001b). Eventually, most American historical archaeologists have come to accept the idea that they study the new version of Ourselves in the Modern World, in sync with Social Anthropology. On the other hand, most American prehistorians have either resisted change or are ambivalent to it, leaving themselves intellectually disconnected from Anthropological colleagues as they continue studying an old fashioned Archaeological Other (Cobb, 2005). This disconnection has triggered a debate about the relationship between archaeology and Anthropology (Gillespie and Nichols 2003) and whether they should stay together.

This situation is also not sustainable. Reflexivity and post modernism within Anthropology have continued to blend Self and Other in every context possible, and are making inroads on re-interpreting prehistory. Additionally, during the 1990s Native Americans and other non-archaeologists interested in community archaeology began strongly influencing the interpretations of their pasts (McDavid, 1997; Watkins, 2001), forcing multilateral interpretative ownership of the past. In particular, Native Americans are proving that they are not living fossils and are fully part of this Modern World; the Kennewick Man debates demonstrated how prehistorians are struggling to maintain the illusion that they still have unilateral rights to interpret the prehistoric past. In reality, this struggle is a negotiation to determine how much authority each interest group will eventually have--this is multilateral archaeology not archaeology versus "alternative archaeologies". This suggests that the microcosm and macrocosm of archaeology are being redefined, by archaeologists and non-archaeologists. American prehistorians are being forced to negotiate a valid Other to study that fits within the parameters left to them by historical archaeologists, Social Anthropologists, and non-archaeologists.

The coming societal shift from inner directed to outer directed will not support a (self perceived) unilateral control of interpretive power over the past by archaeologists because it will be viewed as not civic minded (the opposite of what occurred in the 1940s-1960s when white males controlled American society and archaeology). The next dominant generation, the Millennials, are expected to become the directors over another great age of science. However, science will be gender balanced and ethnically diverse because that generation is the most ethnically diverse generation in American history, science will continue to be viewed as an acceptable career for women and men, and science will be more globally integrated. As institution builders, the Millennials will institutionalize this diversity and a mild form of social libertarianism, and demand conformity to them.

Therefore, the amalgamations of Self-Other and microcosm-macrocosm have serious ramifications for American archaeology because they are identity traps that have to be resolved. This is manifested in two ways. First, prehistorians are in the midst of a wide spread identity crisis. A good example of this is Jay Custer, a Boomer and a prehistorian, who converted from being an avid processual archaeologist into an advocate of Native American rights (Custer 2005a, b). In the old version of Ethnographic Others this close affinity with the Other would have been called "going native." In today's professional environment this behavior is merely the switching of allegiance from one interested party to another as all parties compete for interpretive control of certain resources. The crisis of identity is in the anxiety that comes from sensing that whatever allegiance one chooses could be inadequate because authority to interpret has become fluid. The crisis will be harder on older archaeologists, especially those that have resisted the post modern trend; those that do not adjust will feel increasingly left behind and that their work is increasingly irrelevant. Younger archaeologists are more likely to be accustomed to the interpretive fluidity and will openly seek interpretive partnerships with non-archaeologists. The current secular crisis of the United States is being expressed in archaeology as an identity crisis (Table 5). This crisis also seems to be more widespread than just within the United States as Joffe (2003) offers an international perspective.

The second identity trap is the belief that prehistory will continue as the core of American archaeology. The power bloc of the profession, which currently resides with prehistorians, is swinging to historical archaeologists and will be fully actualized in two decades. Economics supports this change. In culture resource management, beyond generic surveys, historical archaeology is becoming the largest aspect of the industry in many states; in California prehistoric excavations are less common than historic ones (Praetzellis, 2004). Similarly, forecasted expansions in Public Archaeology will also emphasize historical topics rather than prehistoric ones (Moore 2005b). While all of archaeology is being squeezed by outsiders, older prehistorians are getting the worst of it as they now have to accept historical archaeologists as heirs to the profession's main core.

The Purpose of RA

When Self and Other are indistinguishable intense reflexivity is present. This means that formalities and rituals are developing around it and there is an impulse to indulge in theater and acting. For example, technology now allows for field excavations to be filmed and broadcast live into lecture halls. Field technicians can excavate real features, comment on their technique, and answer questions from students many miles away;

meanwhile, professors can comment on the techniques and offer additional explanations of what is happening. Likewise, the recent discovery of an Egyptian royal tomb in the Valley of the Kings, thought to be Tutankhamen's mother, was documented via film and the whole act of discovery became a reality archaeology program. These situations are all choreographed, produced, and can be replayed endlessly.

While reality archaeology will likely continue as educational and entertainment events, the new purpose of RA is to shift archaeology's focus onto its macrocosm, and complete this over the next ten to fifteen years. Concurrently, it has to redefine the boundaries between archaeology's microcosm and macrocosm. Ultimately, this re-marking of the boarders will lead to an expanded definition of archaeology, not a narrower one. The profession already has two useful broad definitions for itself (Reid et al., 1974; Deetz, 1988b) that have not been utilized much. Definitions such as these should take central position in the near future.

Redefining archaeology is tied to resolving the identity crisis that is bubbling within the profession, especially among prehistorians. This shows up in the many Identities described below that archaeologists now have to consider, acknowledging that Identity has replaced culture history, culture process, and post modern critique as the hot topic of the profession.

First, archaeologists study Identity-collective, as in a culture, ethnicity, nationality, and various social groups such as girl scouts and cowboys. This is traditional archaeology extended beyond the search for culture history and process and into the smaller social groups to which people associate themselves.

Second, archaeologists study Identity-personal; how do non-archaeologists relate to material culture, and to the archaeological experience, and, how do archaeologists relate to these as well.

Third, archaeologists study Identity-personal-reflexive; how do archaeologists live with their own identities (do you brag about being an archaeologist or do you avoid telling anyone that you are one? And why?). Archaeologists are now requested to reveal their reasons for participating in the profession, something akin to auto-ethnography; non-archaeologists are requested to discuss their opinions about what an archaeologist is.

And fourth, archaeologists study Identity-collective-reflexive; what are the purposes and roles of archaeology in the twenty-first century? How does the profession interact with outsiders, and in return, get perceived within the broader host society?

All these identities have to be mediated in both the microcosm and macrocosm of archaeology, creating a layered behemoth of multi-dynamic and multi-vocalic identities and perceptions about archaeology. If theatrical analogies are helpful in this effort then using them is appropriate.

RA will negotiate these Identities, putting structure and boundaries on them. Applied Ethnography of archaeological settings and their host communities, along with supporting quantitative surveys, is the best way to get it done. Archaeologists do not have to undergo this change alone; many ethnographers can help because Social Anthropologists have already been through this transformation.

The process of understanding these different versions of archaeological identity has already begun (Hall, 2004; Holtorf, 2005; Ndlovu, 2006; Pokotylo and Guppy, 1999; Ramos and Duganne, 2000; Sandlin and Bey, 2006; Watkins, 2001; Wilson, 2006). *Ethnographies* is an excellent example of this new RA process too. Its essays discuss both the microcosm and macrocosm of archaeology, and, its authors are both archaeologists and ethnographers. Equally important is that most of its authors appear to be Generation Xers conducting pragmatic research. As these scholars continue their work and become masters ten to fifteen years forward, the above items will be resolved and archaeology will be redefined. Concurrently, the reflexive cycle will close as the profession turns its attention to communitas and Public Archaeology.

After Post Modernism

It is a little ironic that Shakespeare's "All life's a stage" is the opening line of a lengthy monologue about the life spans of individuals and generations; he understood the relations between generations and individual life cycles. The social history of American archaeology has been tied to cycles of American history, to current affairs, and the maturing of two generations, Boomers and Generation Xers. The cycle of reflexive archaeology was started by idealist Boomers in their young adult phase and it will be concluded by pragmatic Xers in their mature adult phase; the cycle began as ethical social activism and it will conclude as a tool for redefining archaeology. As the third generation, the Millennials, begins to dominate archaeology the focus of the profession will turn to community connectedness and team issues, individuality will be suppressed, and reflexivity will cycle out of fashion.

Phase two of the reflexive cycle will set boundaries around the microcosm and macrocosm of archaeology, and will resolve the archaeological identity crisis. Afterward, archaeologists will have new roles in society and will embrace multilateral authority, sharing interpretive power with newly re-defined Others. As these changes come about, Post Modernism will no longer be status quo in archaeology; its emphasis on agency will be antiquated. What will be new and in fashion is a civic minded Public Archaeology conforming to new morals about diversity and multilateralism.

With the complete passing of post modernism and reflexivity, the Millennials will lead the next great era of archaeological science, doing advanced comparative studies and constructing general theories about situational dynamics. The elderly Boomers will age gracefully, having found their peace and quiet.

from: Toward a Still and Quiet Conscience: A Study in Reflexive Archaeology. *North American Archaeologist* 27(2): 149-174, 2006.

19 THE END OF PREHISTORY

Recently, I have been writing about ongoing social changes within American society and their effects on American archaeology (Moore 2005a, b, 2006a, b, c). This commentary continues the discussion and focuses on important changes for historical archaeologists. The main forecast is that historical archaeology will emerge within two decades as the premiere archaeological research topic in North America. This change will come at the expense of research on prehistory.

The Useless but Useful Divide

In the past I have argued that the arbitrary conceptual divide between prehistory and history is useless, and even detrimental (Moore 1995, 2001). Those comments tried to unify divergences in American archaeological research such that theories and methods could actually support the argument that the past is relevant to the present and future. I still believe that American archaeology's conceptually segmented research paradigm is useless while conducting research.

However, the social structural divide between prehistorians and historical archaeologists now seems to have significant utility. Historical archaeologists, and their society, SHA, continue to go about their business doing the research they prefer in the way they prefer. Historical archaeologists are more structurally diverse and more involved in public outreach programs than are prehistorians. On the other side, prehistorians go about their business with little regard to outcomes from historical archaeology; they are much more focused on being scientists and most begrudge interferences from outsiders. The Society of American Archaeology, the largest archaeological organization in North America, is open to all professional archaeologists but we all know that it is primarily a bastion of prehistoric interests. Prehistorians have dominated since the beginning of the profession.

We also understand that this divide is a relic of the history of American archaeology. Prior to the inception of SHA in the United States the word "archaeology" usually meant prehistoric archaeology, with an additional nod to contact studies, or, it meant archaeology of some far off continent. This was because, since the inception of American archaeology in the 1830s through the late 1960s, the main topic of American archaeology was prehistoric research. This precedence of prehistory lingers in many ways. Even though SHA was established in 1967, many archaeological surveys continued to make a distinction between "archaeological" sites and "historic" sites well into the 1980s. Even today California archaeologists give priority to prehistoric interests as site numbers for historic sites are suffixed with /H while non-historic sites get numbers that are unmodified (and the irony is that the volume of prehistoric projects there has declined below the volume of historical projects [Praetzellis 2004]). The divide gives us marked and unmarked archaeology. In times past, the marked category has been ignored or treated like an unnecessary appendage to prehistory (Moore 2001b). Wilkie (2005) described the relationship as a soured romance (with undertones of Adam and Eve).

The history/prehistory divide is also a manifestation of a We/They conception of the world dating to the late 19th century when varieties of social Darwinism were rampant. The word "prehistory" was coined in 1851 and by the time Victorians had molded it into social Darwinism values it came to represent the They side of the divide. They, the Other, should be treated as scientific specimens from a fossilized natural world. Victorians, of course, thought of themselves as elites in charge of the world, no different than contemporary prehistorians who believe they have unilateral authority to interpret the archaeological record. For prehistorians the Archaeological Other has always been a Victorian conception. Ironically, the Boasians, who generally denounced social Darwinism and gave us culture history, actually reinforced the divide by hardening the segmentation between Anthropology and history and sociology; they let the "Savage Slot" (Trouillot 2003) become Anthropology's subject.

Since the inception of SHA historical archaeologists have debated the definition of their field. Much of that debate had to do with abandoning that Victorian We/They distinction. Today, historical archaeologists appear to be comfortable with the idea that they do the archaeology of Ourselves in the contemporary global modern world, minus the Victorian divide (Hall and Silliman 2006; Hicks and Beaudry 2006; Little 2006). We understand that We, Ourselves, refers to a heterogeneous pluralistic society that is constantly in motion, a moving target that is hard to define but is still inclusive. History, We, and all of Them have been combined into an lump-all category of humanity. We, contemporary historical archaeologists, also understand that We share interpretive control of the archaeological record with its descendents, and locals, Native Americans, and any interested party that wants into the game (except maybe relic hunters). This is multilateral archaeology. Historians have worked in a multilateral interpretive setting for over a century, so the idea is not new.

Unfortunately, those devoted to prehistoric research are still weighed down by their Victorian divide. And, they are getting beaten up for it. Since the passage of NAGPRA and the subsequent Kennewick Man legal case, prehistorians have been fighting a rear guard action to protect their unilateralism. They continue to propose that they do "archaeology" while others do "alternative archaeologies", that is, marked archaeology. In reality, they have been routed; the process of customization (Moore 2006b) is creating multilateral archaeology, and prehistorians will not be able to withstand this wave of social change. Across American archaeology there are already indications of emerging identity crises, especially among prehistorians (Joffe 2003, Moore 2006c); it's been very hard on one ecological archaeologist who is also a relative of George Armstrong Custer (Custer 2005a,b).

Multilateralism has two implications for historical archaeologists. First, it means that the old divide is imploding. Prehistory and history are no longer in conflict because prehistory is retiring--like an old work horse it is being put out to pasture. In twenty years I do expect archaeologists to study sites that date to several thousand years before present; I also expect that the word "prehistory" will not be used to discuss any of the data, as that Victorian word and all its associated concepts will be purged from the discipline by then.

"Prehistory" is quickly becoming anachronistic. This idea was recently impressed on me while reading a news item about a rare shark captured near Japan (MSNBC.com 2007). The sub caption read "Living fossil species has changed little since prehistoric times." Never mind the fact that these creatures continue to live, breed, and demonstrate scientific theories of evolution in action. Imagine if such statements were used today about living peoples, and the outcry that would come from it. Likewise, do your teenagers really understand what a 'living fossil' is? To my daughter it is an oxymoron; it's not even part of her generation's vocabulary. What this news item identified for me was that "prehistory" is itself a living fossil within our partly fossilized American sciences. A Kuhnian paradigm shift is coming soon and it will be the end of "prehistory."

The second implication of multilateralism, therefore, is that while American archaeology grapples with this significant conceptual change, historical archaeology will become the structural safety net of the profession. Additionally, forecasted expansions in Public Archaeology will emphasize historic topics (Moore 2005b, 2006b) over those associated with earlier eras. The social structural divide between prehistorians and historical archaeologists protects the latter. Thus, there will be a changing of the guard as historical archaeologists take leadership of American archaeology. The Golden Age of archaeology as historical analysis is on the horizon.

Secular Crisis

What would compel scientists to abandon a concept that seems so central to their paradigms? Again, the answer turns on historical change and social transformation.

American archaeology and Anthropology have always reflected the trends in American society (Trencher 2000). The last two decades in America have been an era of strong individualism; anthropologists and archaeologists have appropriately focused on agency, free will, as everyone pursued personal research agendas. From 1946 to 1964 American society emphasized social conformity over individualism; Anthropology emphasized theories that ignored agency (Culturology, cultural ecology, functionalism, and structuralism) and archaeology was a big team event conducting salvage projects under coordinated research plans. From 1964 to 1984 American society had a tug-of-war between conformity and individualism; this dialectic is known in American history as a spiritual awakening. The passion with which archaeologists embraced, then abandoned, the New Archaeology was the same passion that gave American society riots, rage, and rights consciousness. From 1929 to 1945 America endured a secular crisis, suffering from economic depression and then total war. During the war archaeological fieldwork basically stopped; during the depression it was done in management crisis mode as that is the best way to describe how New Deal archaeology was implemented. The four part cycle just described (secular crisis, era of social conformity, spiritual awakening, and era of individualism) is best described by Strauss and Howe (1991, 1997).

Since 9-11, 2001, America has been in a new secular crisis. During secular crises strong individualism continues until the climax when social conformity abruptly takes over. Other traits include severe social and political polarization, governmental and institutional dysfunction, and heightened fear, anxiety, and urgent desires to solve external social problems; the climax of this crisis hasn't come yet. Crisis eras are the great exclamation points of American history: the Depression-World War II (1929-1946), the Civil War (1857-1865), the American Revolution (1773-1794), and the Glorious Revolution (1675-1704). Dramatic social transformation is the outcome of secular crises. If America is in crisis and headed for transformation then so is American archaeology, and American science.

Obviously, political crisis grips America today. We are witnesses to an escalated conflict between the West and most of the Rest. I doubt that it will be the End of the West; more likely it will lead to a stronger multilateralism between the West and the Rest. In the past it's also been said that the non-West didn't have History. But now they do; and they claim the authority to interpret their History as they desire. It has also been said that there would be an End of History. But that too has been wrong as History has been redefined such that its exclusivity has become more inclusive.

As we come to understand the ramifications of these changes it will become apparent that ending "prehistory" is a symbolic concession towards multilateralism. Giving up "prehistory" will be an act of social grace not seen in American science since Anthropology gave up "race" as a biological category for scientific study.

The Little Acorn that Will

I guess the relationship between prehistoric and historical archaeology has always been misunderstood. Maybe we have thought of it as two siblings vying for attention from an Anthropology parent. Or, maybe it was as two combatants eyeballing each other to see who would flinch first; one being the big dog and the other the underdog. Or, we have Wilkie's romantic duo contemplating reunion after drifting apart.

Today, I see the relationship in botanical terms. The great tree of "prehistory" is aged and waning. Its contribution to society is becoming less apparent as each year passes. Soon, all anyone will care about is Paleo, and someday that too will become, like prehistory, passé. They are History.

Historical archaeology is the little acorn that fell from that tree. It is growing strong and waxing elegantly. Its canopy is wide and tall, and will eventually overshadow its parent. Every day that goes by its relevance to society is more evident. It's one of those trees that you just want to lean on as you enjoy the day.

from: The End of Prehistory. *Society for Historical Archaeology Newsletter* 40(1): 26-28, 2007.

20 THE KENSINGTON RUNE STONE
IS A WHITE WHALE

Recently, I have been watching the new Viking show on the History Channel. It is a nine part miniseries about the Viking raids into northern England in the 8th century. It is historical fiction, not a documentary. It is a bloody and lusty tale. I have no idea if the clothing or props are accurate or not. In general, it is good entertainment.

Of course, as a side show, the publicizing of everything Viking or Norse is now ticked up a notch. In the US that means the Kensington Rune Stone, the Heavener Rune Stone and the Newport (RI) Tower get some additional attention.

Years ago, I wrote a piece for the newsletter of the Denver Chapter of the Colorado Archaeological Society about proposed evidence for Viking exploration into North America (Moore 2001). It is reproduced below. Its title was "Hoaxes and the Norsemen of Canada," and was a response to a Viking exhibit that was on display at the Denver Museum of Nature and Science, March 2 to May 28, 2001. I'll have some additional comments afterward.

***

The difference between myth and reality is often a fine line, particularly when the story is too good to be true. No matter how much data is presented or how tight the argument is made some people will believe the version of it they prefer. This often happens with archaeological research. Every now and then, we get to debunk an idea, enjoy the two minutes of limelight, and then our findings are ignored because the other story is more appealing.

Two appealing stories are the continued claims for Viking, or Norse, explorations in the upper Midwest, mostly Minnesota, and in New England. The former is said to have been visited by a Swedish-Norwegian expedition in 1362; the other is linked to the "Vinland Voyages" chronicled in the Norse stories *The Greenlanders' Saga* and *Erik the Red's Saga*. While the sagas do contain useful hints about eleventh century Norse sojourns in parts of Canada, there is little credibility to these "Viking Hoaxes".

These two stories are worthy of attention. The oldest concerns the origin of the Newport Tower in Newport, Rhode Island. The tower is an unusual stone structure commanding the view over the town and bay. In 1837, a Danish professor named Rafn published a book presenting evidence for Norse settlement in the New World. His interpretation of the sagas placed the colony of Vinland within New England. This news led to a flurry of attempts at finding the physical remains of Vikings. Some believed the tower was Norse because it was thought to be different from other English structures from the early days of the town. Others felt that it was English, dating to the seventeenth century. The debate about the tower went on for several years and evidence for Norsemen was brought forth from many places within New England.

To resolve the issue, William Godfrey (1949, 1951, 1955) excavated the area within and around the tower in the 1940. He found numerous artifacts in the builder's trench dating to the seventeenth century and interpreted the structure as a windmill. Even so, people still refer to it as evidence that Norsemen had been in New England.

The other story is a hoax from Minnesota (Guralnick 1982). In 1898, a rune stone was found outside the town of Kensington. Rune stones are rocks that have been inscribed with some message, often a memorial, in the runic alphabet, common in Northern Europe in Medieval times. In some parts of Scandinavia this script was used into the early twentieth century. Many of these stones have been found in Sweden. The Kensington Stone inscription read:

8 Goths and 22 Norwegians on
an exploration journey from
Vinland to the west We
had camp by 2 skerries one
day's journey north from this stone
we were to fish one day after
we came home found 10 men red
of blood and dead AVM
We have 10 men by the sea to look
after our ships 14 day's travel
from this island Year 1362

Certainly, this tale is intriguing. But, soon after it was found, the rock was studied by a linguist and shown to be a fake. Its alphabet is nineteenth century runic not fourteenth, as the date indicates. The language is a dialect of Swedish found only in parts of Minnesota, including the Kensington area. And, the inscription was not weathered, as it should have been if it was older. However, the rock received much attention, and, after a promoter got onto the story, people began to believe that it was real. Suddenly many more rune stones were found. Today, one occasionally hears stories about Vikings in Minnesota.

Not all the stories about Norsemen in North America are hoaxes (Ingstad 1977; McGhee 1984; McGovern 1981, 1990). During the late eighth through the eleventh centuries, there was a major population expansion out of Scandinavia. Norsemen spread across the northern part of Europe and to their west. Iceland was settled in the decade 860-870. Erik the Red colonized Greenland from Iceland in the 980s. By 1500, this colony either was abandoned or had died out, possibly due to Eskimo warfare. About the year 1000, several voyages were undertaken from Greenland to explore further west. Three places are recorded in the Sagas that were either settled or temporarily used: the southern part of Baffin Island, called "Helluland," the coast of Labrador below the medieval tree line, named "Markland," and the northern part of Newfoundland, the legendary "Vinland".

Archaeological evidence for Norse settlements or contacts in North America is sparse but they definitely did land in parts of Canada. The best known site is L'Anse aux Meadows, located along the northern coast of Newfoundland, which was excavated in the 1960s by Anne and Helge Ingstad and by Parks Canada in the 1970s. There, the remains of ten houses, four boat sheds, refuse heaps, and two cooking pits were recovered. The houses were medieval Norse long houses, similar to ones found in parts of Iceland and Sweden. Some of the artifacts, such as a spindle whorl and some rivets are typical Norse products. Twenty-one carbon dates clustered around the early eleventh century, correlating well with the Sagas. Anne Ingstad is cautious about calling this site the Vinland colony. However, it is a very good chance that it is.

Relations between the Norse and American natives, or "skraelings" as they called them, were mostly hostile. Three groups were probably encountered: the Dorset Eskimos in northern Labrador, the Thule Eskimos in Greenland and eastern Arctic Canada, and the people of the archaeological complex called Point Revenge, found in southern Labrador and Newfoundland. The Dorset and Thule Eskimos differed in their material culture, the latter having a more complex marine technological system. The Point Revenge people may be the ancestors of the historic Algonquian speaking Naskapi, Montagnais, and Beothuck tribes.

Fascinating as this archaeology may be, the Norsemen did not leave much of an impact on the New World. The modern stage of North America does not start with their presence. There is no evidence for major epidemics, battles, or changed economies. All of that would come later. The existing evidence suggests sporadic and wide-ranging contact between Norse and Native Americans, whose legends apparently do not remember them. Their memory lives on in our culture in the form of runic stones, strange towers, and the all too often vague line between fact and fiction.

***

Since 2001, there have been many claims that these two "hoaxes" are in fact truth. The Newport Tower has been featured in recent cable shows (e.g. *America Unearthed*), once again arguing for a Viking or a Knights Templar connection. Godfrey's research can't be accepted because it is too boring; people just want more. I admit I shouldn't have called the tower a "hoax" because the structure is very authentic. It was built for a real purpose, as a windmill, a gristmill, built in the 17th century. Those perpetuating the "fringe" interpretations about it are con artists trying to make a buck or a name from selling silly ideas.

However, the Kensington Stone has actually gained some respectability in the last few years. Two recent books (Kehoe 2004; Nielson and Wolter 2005) sum up the sordid story and argue for the stone's authenticity. Nielson has done much new research on the linguistics and history of runic writing in Scandinavia. He actually documents that many of the linguists who first looked at the stone were wrong in their understanding of runic history. His research seems like a valid contribution to the case.

Wolter's contribution to the story is his petrographic analysis from which he argues that the inscriptions are older than when the stone was found; in other words, it had to be older than 1898. Unfortunately, petrographic analysis isn't an established dating method, so he can't tell us when the stone was inscribed. He assumes the date on the stone is correct.

Since their joint publication in 2005, Nielson and Wolter have soured their relationship. Several physical scientists have waded in on the discussion and Wolter's petrograhic analysis is considered to have failed. The best evidence against Wolter is now found on Nielson's web page, http://www.richardnielsen.org/Welcome.html, under the Discussion tab. Wolter has gone on to be a shill for the Knights Templar/Holy Grail in America theme, using both the Kensington Stone and the Newport Tower as a backdrop.

Into this fray came well respected Anthropologist and archaeologist Alice B Kehoe who argued for the stone's authenticity and supported

Nielson and Wolter in her own book and by writing the Forward to their 2005 book. In the Forward, Neilson and Wolter are described as "hard scientists" with appropriate resumes.

One has to wonder about Kehoe's stance in this controversy. She has spent much of her professional life arguing for a multitude of pre-Columbian contacts from the Old World to the New, and across the two continents of the New. She seems to particularly dislike the idea that Columbus "discovered" America. Two essays summarize her position (Kehoe 2003; 2010). Today, it is widely accepted among archaeologists, myself included, that Polynesians, Basques, Chinese, and others came to the New World long before Columbus. I would love to see a rigorous analysis that Jomon Japan is connected to Mesoamerican antiquity. Kehoe seems to ignore this commonly held view and acts as if opinions like mine don't exist.

The Norse certainly lived in Newfoundland; the Chumash probably saved the lives of some Polynesians and adopted their boat making skills and words; and the Basques left words in Micmac. But none of these events changed the world the way Columbus did. Archaeologists don't have to prove that fact.

If Kehoe and others want to argue that pre-Columbian cultural contacts were indeed momentous events then the burden of proof is on them. Find the evidence, make a good presentation, and convince us that Columbus wasn't THE watershed event.

Unfortunately, the Kensington Stone has fallen into a terrible state of affairs. Around 2002 a cast of the stone was made and now a black silicon layer covers the stone. Physical analysis isn't possible until the contamination is removed. Moreover, it is not clear on how to do this without destroying underlying patina and the surface of the stone itself.

Like Indy, all I can say is the stone belongs in a reputable museum. Regardless of its authenticity, the story of the Kensington Stone is wonderful American folklore that continues to inspire people to do inspiring things. It shouldn't be treated as some commercial object.

This whole sad discussion reminds me of the book *Moby Dick* by Herman Melville. There, the scarred, tortured, and obsessive character of Captain Ahab chases the elusive goal, destroying his life and everyone else around him. He never really catches the whale but becomes tied to it, cannot escape, and goes down with it. Only the narrator, Ishmael, survives. Perhaps that is Neilson.

from: The Age of Intuition, March 25, 2013.

21 ANTHROPOLOGISTS
LOST IN A POST SCIENTISM WORLD

It seems that the American Anthropological Association (AAA) is having spasms again. This time it is due to their leadership folks deciding to drop the word "science" from the AAA mission statement. The word is too hot, if you will, because it reeks of colonialism and such. The debate seems to have crumbled into the clean pro-science bunch verses the science haters (dirty ugly postmodern types). That's their characterizations, not mine.

There are several people hitting the issue. A story by Berrett (2010) is in *Higher Education* and excellent blog coverage is Lende (2010) and Smith (2010).

I am compelled to offer my two bits because a few years ago I told my colleagues in archaeology that science just wasn't what it used to be (Moore 2007b). I'll get to that essay in a minute.

Let's start by understanding the term "scientism." From the online version of the *American Heritage Dictionary* come the two following definitions:

- The collection of attitudes and practices considered typical of scientists.
- The belief that the investigative methods of the physical sciences are applicable or justifiable in all fields of inquiry.

Next, let's add another from the online Merriam-Webster Dictionary:

- An exaggerated trust in the efficacy of the methods of natural science applied to all areas of investigation (as in philosophy, the social sciences, and the humanities)

Scientism is about the value of and use of science in society. Nonscientists often use the term pejoratively because scientism is an ideology, an ethos, that can replace religious faith. It describes many peoples' blind faith or exaggerated trust in science, including the faith that scientists often have about their own work. Don't confuse it with science itself.

Richard Dawkins is a good example of a scientist who has blind faith in science. In his 1997 essay "Is Science a Religion?" he argues that science is not a religion because

> Science...is free of the main vice of religion, which is faith. But, as I pointed out, science does have some of religion's virtues. Religion may aspire to provide its followers with various benefits; among them explanation, consolation, and uplift. Science, too, has something to offer in these areas.

So, to him, faith is the ugly bugger that separates science from religion. Dawkins also tells us the following:

> I believe in the fact of evolution. I even believe in it with passionate conviction. To some, this may superficially look like faith. But the evidence that makes me believe in evolution is not only overwhelmingly strong; it is freely available to anyone who takes the trouble to read up on it. Anyone can study the same evidence that I have and presumably come to the same conclusion. But if you have a belief that is based solely on faith, I can't examine your reasons. You can retreat behind the private wall of faith where I can't reach you.

It is widely known that witnesses to a crime usually have extremely different opinions about what happened. People looking at the same evidence rarely have the same conclusions. Sadly, Dawkins hides behind the word "fact" because he has no other place to go. He hides behind logic and evidence as if their correctness was self evident, like magic. Viscerally--faith, fact, what's the difference? It demonstrates he is a shill for science. He is a "believer." I don't like shills of any kind, no matter what they are selling.

If evolution were fact, scientists would call it a Law like gravity. Evolution is a Theory. It may be a good theory and it may have withstood strong critiques. However, as a Theory it is always open to the possibility that some other theory will replace it.

Let's add a new definition to scientism: scientists who believe their theories are facts are religious folks who approach science with the same fervor and dogmatism that other religious fundamentalists do. Scientists have their evangelical epiphanies and their revivals too. Science is not a religion; scientism can be a religion.

178

For most of the Modernist era (1890-1990), especially the post war period (1945-1987), science was revered and scientists given high prestige in society. If you went to graduate school in the 1970s and 1980s some science professors were more than Professors, they were Prophets--noting the shared root. In the 1980s archeologists James Deetz and Louis Binford were treated like gods. (I knew Deetz and remember that he despised being treated that way; he also handled it with grace).

This reverence for science was one of the defining characteristics of modernism. That is why historian and sociologist of religions William McLoughlin proclaimed the 20th century as the Era of Scientism (McLoughlin 1978:42). He recognized that in doing intellectual history the separation between science and religion was arbitrary, only meaningful to those professions built around them.

My 2007 essay was about the decline of scientism--understood in all the versions above--in American culture that occurred through the 1980s and 1990s. The tipping point of the decline was the Challenger disaster of 1986 wherein scientists demonstrated gross incompetency. After that, there is much less reverence for science in American culture, and the prestige was gone. Today, scientists are average people with all the foibles that anyone else has--they are not the legends and heroes that Old Modernism made them out to be.

For American archaeology, I have already offered my opinion that the profession is in an identity crisis and that the word "prehistory" should be abandoned, perhaps to be replaced by "antiquity" or something similar (Moore 2006c, 2007a). If you drop "science", I won't care. We'll just call our work *inquiries* or something else.

My advice to the AAA is to recognize that they are in an identity crisis (along with the rest of the United States, by the way). The membership needs to have a serious discussion of why they should or should not use the word "science" in their mission statement. Maybe the compromise is to just redefine what it means.

However, today, America is a Dionysian high context culture; it has shed much, but not all, of its Modernist Apollonian low context culture. If Anthropologists choose to drop the term "science" then recognize that this is a Dionysian impulse. It would be another insult to Apollo. Does anyone really care? I suspect most Americans don't care what Anthropologists call themselves--their faith in science has already eroded greatly.

from: The Age of Intuition, December 5, 2010.

22 ANTHROPOLOGY
AFTER BITTER COMES SWEET

In December 2010, members of the American Anthropological Association had a little tiff about "science" in their profession. Three months later, it is still playing out as some have turned to redefining (and marketing) Anthropology. Others are discussing "What does Anthropology mean to me". And thirdly, people are writing "loves letters" to Anthropology, in honor of Valentine's day, as a way to get passed the bitterness of the tiff. All this is good, as it offers catharsis.

My intent here is to be participant observer. Note that the two web sites *Savage Minds* and *Neuroanthropology* are leading these efforts. These two sites, and the Open Anthropology Cooperative, are currently leaders in the Anthropology blogosphere. Both sites are collaborative projects by people who are roughly in the same age groups, generally known in the United States as Generation X.

I cannot reiterate the Generations Model as it would be too long. America is in cultural crisis, an era that will last about 20 years; we have many years to go before it completes [1]. The leadership of the idealist generation, in this case, the Boomers, starts the crisis. Idealist generations are the recurring polarizer's of American culture and they have begun every major crisis in American history (Glorious Revolution, American Revolution, slavery debate and Civil War, depression and World War II, and the current crisis).

The crisis era closes as the next generation, the reactive nomads, today's Gen X, leads the way out. During the crisis era, some nomads become commanders who take pragmatic leadership roles in many institutions and politics. If they arrive too early and push too hard like autocrats, they eventually are vilified and burned [2]. If they go slow, they can become great leaders and much admired. I discussed this for archaeologists (Moore 2009).

However, reactive nomads make poor visionaries. The one example of a reactive visionary is Hitler, obviously not a good role model for Gen Xers. Reactive commanders do best when they have a clear destination in mind and are allowed to go after it. They themselves likely will not conceive of the destination but will receive it from another.

The latter half of the crisis era instills a vision of the future that becomes the founding principles of a revitalized, "reborn", culture. In the past, an idealist known in generational theory as the Grey Champion (GC) has always provided that vision (John Winthrop, Benjamin Franklin, Abraham Lincoln, and Franklin Roosevelt). In our current national crisis the GC has not emerged; it's not Bernanke as he is one of the culture destroyers. Maybe Hilary Clinton or Ron Paul will get to play the role but I suspect it will be someone less well known.

Institutions and professions also need their Grey Champions. Anthropology currently needs one. Anthropology died and was reborn previously in the years 1925-1945; the Boasians were marginalized as the modernists with their general system theories and evolution became mainstream. The GC for the modernists was likely Ales Hrdlichka. Today, the modernists have been marginalized but no one is standing up offering a prophetic vision for the future of Anthropology.

I have looked hard at the Boomer class of Anthropologists and none seems to stand out. Too many of them want to fight the culture wars or are jaded from those battles.

The title of Lende's (2011) recent essay sounds like its offering a vision. But, in true Xer fashion, he can only say:

> We are pragmatists -- we recognize the need to rewrite an outdated long-range plan and the need to be inclusive. We are sadder-but-wiser, ready to get on with things, but not really clear where we need to be getting to...Anthropologists do seem to be searching for a new identity, something to lend us vision, a plan of action for the future.

His essay is more a quest than a revelation. He'll make a great commander but not a prophet.

Anthropology needs direction and a destination. I offer these humble clues to what the destination is:

1. Let the Enlightenment go--it is no longer needed.
2. Say No to Descartes--the mind/body is one system; nature/culture is one system.
3. Embrace chaos and complexity--the world is rarely linear.

4. Embrace the philosophy of Pragmatism.
5. Create an inquiry of situational behavior (includes non-situational and desituated).
6. Enjoy the next 50 years of Dionysian dance; Apollo can return later.
7. Our goal is to develop Old Masters, and, we can enjoy the young geniuses as they do their one-hit-wonder routine.

How do we get there? I don't know; I'm not the GC and don't want the job.

There are Boomers out there that offer a way forward. Lakoff and Johnson's magnum opus *Philosophy in The Flesh: the Embodied Mind and its Challenge to Western Thought* is a place to start. Johnson followed it with *The Meaning of the Body: Aesthetics of Human Understanding*. (Lakoff has returned to being a culture warrior). The Strauss and Howe model mentioned above is also useful, as is the work of Robert Shiller in economics. There must be more out there but I don't see any Boomer Anthropologist that fits the role of GC. Let's hope that someone steps forward and publishes the path ahead.

Notes:

1. Some argue that the crisis started with 9/11/2001, others in August of 2007 with the credit crisis that becomes the global financial crisis. Either way, we have many years to a resolution, circa 2022-2027. And, hell lays in between. Remember, the culture has to ritually die before it's reborn.

2. Think of Michelle Rhee for Washington DC and maybe what's coming for Scott Walker in Wisconsin; and never forget Jacob Leisler, a hanged nomad of the Glorious Revolution. Obama has been less forceful; all he knows how to do is jump from one idea to another, like a fart in a skillet. The GC will have strong convictions and will hold fast when facing hell, something a nomad is unlikely to do.

from: The Age of Intuition, February 21, 2011.

23 SECULAR CRISIS, IDENTITY CRISIS AMERICAN STYLE

The recent flare up at the American Anthropological Society (AAA) about whether or not they would use the word science in a mission statement reminded me that I haven't clearly articulated the concept of secular crisis. In my first essay (chapter 20) about the AAA problem I made the comment that they were in an identity crisis. Let's take a look at what this means.

In the context that I am using the phrase, *identity crisis* is a social problem. AAA is an organization whose members join freely because they have some common ground that unites them. The crisis occurs because that common ground is shaken by new ideas and new power structures among members--the overall trust that exists within the organization becomes mistrust. The group no longer has unified goals and objectives. The crisis is resolved when some resemblance of trust is reestablished; they may or may not redefine their goals and objectives.

Sometimes an identity crisis can be transformative. In the 1970s-1980s the industry of medicine went through an identity crisis that led to the de-professionalization of medicine. In those years, the roles and responsibilities of doctors and nurses were redefined (probably due to insurance companies getting more power over the industry). Part of the resolution was the wider acceptance of other roles (the physician assistant and nurse practitioner) that previously had been minor within the industry.

Likewise, the profession of journalism is currently in an identity crisis. Journalists are fighting the same battle as AAA. The recent debate between Ted Koppel and Keith Olbermann was about those who adhere to the ethos of Modernism (Koppel) and those who don't. Olbermann is similar to the Romantic scientists--he claims to be doing good journalism without adhering to the narrow strictures of old Modernism. Romantic scientists pursue a expanded version of science and don't limit themselves to narrow causality or positivism. Within AAA it's the Modernist scientists who feel that they are marginalized while the Romantic scientists and non scientists are fine with the way things are. Remember, Modernism is fading in American culture while Romanticism is raging.

Additionally, journalism is de-professionalizing. The rise of the internet, the rise of bloggers, the decline in newspaper readership, and the decline in TV viewing, all point to the transformation of journalism. Will it survive? I don't care and I don't expect Modernist journalism to rebound.

Now, take the idea of identity crisis, and step up a whole level of scale, and think about a whole society that is undergoing an identity crisis. Do the majority of Americans still believe we are Number One in the world? Are we still a superpower? Is the US dollar still the most powerful currency? Is the US military still the best functioning weapon in the world? Today, it seems that there is much doubt about positive answers to all these questions. America is in secular crisis.

A secular crisis is a culture wide identity crisis. However, it has other attributes that make it different from other eras, such as: it is transformative because a status quo will be changed, genocidal warfare is common, and it is recursive in American culture history. The secular crisis is winter. Let's review the previous American crises.

The Glorious Revolution (ca. 1676-1700) from the perspective of colonists
- Identity question: do English colonists have full rights as English citizens?
- Events: King Philip's War (genocidal); governors from all colonies were evicted via several rebellions; Connecticut, Massachusetts, and Rhode Island colonial charters were terminated--all three were combined into a provisional colony called New England; Salem witch trials.
- Status Quo change: King James dethroned with William and Mary seated jointly; new colonial governors seated.
- Identity resolution: Colonists were not English citizens with full rights; colonial charters were rewritten.

The American Revolution (ca. 1763-1794) from the perspective of colonists
- Identity question: do English colonists have full rights as English citizens?
- Events: Succession (independence); civil war (Continentals v Redcoats); genocidal warfare on western front against Indians, and, in the Carolinas as guerilla fighting.
- Status Quo change: "these" United States created out of the British empire.

- Identity resolution: Americans are free of British control; Tories were evicted.

Slavery Conflict--Civil War (ca. 1854-1876)
- Identity question: can Americans have slavery and believe in freedom too?
- Events: Bleeding Kansas, succession and civil war with widespread genocidal behavior; reconstruction.
- Status Quo change: The Southern political power block that had prevailed since the 1790s was overthrown; the federal government became more powerful.
- Identity resolution: Americans believe in freedom; slavery abolished; "these United States" became "the United States".

Depression--WWII (ca. 1929-1946)
- Identity question: Are Americans isolationists or are they a superpower?
- Events: depression; WWII with genocide in the Pacific theater.
- Status Quo change: Power center of Western Civilization shifts to US from Europe.
- Identity resolution: the US is a superpower.

Our current Crisis of Confidence (ca. 2001 to about 2025)
- Identity question: is US still Number One?
- Events: World Trade Center attack; War on Terrorism, Great Recession; FED owns everything; Americans can expect an episode of genocidal warfare.
- Status Quo change: US Dollar replaced as reserve currency? Decline in American economic and political influence? Will some wealthy folks be lynched?
- Identity resolution: America either will become a more powerful Superpower, a fallen one, or will share power with a competitor.

Our current crisis is still unfolding. I tend to see it as being similar to the Glorious Revolution and the Civil War eras since those too played out during Dionysian times. There will be many seemingly isolated events that take place that actually are connected reciprocally or reflexively (but not in a cause/effect way). Thus, I can foresee rebellions in several states with the governors and elected bodies being replaced wholesale like. I can foresee many wealthy families leaving the country or lynched. This could all happen as WW3 plays out overseas and our need for collective emotional release allows for some genocidal events. Resolution will come when there is a sense that fairness is returned to the population; America will either become a more powerful Superpower, a fallen one, or will share power with a competitor, such as China.

Stepping back down to the organization level, AAA isn't likely to go through a blood bath. They agree to either get along or break up. Years ago at Stanford they chose to break up and now, they have two Anthropology programs there, the scientists (Department of Anthropological Sciences) and the non-scientists (Department of Cultural and Social Anthropology). It must be nice to have the luxury to afford both.

from: The Age of Intuition, December 18, 2010.

24 ANTHROPOLOGY, ECONOMICS AND THE PRACTITIONER'S ROLE

Earlier this year Anthropologists had a debate about the status of Anthropology as a science (Lende 2010). Now, economists are having one too. Here is a list of blogs asking the basic question; the comments are good too:

- "Weakonomics"; Is Economics as Science? March 17, 2011; http://weakonomics.com/2011/03/17/is-economics-a-science/
- Adam Ozimek; Is Economics a Science? March 17, 2011; http://modeledbehavior.com/2011/03/17/is-economics-a-science/
- Paul Krugman; Economics as a Science: A Bad Example, March 17 2011; http://krugman.blogs.nytimes.com/2011/03/17/economics-as-a-science-a-bad-example/
- Jim Manzi; Is Economics a Science? March 18, 2011; http://www.nationalreview.com/corner/262473/economics-science-jim-manzi
- Brad DeLong; Is Economics a Science? March 18, 2011 http://delong.typepad.com/sdj/2011/03/is-economics-a-science.html
- Jim Manzi; Jim and Noah's Excellent Adventure, Part I, March 19, 2011; http://theamericanscene.com/2011/03/19/jim-and-noah-s-excellent-adventure-part-1

I don't care what their opinions are, yeah or nay. Obviously, the debate is similar to what Anthropologists have been doing. The topic also comes up regularly in economics; here are some older ones:

- Alex Pollock; Is Economics a Science? November 6, 2010; http://www.american.com/archive/2010/november/is-economics-a-science
- Greg Mankiw; Is Economics a Science? May 17, 2006; http://gregmankiw.blogspot.com/2006/05/is-economics-science.html
- Alvin Roth; Is Economics a Science? (Of course it is), May 1999; http://kuznets.harvard.edu/~aroth/econsci.html

I find all of this rather silly, especially from people who are well educated and have prestigious awards such as the Nobel Prize (Krugman).

Other than Roth above, don't people of this caliper understand the basics of classification? When you define something, you are doing simple sorting. Some things go into Box A and some things don't go into Box A because of how Box A is defined. If your standard for science is Physics then only Physics goes in the box called "science". Nothing else qualifies.

Trying to argue that there are degrees of science just muddles the discussion, as in hard versus soft science, pure versus less-pure science, and proper versus less proper. These distinctions are childish, like fifth graders at recess: I dare ya to be a soft scientist... no, I double dare ya...

There is no wisdom in these conversations.

For many, the claim to be a scientist has become political posturing or advocacy for special interest groups, or perhaps even for themselves as they think it will make them better positioned during upcoming budget cuts or grant awarding.

If we really need science in our lives then I recommend that it be defined broadly such that the usual and accustomed suspects are put into the box. Since we typically divide professions, and thus occupations and job postings, by subject matter (physics, chemistry, biology, economics, etc.) then those subjects that have been traditionally viewed as science can continue the claim as long as they meet simple criteria.

Science is the systematic and comparative study of observable phenomena.

1. Systematic means having a widely accepted set of methods, techniques, and standards that are used to study events and phenomena.
2. Comparative in that the results of numerous singular studies are used to make generalized explanatory and/or interpretive

summations.

3. Observable in that one can witness directly or indirectly-(via-tools like microscopes) an event or phenomenon, and, observations can be used to reasonably infer the presence of something not observable (no one sees gravity or magnetism; we infer them by observing their regular and recurring affects).

Most professions that have traditionally been classified as a science will qualify because they meet 1, 2 and 3.

Historians aren't scientists because they do particularistic studies; from what I've seen, comparative history is not strong; they don't do #2. Chefs aren't scientists because they, too, likely don't do much of #2. However, "culinary science" is the science and technology behind meal planning, preparation, processing, and service for a global consuming public. A chef makes food. Culinary applied science is integrated, matrixed, into business models by those trying to operate restaurants as profitable businesses.

Science isn't just for academics looking for Truth. Most of it is used by corporations to make a buck and by governments trying to regulate or manage something. In most cases, science is a means to an end; it generally is not an end unto itself.

Back in the days of strong modernity, ca. 1920-1975, science was mostly segmented and rigid. By that I mean biologists did biology, chemists did chemistry, and "interdisciplinary work" was generally frowned upon. In today's post-modernity the work environment--outside of academia--is just the opposite. Segmentation has been replaced by integration; rigidity by flexibility. In the federal government, most environmental compliance biologists have to know something about archaeology and air pollutants. Environmental planning tries to be holistic, not segmented, and resource management plans are "Integrated". Segmented academia is looking more archaic every day.

Instead of debating whether a profession is science or not I suggest people focus on what roles people have and when is it appropriate to say that someone's role is "scientist" or not.

Here are some roles (in no particular order of significance):
1. Scientist: a person who regularly does research that meets the definition of science given above. If you are not actively doing scientific research then you are *not* a scientist. A scientist is a producer of science.
2. Technician: a person who gathers scientific data and may conduct initial analyses'. They are typically well trained in scientific methods and techniques, and may have good understandings of theoretical issues. Examples: x ray techs, engineering techs, geo-technical

specialists, and the popular science folks as seen on the cable show *Myth Busters*.

3. Teacher: a person who regularly teaches. Teachers of science can also be scientists if they are also actively doing research. Most high school science teachers only teach; many science professors are teachers.

4. Professional/Practitioner : A person who does not do research but uses a body of scientific knowledge to solve problems and/or set policy (e.g. physicians, engineers, corporate executives, consultants, government employees). They are consumers of science.

I am an Anthropological archaeologist by training but I do "cultural resource management" for a federal agency. That is, I ensure that my agency complies with federal laws about historic preservation, which is a part of the overall environmental compliance sector. While I know that some federal archaeologists have done science, I, as a federal employee, have never been able to do it. In fact, most of my job is about the avoidance of doing archaeological research. I am a practitioner.

Let me elaborate. Coming this week there will be an archaeological study done in Oregon sponsored by my agency. Federal environmental specialists, state environmental specialists, environmental and archaeological consultants, and I, have planned the study. The purpose of it is to determine the presence or absence of archaeological sites within a defined number of rangeland acres, approximately 1700, that may become developed. The study is a survey not an excavation. The actual work will be done by archaeological consultants supported by archaeological technicians. The purpose of the study is to provide descriptive data such that federal bureaucrats can make decisions about land use. It is also being done under the umbrella of an Environmental Impact Study and will become a component of that assessment.

The result of this archaeological survey will be a technical report, a singular study. There is no intention of doing any comparisons, there are no hypotheses to be tested, and there will be no attempts at determining ancient land use patterns. In this specific case, science is not required to meet the needs of making land use decisions related to historic preservation. My final involvement is to ensure that the technical study does meet certain minimum standards. Having a solid background in archaeological science helps me in determining the quality of technical reports. Most technical studies produce average reports and few are excellent. I accept average or better and reject crap.

Most American archaeologists are practitioners or technicians who produce or consume technical reports. Their work falls short of being classed as science. The contexts and conditions in which they work rarely compel them to do the comparative work that is typically viewed as "science". In the last ten years, I have done archaeological science twice (Moore and Busch 2003; Moore and Hurst 2005) and both those projects were done as volunteer efforts, on my own free time. In addition, there is nothing bad or wrong about producing or consuming technical reports. Archaeological science cannot be done without good technical reports.

Returning to the economics debate: those folks make an interesting analogy that economics is "like engineering". Obviously, this analogy is emphasizing the practitioner role of economics. They can't see this because their scientism obscures their ability to distinguish the role of scientist from practitioner, producer from consumer. I guess they like the idea because they believe they are engineering the economy and society, a common illusion among highbrow types. They are holding onto what's left of modernism. I suspect that many economists are actually practitioners or technicians who don't get to do science.

To me the word engineer brings up other images. I am reminded that 'waste engineers' used to be called garbage men, and, in some parts of this world, archaeologists are thought of as waste engineers.

I am not a waste engineer.

from: The Age of Intuition, March 20, 2011.

25 WELCOMING GENERATION X

Generational models of social change are common today. I'll relate one to archaeology. Winograd and Hais (2008) recently argued that the emerging Millennial generation (Table 25-1) will transform American society and politics, and dominate these for most of the twenty first century. Their claim is based on the premise that the Millennials are like the G. I. generation of World War II fame as they are both civic minded heroic generations. I have no argument with this claim other than it comes early in the generational secession process. The G. I. generation was led and mentored by their next elders, the Lost Generation. Likewise, the Millennials will be led and mentored by Generation X (in Europe called Baby Busters or the Seventies Generation). Thus, we need to understand the Xers as they are transitioning into senior leadership roles. This essay briefly summarizes their generational type and outlines what can be expected of them as leaders; it also recognizes the mythological relationship between Gen X and Indiana Jones.

The Generations Model
Strauss and Howe (1991, 1997) provide a model of four generational archetypes that rotate over approximately eighty years. The types are idealist, reactive, civic, and adaptive (Table 25-1); they are also known as prophets, nomads, heroes, and artists. Gen X is the reactive nomad type. Different endowments characterize the four types. Idealists focus on principles, religion, and education. Reactive generations focus on survival, pragmatism, and liberty. Civics focus on community building, technology, and affluence. Adaptive generations promote pluralism, social justice, and expertise. Civics and Adaptives are collectivists focused on social cooperation. Idealists and Reactives are individualists pursuing self interests.

Table 25-1: Recent generations with their types and examples.

Name	Type	Birth years	Examples
Transcendentalist	idealist	1792-1821	Charles Darwin, Herbert Spencer, Henry Schoolcraft, Lewis H. Morgan, E. G. Squier, Abraham Lincoln, Susan B. Anthony
Gilded	reactive	1822-1842	Daniel Brinton, Edward B. Tylor, Albert S. Gatschet, Hubert H. Bancroft, Samuel Clemens, Louisa May Alcott
Progressive	adaptive	1843-1859	Sigmund Freud, William H. Holmes, Franz Boas, C. B. Moore, Woodrow Wilson, Arthur Conan Doyle, William H. Jackson
Missionary	idealist	1860-1882	Alfred L. Kroeber, Hetty Goldman, Howard Carter, H. B. Hawes, Edgar Lee Hewitt, Franklin D. Roosevelt, Julia Morgan
Lost	reactive	1883-1900	Ruth Benedict, Edward Sapir, Alfred. V. Kidder, Ann A. Morris, Winifred Lamb, Dorothy A. Garrod, Neil Judd, Luther Cressman, William C. Holden, Carl Guthe
G. I.	civic	1901-1924	Waldo Wedel, Betty Meggars, James Griffin, Mary Leakey, Kathleen Kenyon, Gordon Willey, James Ford, Bruce Goff
Silent	adaptive	1925-1942	James Deetz, Cynthia Irwin-Williams, Lewis Binford, Alice B. Kehoe, Thomas King, Dean Snow, James N. Hill, Mark Leone
Boomers	idealist	1943-1960	Linda Cordell, Ian Hodder, Deborah Pearsall, Kenneth Ames, Michael Shanks, Alison Wylie, Michael J. O'Brien

Gen X	reactive	1961-1981	John Kanter, Andrew Duff, Laurie Wilkie, Cornelius Holtorf, Kelly Dixon, Shannon Dawdy, Troy Lovata, Julie Schablitsky
Millennials	civic	1982-2002	Celebrity ladies currently reign: Mandy Moore, Scarlett Johansson, Paris Hilton, Lindsay Lohan, Britney Spears, Miley Cyrus
New Progressives	adaptive	2002-	Toddlers and elementary school kids

Adapted from Strauss and Howe (1997). The post WWII baby boom was a spike in the birth rate from 1946 to 1964; the Strauss and Howe model defines generations based on social cohort differences not changes in birth rates.

In academia, Idealists moralize a complicated world, Reactives simplify it into manageable fragments, Civics offer simplistic grand narratives, Adaptives add complexity and nuance to simple grand narratives, and the cycle repeats. Since the European colonization of America there have been nineteen generations living through five rotations that have influenced American culture and history. Table 25-1 lists recent ones of interest to archaeology.

As sociological concepts, generational types assist in understanding collective history and individual behavior. Civil War historians often contrast the leadership styles of Robert E. Lee and Ulysses S. Grant. It is useful to know that the former was an Idealist (Transcendentalist) and the latter a Reactive (Gilded) because it informs why they did what they did. Lee initiated campaigns into enemy territory (Antietam, Gettysburg) in the belief that a victory there would be symbolic enough to end the war. Grant preferred to use his larger force in sustained engagement until his smaller opponent was subdued (Vicksburg, Petersburg). The generational types of Lee and Grant reflect the leadership styles of Boomers (values driven) and Xers (pragmatic) that are nearly opposites.

Reactives are Free Agents

Reactive generations are the roughest in American history; they are the "bad" generations, using that word in all its variations. They generally come of age during moralistic culture wars and they suffer economic hardship most of their adult lives; many live a boom and bust life. Gen Xers have been caught in the midst of age-graded wage stagnation. Despite economic growth, the standard of living for a 30 year old in year 2000 was much less than it was for a 30 year old in 1970 because real median income (inflation adjusted) has stagnated in the United States since the 1970s and personal savings rates have hit lows not seen since the Great Depression; meanwhile household debt ratios have risen to new highs (Kemenetz 2006; Krugman 2007:124-152; Mooney 2008; O'Shaughnessy 2008; Strauss and Howe 1997:236). The tough economic times that Reactives live through, and the culture wars they try to avoid, casts them as survivalists, bottom line realists, and scrappy innovators and entrepreneurs. Their values are in stark contrast to prior generations: a career is not the most important thing in their lives, they cannot imagine working for the same company or in the same line of work for their entire lives, they expect to be respected, they are reluctant to commit to much of anything, and they expect to get as much as they give (Peters 2001:48-49).

As survivalists Xers are not beholden to any moral agenda other than individualism and eclecticism. Unattached as they are to the agendas of their next elders they are called nihilists which, of course, is inaccurate because what they are doing is not engaging in the culture wars of their elders; they are apathetic toward and tired of those crusades. The generational tiff between Boomers and Xers is real. The former look upon the latter as amoral slackers too focused on rascally fun (These losers will run society some day? God forbid!). Xers view Boomers as hypocritical culture warriors too incompetent to manage society (Will they ever shut up and stop arguing?). Living in the wake of the Boomers has not been pleasant; so they write about it (Coupland 1991; Gordinier 2008) waiting for their turn at leadership.

Xers have already made lasting impressions on American culture and archaeology. First and foremost, they are interested in having fun. Xers are simplifying the complicated moral world of the Boomers and they are focusing on enjoyable learning experiences. To them, archaeology is fun-- it's not a moral crusade, it will not change the world, and debating its status as a science is a wasted effort. Xers are also extremely physical giving America extreme sports, bungee jumping, snowboarding, and the now popular fist bump. Many Gen X women like digging and surveying, and can do them as well or better than men. Within the generation there is gender parity in terms of employment; in historical archaeology, employed women may outnumber men. Gen Xers are also the most tattooed and pierced generation in American history. Colorado archaeologists are having fun with it (http://www.coloradoarchaeologists.org/Funstuff.htm, accessed July 26, 2008). As strong romantics Gen Xers are changing popular culture toward super athletic *and* pleasantly plump characters because curves, firm or soft, are more appealing than rational slimness and angularity. (Millennials will take plumpness even further as romanticism climaxes; Venus figurines anyone?). In archaeology Xers live up to their nomadic ways. They embrace the life of shovel bumming with a sense of irony, caricature, and nobility (de Boer 2004). The shovel bum novel *Swamp* (Pachinco, 1997) is both a great description of contemporary CRM archaeology and of the life style of low income Gen Xers. Their hard hitting commercialism is seen in companies like Amazon, eBay, Google, Yahoo, and Dell, all founded by Gen Xers. What the entrepreneurs of these companies did was take something that already existed for corporations and made it efficiently available to individuals because their focus is on personal satisfaction, fun, and survival. As it is done today, archaeological research could not be done without the services of companies like these.

Previous reactive generations offer clues to what Gen Xers may be like in senior leadership roles. American presidents George Washington, John Adams, Grant, Hays, Garfield, Arthur, Cleveland, B. Harrison, Truman, and Eisenhower were all Reactives. The traits that connect them are pragmatism, fiscal conservatism, and a low tolerance for risk taking while in office. They were also generally unpretentious. These presidents had had prior military service and several had been generals. They all took their leadership roles during or directly after American culture was in secular crisis (the Revolution, the Civil War, and the Depression-WW II). Since 9/11 2001 America has again been in secular crisis and the midlife reactive generation is standing up. Additionally, Reactives attaining high office fairly young may tend toward autocracy (Sarah Palin, Michelle Rhee) which likely moderates with age. The nomadic type also has its flamboyant characters such as Barack Obama, George Custer, and Sir Mortimer Wheeler.

Reactives are best understood as Nomads and Commanders with keen analytical, management, and writing skills. Nomads wander geography, but also the mind, the soul, and the heart. As they have no cultural agenda other than survival they are not wedded to any theory or methodology. Nomads will pursue concepts that are productive toward planned goals; they will even abandon useful concepts in the desire to experiment with others. Previous reactive scientists include biologists Alfred Wallace, Thomas Huxley, Julian Huxley, and Francis Galton, economists Friedrich Hayek and Karl Polanyi, and geographer Carl Sauer. There is nothing wrong with being classified with these thinkers even as some of them pursued concepts that are generally unacceptable today (Social Darwinism, eugenics). More than other generations, nomads explore all corners of life, its wonderful pleasures (Mae West) and its darkest powers (Adolf Hitler).

The Lost Generation of archaeologists left a strong imprint on the profession, most notably because they were the core group of journeymen who founded SAA (c.f. Guthe 1967). They also established the basic outlines of regional chronological sequences and provided richly described reports. Their theories are largely forgotten and their methods and categories (the Direct Historical Approach, the Pecos Classification System, and the Midwestern Taxonomic System) are embedded in today's research. A roll call of the generation provides a few famous mentors and many forgotten ones: V. Gordon Childe, A. V. Kidder, W. C. McKern, Frank H. H. Roberts, William Duncan Strong, Ann Morris, William Albright, Gertrude Caton-Thompson, Raymond Dart, Dorothy Garrod, Winifred Lamb, Matthew Stirling, Helge Instad, and many more. The Gen X legacy will be similar to the Lost, unpretentious, generally non-ideological, and grounded in data. Archaeology will take a strong pragmatic turn in the next few years.

Reactive Mythology

Reactive generations are also the source for America's most iconic archaeologist, Indiana Jones, whose plotline places him within the Lost Generation (Table 25-2). This icon combines several reactive traits. From the Gilded Generation Indy takes the cowboy and gunfighter images, the nomadic lost souls of the Old West (Wild Bill Hickock, Buffalo Bill Cody, and Wyatt Earp). From the Lost Generation he takes the images of adventurers and explorers (F. A. Mitchell-Hedges, Roy Chapman Andrews) and blends them with characters from Lost mystery writers (Agatha Christie, Raymond Chandler, and Dasheill Hammett). As an anti-hero Indy is an Archaeologist-Detective and Archaeologist-Adventurer (Holtorf 2007: themes A and D). He is Hammett's Sam Spade but not Arthur C. Doyle's Sherlock Holmes (an adaptive character). Indy, of course, does not reflect the full range of reactive traits. In the Indy movies he is mostly a nomad. There are brief scenes where his commander side is shown but it is not the focus of the movies. Action movies with reactive main characters do best commercially when the nomadic image is emphasized.

Contemporary Western mythology has provided audiences with several stories--Harry Potter, Lord of the Rings, and Star Wars--that typecast the reactive commander role. In these apocalyptic tales the young civic heroes always come in teams with a team leader (Harry Potter/Hermione/Ron; Frodo/Sam/Merry/Pippin; Luke Skywalker/Princess Leia). These heroes are the focus of the stories and their exploits are legend. However, they cannot succeed without help from the next elder generation, as mentors, teachers, and leaders (Snape/Hagrid/the Dark Arts teachers; Aragon/Arwen/Boromir/Gimli/Legoas; Han Solo/Chewie/robots). In the commander role Reactives are often military officers or people of action but they can also be teachers and defenders of culture (Holtorf 2007: themes R and C). Reactives live nomadic and dangerous lives while young; they may even be iconoclasts. They mature into careful, pragmatic, and conservative leaders who enable the younger civic heroes to greatness.

Table 25-2: Mythical characters and generational types.

Idealists / Prophets	Reactives / Nomads
Jesus, Mohammed, Moses, Gandalf, Dumbledore, Obi-Wan Kenobi	Huck Finn, Indiana Jones, Lara Croft, Sam Spade, Snape, Aragon, Han Solo
Adaptives / Artists	**Civics / Heroes**
Buddha, Confucius, Merlin, Yoda, Sherlock Holmes, James Bond	Superman, Batman, Wonder Woman, Harry Potter, Frodo, Luke Skywalker

Every generation has a sociological function, its mythic destiny, and they can succeed or fail. Heroic generations provide the critical mass that pushes a crisis laden society to greatness; afterwards, they are the builders of a new society. Adaptives are the social reformers who spread elegance and grace through society; and yet they may compromise it through indecision. Idealists are culture warriors who polarize and potentially destroy society; from within their chaos comes a visionary offering a new moral order. Reactives wander a cultural wasteland and then they redeem it, assisting its rebirth. For Generation X history has charged them with the task of demonstrating that Americans can still enjoy "life, liberty, and the pursuit of happiness" without letting the world fly to pieces, without bankrupting the nation, and without squandering scarce global resources. They get to do the dirty work, have a little fun, and help the heroic kids behind them (Howe and Strauss 1993:228).

The Eternal Return

America in the '00s has been a fearful place. Since 9/11 we have been afraid of terrorists, of blue and red states, of our inept leaders, and of the economy. Two Boomer presidencies (Clinton and Bush Jr.) have wracked the culture off its moorings, letting it flounder in a crisis of confidence. The economy is in systemic crisis. The collapse of the Bush administration in 2006 sent the conservative movement into shock and Boomers everywhere are anxious because the failure of one part suggests the failure of the whole generation that believed it could change the world. They are, actually, living out their destiny as culture warriors who may be destroyers. Mythology helps to sway the fears because during the apocalypse there is always a prophet giving moral courage and guidance to the younger generations. Harry, Frodo, and Luke all had steely eyed gray haired champions to look up too (Dumbledore, Gandalf, Obi-Wan Kenobi). This gray champion has yet to emerge from the Boomer generation. History suggests that he or she will as they always have in the past (Franklin D. Roosevelt, Abraham

Lincoln, and Benjamin Franklin). This secular crisis is far from over. There is time for a Boomer to stand up, deliver a vision of a new moral order, and complete a generation's destiny.

Gen Xers are also doing their part; they are entering upper management positions and tenured professorships. They bring to archaeology pragmatism, flexibility, fiscal conservatism, and keen analytical abilities. They are unpretentious and mostly non-ideological. They are not culture warriors but are redeemers of culture. Nearly 80 years after the creation of SAA, Reactives are here again to assist in the reinvention of archaeology, something that Millenials will fully materialize (and get all the credit for). As it stands now CRM is the part that needs the most help. It, like life in general for Gen Xers, is a swamp of inequity and foolishness that needs redemption. Gen Xers can do it as it is their destiny.

Welcome back Indy.

from: Nomads and Commanders: Welcoming Generation X. *The SAA Archaeological Record* 9(5): 33-36.

26 ARCHAEOLOGISTS SHOULD DIG MORE

The recent essay by Anderson, Card, and Feder (2013) encourages us to chase pleasant distractions. They urge us to fight the forces that have "hijacked" (p.27) the public's perception of archaeology, and outline a process to do this. I'm uncertain that archaeologists ever had a claim on those perceptions, or should have one. As long as professional opinions are viewed as *mainstream* and the other side as *alternative* then no hijacking has occurred. Further, other fantasies are more threatening.

First, our knowledge of why people believe fantastic theories has been much improved by the research they have compiled. There is enough evidence to support the generalization that humans don't live on facts, truths, or science, alone. They also use religion, superstition, fiction, lies, misinformation, and metaphors to create meaning in life. Honestly, it would be a bland ugly world if facts and truth were all we had to sustain us. Fantasy is useful. Certainly, Feder has made a career out of jousting with the con artists and snake oil salesmen; it adds purpose to his life.

I do wonder about scientists who can't see the world in anything but literal terms. Ghosts, angels, werewolves, and vampires are metaphors for those people, things, and processes in life that challenge us, make us afraid, or feel wonderful. There is nothing wrong with calling your car a *guardian angel* if it saved your life. A vampire is someone or something that drains your energy, ambition, motivation, such as unpleasant people or governmental red tape. They are everywhere.

As threats go, the sellers of alternative ideas are minor compared to the oligarchs and politicians draining resources away from our potential use.

Our nation's economic crisis continues and the worst is still likely to come because the credit crisis of 2008-2010 was the vanguard of a much larger problem. In comparison, jousting about the origin of rune stones is a pleasant distraction.

American archaeology also has an internal threat. Like most vampires, this one is seductive, provocative, and promises to give eternal life (job security). Its name is historic preservation. With the rise of the preservation ethic in the 1980s, followed by the SAA ethics revision in 1996, and then topped off with the 2004 revision of the 36 CFR 800 regulations implementing Section 106 of the National Historic Preservation Act, the preservation ethos has consistently worked to reduce archaeological excavations. We used to dig more than we do now.

I, too, have participated in this. In the early 1990s, while working for Fairfax County, Virginia, I always had an excavation underway or planned, and I enabled many others. In federal service for the last eight years, I have facilitated zero excavations. Every day, I seek to avoid effects to most sites, especially adverse effects to significant ones. CRM archaeology has been diminished to locating, recording, and avoiding sites. Excavation is generally a last resort or the result of an inadvertent discovery.

In 2004 archaeological excavation became an adverse effect under the revised 36 CFR 800 regulations (as a logical consequence of proclaiming archaeological research an undertaking requiring Section 106 consultation). This rapidly became an indictment against excavation. At the Meta level it simply connotes that excavation is morally wrong or is too much of a burden (added costs, time, and planning). Regardless of the procedures guiding us to resolve adverse effects, most developers and planners choose to not have adverse effects because of the negative perceptions about creating them or the sense that they are too burdensome. At a macro level, the indictment equates excavation with those other adverse effects that archaeologists despise, such as bull dozing without research. We know that excavation is destructive but now we also damn ourselves for it. At the micro level, excavation potentially creates one of the most absurd situations possible in CRM. Since excavation is still viewed as an acceptable mitigation technique, it is now possible to use an adverse effect to mitigate another kind of adverse effect. The best response to this is to avoid adverse effects of any kind.

That creepy feeling that we are not connecting with and influencing the lay public in ways we expect or desire will continue even if we joust with con artists because we are not listening to the public. The SAA sponsored Harris Interactive study (Ramos and Duganne 2000) identified that the primary association lay people have with archaeology is the image of *digging*. And most of us are doing less and less of the one thing the public associates with us--digging. There is no need to blame others for our social clumsiness.

The best way to connect with the lay public, and to undermine alternative views, is to increase excavations, everywhere possible, using the new Gemeinschaft perspectives. Preservation should be an ally, not our master.

from Letter to the Editor, *SAA Archaeological Record* 13 (4): 3, 2013.

27 American Archaeology, Circa 2013

It's been thirty years since I began thinking about archaeology as a subject of sociological inquiry. It's time for some reflection, a summation of a long process. To me, archaeology just isn't what it used to be. It's not "happening" as much as it should.

In the early 1980s I played the role of ethnographer. In the summer of 1983 I did my first ethnographic stint at an archaeological field camp. I returned in 1984 as well. After that, I went to work as an archaeologist because it was the easiest way to find employment, and more graduate school was not appealing. The late '80s was when I became an "archaeologist," although I never really thought of myself as that. I was, and always have been, a "student of the human condition." Ethnography, archaeology, financial services, are windows into it.

Initially, I started out as a migrant field technician—instead of *shovel bum*, we had a more derogatory term for ourselves in those years (*dig-roes*, not very polite, then or now). By 1988, I became the vaunted Principle Investigator or PI. From 1989 through 1996, I dug--meaning I directed large crews in the excavation of--several sites, mostly block excavations or trenches. I became a master of soils, stratigraphy, and features. Today, my trowel is rusty but I still know good archaeology when I see it. As they say, "once a PI, always a PI".

A new show on the National Geographic channel (*The '80s: The Decade That Made Us*) glorifies that decade. As a nation, we went from people mostly living within their means--plain living and high thinking--to "shop until you drop" with Madonna screaming that she was a material girl. We went from Apollonian intellectualism to Dionysian crass materialism. Dionysian intellectualism was a possible option but big corporations and the political far right chose to take us into crass materialism and anti-intellectualism. Science was taken off its pedestal and stomped on by everyone (except those few scientists who continued to believe in its righteousness). If you believe in scientism today, you are on the fringe.

In the '80s, America was in the last third of the Fourth Awakening. Collectively, our brains were on fire with the right and left hemispheres fighting for control. Entropy was high. Like the two decades before, it was a tumultuous time. I remember some riots and, at graduate school, even marches and demonstrations for some unremembered cause. In Montana, there were anti-government skinheads blowing up cars in Missoula and they shot a cop. In '85 or '86 , while out to do an archaeological survey for a timber sale, I got to drive a nice green Forest Service truck into a camp of skinheads, wearing bandoliers, and grinning as they generally pointed their guns my way. I didn't stay. After the Ruby Ridge incident, the Northwest quieted down.

Obviously, the big mega change has been the transformation from an Apollonian culture of circa 1920-1960 to our now fully Dionysian one, 1990-present. (The Fourth Awakening was 1960 to 1990). The right hemisphere won the struggle. Today, intuition rules everything we do. The second age of reason, modernism, is 90 percent gone. The last ten percent is legacy stuff. No one really cares about critical thinking or building a good linear argument. Such things reek of days gone by.

In archaeology, many things have changed since the '80s. In terms of techniques and technologies, the big change has been computers. We used to make field notes by hand with pen or pencil; now there are computers in the field. We once wrote field diaries; I haven't heard that idea in a long time. We used to use typewriters to do our reports; now it is all computers. We once tried to be good photographers, using expensive cameras, and knew the usages and settings of color, black and white, and slides. Today, we use cheep digital cameras and just point and shoot. In the '80s people dabbled with clunky video cameras; now every small cell phone is a movie maker. We were once amateur mapmakers, using leveled transits and rod. Then came laser transits and rod. Now it is just all about GPS and GIS. Once we were excellent at land navigation, could read a topographic map, use a compass, and used our cognitive maps to find our way home. Today, we depend on gizmos.

In the '80s large excavations with large crews used to be common. In 1987, at the Fort Union project, we had about 45 people. Next, at Addison Plantation, there were a few more. Large open area excavation was the way to get it done. I continued that with my own projects. Next, briefly, we used widespread random testing (because random sampling was scientific). Today, we do limited targeted testing, or nothing. A few academics do small excavations; in the world of CRM, excavation is done only in emergencies or for inadvertent discoveries.

In the 1980s there wasn't a collections or curation crisis. We had plenty of space because we put stuff anywhere we could, in garages, basements, or storage sheds. Then came 36 CFR 79, in 1990, and everyone had to comply with professional museum standards to store collections. Since compliance to these standards is expensive, few facilities were built and a crisis was created. Lack of compliant storage space also supports our decision to not excavate. I am not opposed to museum standards but much of the stuff we excavate doesn't need to be stored forever or doesn't need climate controlled space.

In the '80s we once thought that chemical and biological studies would be extremely helpful. The answer is a mixed bag. We used to take soil acidity samples, sampled for phytoliths and pollen, and wished that blood residue studies would come back with "human" rather than the ubiquitous "deer". When you make a big effort to find seeds in hearths and all you ever get is chenopodium, then what good is it? Maybe these studies are just a luxury now. Since excavation is now limited, so are the extra studies.

The perspectives of archaeology have changed as well. There was a big debate, the processual versus post-processual one. Of course, that was the shift from Apollo to Dionysus as a leading metaphor. Some folks still call themselves scientists but the kind of science conducted is different. Dionysian science allows the nonlinear and chaos perspectives to thrive. In the old days, the Clovis First theory was paramount; now it is widely accepted that some type of pre-Clovis occupations occurred in North America. Tied to this conception is the mono or multi migration route debate. Once I understood that Australia was inhabited 60 thousand years ago, the mono route via the Bering Strait made no sense and I agreed with the multi route perspective and with a multitude of pre-Columbian contacts. People don't stay put. They move around.

Some perspectives haven't changed. Archaeologists are still of the mindset that older is better; most struggle with the material culture of the twentieth century. Additionally, like most Americans, they fuss about the moral and ethical issues around the concept of Firsts. If someone is a First what claims do they have? Should they have any claims? First born, first to scoop the story, First Americans--Why does First matter?

Today, the social context of archaeology is very different. In the '80s the GI and Silent generations were still very active; as collectivists they portrayed a sense of common purpose across the profession. Now, with the Boomers and Gen X generations dominating the field, strong individualism undermines illusions of common purpose. Additionally, back then, archaeologists were heroes because Indy was new and popular; now they are shovel bums with fedoras wishing Indy wasn't so old. Indy is a powerful icon but another can replace him. Lara Croft won't do it; she is too sexy and is a thief of time. For a while Daniel Jackson of the *Stargate* franchise seemed to be appealing because he is actually a good metaphor for CRM archaeology (archaeological consultant to the government who helps solve everyday problems). Unfortunately, CRM has become stale and directionless, a jobs program, another example of the ponzie schemes rampant in America.

After the economic scare of 2008-2010 that unemployed so many archaeologists, it seems that most are working again. Or, another way to put it, I don't know any unemployed archaeologists at the moment. Good for all of us, we have jobs. I still believe the profession is at risk from severe external forces, that political-economic hell is coming. The earlier shock was a vanguard; the next one will be the great test. We may not have jobs in the future.

However, working as an archaeologist also isn't what it used to be. In the early 1990s I worked for Fairfax County, Virginia; my title was initially Historian, then it changed to Heritage Resource Specialist. I did my best to always have an excavation underway or planned, and I enabled others to do excavations. Archaeology was about digging and research. I didn't care what my title was. I wasn't a preservationist.

Today, ironically, I have a job title and a business card that say I am an archaeologist. My job is best described as heritage resource specialist. I work in the preservationist world. Along with many other things, I do think about and assess archaeological sites, I review survey reports, I communicate with tribes, I draft environmental documents, and I research issues of historic preservation law. In depth archaeological research is incidental to my duties and I do my best work when I ensure that archaeological excavation does not happen. In the eight years I have been a federal "archeologist" (without the "a") there have been many surveys and a few test projects but no excavations enabled by me. I have done my preservationist job and ensured that sites have been avoided and preserved in situ (in place).

Today, CRM archaeology is all about pedestrian survey with a little bit of test units on the side. CRM has been reduced to locating and avoiding archaeological sites because, under historic preservation guidelines (36 CFR 800), excavation is considered an adverse effect, no different from destruction by bull dozing. And avoiding adverse effects is what we in the preservation field do.

I also notice, at conferences, that academics are spending more time re-studying old collections than making new ones, especially if the project is about Native American antiquity.

It seems that excavation has fallen out of favor in American archaeology. The preservation ethos, the adverse effect indictment, the sensitivity to tribes, and the curation crisis, all lead to the decision of "don't excavate." American archaeologists just don't make it happen, contrary to what European archaeologist Martin Carver (2011) advocates.

I wish I had numbers to compare the '80s to today but I don't. My gut feeling and my anecdotal evidence is that the amount of dirt excavated today is minuscule compared to what it used to be. It's possible that we are surveying more acres than then but we aren't doing the digging we once did. It is a sad observation.

Like most Americans, I believe that archaeology is about digging. It isn't about survey, record, and avoid. Preservation isn't archaeology.

from Age of Intuition, April 7, 2013.

28 ENCHANTED AMERICA, ENCHANTED ARCHAEOLOGY

Morris Berman is a disenchanted American studies scholar and social critic. He thinks America has failed and that there is no hope for a turnaround (Berman 2012). In a recent essay (2013), he starts by discussing older thinkers who worried about how our "rational" world was non-harmonious and disenchanted:

> The notion that there was a way of life characteristic of modern (or industrial) societies that was qualitatively different from the way of life found in pre-modern (or folk) societies goes back, at least, to the German sociologist Max Weber [2009]. Modern societies, said Weber, are governed by bureaucracies; the dominant ethos is one of "rationalization," whereby everything is mechanized, administered according to the dictates of scientific reason. Weber famously compared this situation to that of an "iron cage": there was no way the citizens of these societies could break free from their constraints. Pre-modern societies, on the other hand, were permeated by animism, by a belief in magic and spirits, and governance came not through bureaucracy but through the charisma of gifted leaders. The decline of magic that accompanied the transition to modernity Weber called die Entzauberung der Welt—the disenchantment of the world.

He goes on to mention other thinkers who have made similar distinctions, such as the Gemeinschaft [community based on good social relations] and

Gesellschaft [society based on contracts] cultures of Ferdinand Tönnies (2002), the Genuine [contented, satisfied] versus Spurious [frustrated, dysfunctional] cultures of Edward Sapir (1924), and the moral versus technical order of Robert Redfield (1963). These are all simple, old fashioned, distinctions about modern culture versus "pre-modern" with the emphasis on the non-modern as being a more humane way of life. It is them looking over the fence and seeing greener pastures.

Of course, he could have added Nietzsche (1967 [1872]), Ruth Benedict (1934) and E. T. Hall (1976), who also divided cultures into two types, the Apollonian-Low context cultures versus the Dionysian-High context ones. While there is no doubt that Hall's Low Context Culture resembles a spurious technically ordered society, it is hard to say that Dionysian cultures are always moral orders full of community minded folks. After all, Dionysians can be genuinely nasty. I, of course, prefer this distinction and emphasize that it does not force a moral valuation of one over the other. The distinction is a good way to describe cultures without judging them.

To be disenchanted, one must believe the basic premise of modern versus pre-modern, and then draw a moral distinction. One supposedly seems better than the other based on some yardstick of warm, sweet and cuddly versus cold and impersonal. Certainly, Weber's work has been debated greatly. Does rationalism and technological change really disenchant? Some folks don't think so (Jenkins 2000; Landy and Saler 2009) and I don't think so. When people become enchanted with science and rationality, the magic of it all isn't called magic but something else, such as "it's an elegant theory" or "it's a no-brainer".

However, let us suppose that Berman is correct and play along with him. Is America disenchanted based on the criteria outlined above? Let's look at animism, belief in magic and spirits, and governance via the charisma of gifted leaders. First, we do have a bureaucracy without charismatic leaders. In my adult lifetime, back to Reagan, I can't think of a single person in the political realm who inspired me. Martin Luther King was inspiring but he wasn't a political leader. So chalk one up for being disenchanted with our leaders.

Does American culture have animism, magic and spirits? They dominate our popular culture. In the last year, every commercial for Jaguar cars has been animistic; this month, the tag line for the newest commercial is, the car is "Alive as you are." Our entertainment is full of wizards (*Harry Potter*) and ghost hunting (*Ghost Hunters, Ghost Adventures, Haunted Collector*). Moreover, if ghosts don't get your attention then vampires, werewolves, zombies, and angels are there to fill the void. The basketball player called "Magic" Johnson didn't get his name because he plays like a machine but because his movements are "magic." By any standard, American popular culture is as enchanting as any recent Brazilian carnival.

Some critics might say that popular culture doesn't reveal the "real" culture. This is foolishness, typically coming from older modernists who still glorify intellectualism and "high" culture. Pop culture is our folklore, our mythology, our soul.

To make this point a little deeper, let's look at a subset of American culture, the profession of American archaeology. Do archaeologists believe in ghosts and spirits? Some of them do. Most of them do not have cold-blooded clinical mentalities. Archaeologists go into strange unusual places and they tend to find ones that were once sacred. They are human, all too human, and many of them are susceptible to their emotions, their imagination, and the heebie-jeebies. Many will tell stories of places that spooked them so much they had to leave; others talk of having nightmares while excavating graves. Many a lab technician has heard things go bump in the night and day, especially when human remains are on tables or in boxes nearby. Spookiness and archaeology go together.

Does archaeology have animism? Very much so, it's everywhere. Whenever archaeologists discuss artifact assemblages you will likely hear phrases such as "these are objects of change" or "vectors of change" or "this artifact symbolizes." Archaeologists reify and animate objects with regularity because it's the way Americans communicate. Animistic statements are complex metaphors that tie us to our natural world. Objects and technology are part of our natural environment. Tools, all material culture, are extensions of us. Why shouldn't we talk about them and interact with them as if they were alive? Likewise, we talk about abstractions as if they were alive: statistics "speak for themselves," cultures "move" from one place to another, and America is said to "fail". How can America "fail"; is it alive with agency? Just as in "pre-modern" cultures, it is customary for Americans to communicate in this way.

For archaeologists artifacts have magical powers. Not every artifact or site does, but some do. If you dig a hundred shovel tests and find only one arrowhead then that moment of discovery may be magical, special. Most archaeologists are connected to the tools of the trade. Many have their special trowel that symbolizes their professionalism, like a red badge of courage. Field vehicles are old friends, held onto for many years. Just as the cable show *Warehouse 13* demonstrates, some artifacts are imbued with meaning and power such that they can be transformative. Find the right type of site or artifact and it can change your life, your career, no different from winning a large lottery. Ideas are also magical. Coming up with a new and compelling interpretation or explanation can be career enhancing.

Moreover, many archaeological ideas are coyote tales, full of trickery and suspension of disbelief. Given a couple hundred artifacts and a few radiocarbon dates, an archaeologist can reconstruct the life way of a culture. Do you really believe it? Archaeologists have also held many debates over the "realness" of their artifact typologies. It doesn't matter that sand tempered cord marked pottery from Virginia likely resembles sand tempered cord marked pottery from Nebraska; they have to be different based on the archaeological mentality. Many a thesis or dissertation has been written based on the analysis of a few ceramic shards or a shoebox of "projectile points" (many of which were likely knives or scrappers). Nevertheless, who cares? A compelling statement is what matters. Archaeologists are sometimes magicians.

Currently, there are a few charismatic characters in archaeology. However, none of them is leading the profession. In the recent past, there were charismatic leaders, especially in the 1960s and 1970s. In those years, America was transforming from an Apollonian culture steeped in rationalism into a Dionysian one based on intuition. This transformation was the Fourth Awakening (McLoughlin, 1978) that was a revitalization movement (Wallace 1956). It was a frenetic era with social unrest and an unpopular war. These years are marked in archaeology as the New Archaeology era. During this time, Louis Binford introduced a narrow form of positivism into the profession, the idea caught fire in popularity with minimal disbelievers, and the profession rode the wave of "rational" ecstasy for twenty years, until it burned out. It also coincided with the broader love fest for science that was underway in the social sciences at that time, such as the New Ethnography, Enthnoscience, the New History, the New Geography, and monetarism in economics.

The New Archaeology had all the traits of an old-fashioned religious revival movement (McLoughlin, 1978). Led by a charismatic leader, it used something old and abandoned, positivism, to make corrective changes within the profession, to make it more scientific. In the face of rising intuitive processes and complex metaphors it was a retro, conservative, effort to continue rationalism that ultimately failed, as all revivals do, because it didn't instill long term change. When the New Archaeology flame burned out scientism crashed in American archaeology, as it did in all of American culture in the late 1980s and 1990s.

The irony is that the New Archaeology was a Dionysian process, a slight of the hand, or the brain, if you will. It is well known that left hemisphere processes (McGilchrist 2009) direct Apollonian cultures; the control, order, hierarchy, and temporal aspects of life are emphasized over their opposites. Rationalism is a left hemisphere complex metaphor. But, what happens when the right hemisphere plays with it? You get eye dazzlers.

Apollonian artifacts usually have geometric designs and they are simple and elegant--think of the popular late modernist corporate buildings from 1970s with all the rectangular glass. Next, take all those rectangles and compound them so much that the positive and negative fields are blurred. You get a design that shimmers as patterns go back and forth. It becomes an eye dazzler. The same thing happens with our concepts and ideas. Take conceptual linearity too far and you get conceptual bedazzlement. The New Archaeology, with its hypothetical deductive argumentation, was a coyote tale of bedazzlement, enchanted by its supposed rationalism.

Today, American archaeology is fully Dionysian. There are a few elder modernists holding on to their left brained science but they live at the margins. Right-brained science and non-science are in control; Post Modernism and Romanticism are the buzzwords of the day. Other warm and fuzzy concepts are widely used such as collaboration and "community archaeology". The preference is Gemeinschaft as a way of approaching archaeology, a desire for a moral order that is genuine and democratic, leaving everyone satisfied and fulfilled. It is enchanted archaeology.

There are problems within archaeology. While many likely believe that historic preservation compliance is the redeeming feature of the profession, because it drives the majority of work, it actually is a vampire sucking the soul from the profession by reducing the total number of excavations done every year. Digging is the true life-blood of the profession. It is what the majority of the public wants from us; not site preservation. Archaeologists can break free of this cage if they choose. But since they have not done so, the need is not dire enough for it to happen.

Maybe the troubles of America that Berman documents so well in his books could compel archaeologists to switch gears and go another direction. I'm all in favor of it. However, an "iron cage of rationality" is not one of those troubles. America is fully Dionysian and enchanted; its troubles stem from the wild impulses emanating from our right hemispheres. This will continue until the next Awakening, some forty years hence. Meanwhile, resolving immediate problems will have to be done by tickling the right hemisphere, and the solutions will be based in reciprocity and reflexivity, not cause and effect.

There is no reason to be disenchanted when life is such a wonderful carnival.

from: The Age of Intuition, February 24, 2013

REFERENCES

Adams, H. (1988). *The Academic Tribes* (Second ed.). Champaign, IL, University of Illinois Press.

Agar, M. H. (1996). *The Professional Stranger: An Informal Introduction to Ethnography* (Second edition ed.). Orlando, FL: Academic Press.

Alsen, E. (1996). *Romantic Postmoderism in American Fiction*. Atlanta, GA: Rodopi.

Anderson, D., Card, J. J., & Feder, K. L. (2013). Speaking Up and Speaking Out: Collective Efforts in the Fight to Reclaim the Public Perception of Archaeology. *SAA Archaeological Record, 13*(2), 24-28.

Armstrong, D. (2001). Attaining the Full Potential of Historical Archaeology. *Historical Archaeology, 35*(2), 9-13.

Arnold, D. A. (2002). *The Great Bust Ahead: The Greatest Depression in American and UK History is Just Several Short Years Away*. New York, NY: Vorago-US.

Association Research, Inc. (2005). *2005 Salary Survey for the Society for American Archaeology*. Rockville, MD: Association Research, Inc.

Augilar, J. (1981). Insider Research: An Ethnography of Debate. In D. A. Messerschmidt (Ed.), *Anthropologists at Home in North America* (pp. 15-26). New York, NY: Cambridge University Press.

Babcock, B. (1980). Reflexivity: Definitions and Discriminations. *Semiotica, 30*(1-2), 1-14.

Barret, R. A. (1984). *Culture and Conduct: An Excursion in Anthropology*. Wadsworth, CA: Belmont Publishing Company.

Becher, T., & Trowler, P. (2001). *Academic Tribes and Territories: Intellectual Enquiry and the Cultures of Discipline* (Second edition ed.). Philadelphia, PA: Open University Press.

Beck, U., Giddens, A., & Lash, S. (1994). *Reflexive Modernization: Politics, Traditions and Aesthitics in the Modern Social Order.* Stanford, CA: Stanford University Press.

Bell, D. (1967). *Marxian Socialism in the United States.* Princeton, NJ: Princeton University Press.

Bender, B., Hamilton, S., & Tilly, C. (Eds.). (2006). *Stone Worlds: Narrative and Reflexivity in Landscape Archaeology.* Walnut Creek, CA: Left Coast Press.

Bender, T. (1978). *Community and Social Change in America.* Piscataway, NJ: Rutgers University Press.

Benedict, R. (1934). *Patterns of Culture.* New York, NY: Houghton Mifflin.

Berman, M. (2012). *Why America Failed: The Roots of Imperial Decline.* Hoboken, NJ: John Wiley and Sons.

Berman, M. (2013, February 8). *The Moral Order: A Dying Civilization.* Retrieved February 22, 2013, from CounterPunch: http://www.counterpunch.org/2013/02/08/the-moral-order

Berreman, G. D. (1962). *Behind Many Masks: Ethnography and Impression Management in a Himalayan Village.* Society for Applied Anthropology, Monograph No. 4.

Berrett, D. (2010, November 30). Anthropology Without Science. *Inside Higher ED.*

Beteille, A. (1986). Individualism and Equality. *Current Anthropologist, 27,* 121-134.

Binford, L. R. (1962). Archaeology as Anthropology. *American Antiquity, 28,* 217-225.

Binford, L. R. (1987). Data, Relativism and Archaeological Science. *Man, 22,* 391-404.

Binford, S. R., & Binford, L. R. (Eds.). (1968). *New Perspectives in Archaeology.* Chicago, IL: Aldine Publishing Company.

Bohannan, P. (1963). *Social Anthropology.* New York, NY: Holt, Rinehart, Winston.

Bouchard, M. C. (2004). The Current Decline in Archaeological Society Memberships in Connecticut: Causes, Effects, and Possible Solutions. *North American Archaeologist, 25*(3), 239-249.

Bourdieu, P., & Wacquant, L. (1992). *An Invitation to Reflexive Sociology.* Chicago, IL: Chicago University Press.

Bousquet, M. (2004). Academic Labor and the Reflexive Turn in Literature and Cultural Studies. *College Literature, 31*(4), 172-180.

Buber, M. (1949). *Paths in Utopia.* Boston, MA: Beacon Press.

Buber, M. (1971). *I and Thou.* (W. Kaufmann, Trans.) New York, NY: Touchstone Publishing.

Burns, A. F. (1983). Obituary: Solon T Kimball, 1908-1982. *Anthropology and Education Quarterly, 14*(2), 148-157.

Butler, W. B. (1976). Archeology and Prohibition. *Plains Anthropologist, 21*(71), 67-72.

Calabrese, C. (1994). Investigating Mass Graves for the U.N. *Federal Archeology, 7*(2), 9.

Campbell, C. (1987). *The Romantic Ethic and the Spirit of Modern Consumerism.* New York, NY: Blackwell Publishing Company.

Carman, J. (2006). Digging the Dirt: Excavation as a Social Practice. In M. Edgeworth (Ed.), *Ethnographies of Archaeological Practice: Cultural Encounters, Material Transformations* (pp. 95-102). Lanham, MD: AltaMira Press.

Carver, M. (2011). *Making Archaeology Happen: Design Versus Dogma.* Walnut Creek, CA: Left Coast Press.

Castaneda, Q. E. (1991). *An "Archaeology" of Chichen Itza: Discourse, Power and Resistance in a Maya Tourist Site.* PhD Dissertation, State University of New York, Albany.

Chadwick, A. (2003). Post-Processualism, Professionalism and Archaeological Methodologies: Towards Reflective and Radical Practice. *Archaeological Dialogues, 10*(1), 97-117.

Claes, T. (1996). Theorizing the West: A Second Look at Francis L. K. Hsu. *Cultural Dynamics, 8*, 79-99.

Clarke, D. L. (1973). Archaeology: A Loss of Innocence. *Antiquity, 47*, 6-18.

Cleland, C. E. (2001). Historical Archaeology Adrift? *Historical Archaeology, 35*(2), 1-8.

Cleland, C. E., & Fitting, J. (1968). The Crisis of Identity: Theory in Historic Sites Archeology. *The Conference on Historic Site Archaeology Papers, 1967, 2, part 2*, pp. 124-138.

Cobb, C. R. (2005). Archaeology and the "Savage Slot": Displacement and Emplacement in the Premodern World. *American Anthropologist, 107*(4), 563-574.

Coupland, D. (1991). *Generation X: Tales for an Accelerated Culture.* New York, NY: St. Martin's Press.

Covey, S. R. (1990). *The Seven Habits of Highly Effective People: Powerfull Lessons in Personal Change.* New York, NY: Simon and Schuster.

Cressey, P. J., Reeder, R., & Bryson, J. (2003). Held in Trust: Community Archaeology in Alexandria, Virginia. In L. Derry, & M. Malloy (Ed.), *Archaeologists and Local Communities: Partners in Exploring the Past* (pp. 1-17). Washington, DC: Society for American Archaeology.

Custer, J. F. (2005a). Ethics and the Hyperreality of the Archaeological Thought World. *North American Archaeologist, 26*(1), 2-27.

Custer, J. F. (2005b). Haunted by Pehin Hanska. *The American Indian Quarterly, 29*(3-4), 675-690.

Dalton, R. (2011, May 20). *Scientists Fight University of California to Study Rare Ancient Skeletons.* Retrieved March 16, 2013, from Wired.com: http://www.wired.com/wiredscience/2011/05/ucsd-skeleton-fight/

Darvill, T. (2004). Archaeology in Rock. In N. Brodie, & C. Hills (Eds.), *Material Engagements: Studies in Honour of Colin Renfrew* (pp. 55-77). Cambridge: McDonald Institute for Archaeological Research.

Dawkins, R. (1997, January/February). Is Science a Religion? *The Humanist.*

de Boer, T. (2004). *Comix of Archaeological Field Life.* Walnut Creek, CA: Altamira Press.

Deagan, K. (1988). Neither History nor Prehistory: The Questions that Count in Historical Archaeology. *Historical Archaeology, 22*(1), 7-12.

Deagan, K., & Scardaville, M. (1985). Archeology and History on Historic Hispanic Sites: Impediments and Solutions. *Historical Archaeology, 19*, 32-37.

DeCorse, C. R. (1987). Historical Archaeological Research in Ghana 1986-87. *Nyama Akuma, 29*, 27-31.

DeCorse, C. R. (1992). Culture Contact, Continuity and Change on the Gold Coast, AD 1400-1900. *African Archaeological Review, 10*, 163-196.

Deetz, J. F. (1977). *In Small Things Forgotten: The Archaeology of Early American Life*. Garden City, NY: Anchor Press/Doubleday.

Deetz, J. F. (1983). Scientific Humanism and Humanistic Science: A Plea for Paradigmatic Pluralism in Historical Archaeology. *Geoscience and Man, 23*, 27-34.

Deetz, J. F. (1988a). Material Culture and Worldview in Anglo-America. In M. P. Leone, & P. B. Potter (Eds.), *The Recovery of Meaning: Historical Archaeology in the Eastern United States* (pp. 219-233). Washington, DC: Smithsonian Institution Press.

Deetz, J. F. (1988b). History and Archaeological Theory: Walter Taylor Revisited. *American Antiquity, 53*(1), 13-22.

Deetz, J. F. (1991). Introduction: Archaeological Evidence of Sixteenth and Seventeenth Century Encounters. In L. Falk (Ed.), *Historical Archaeology in Global Perspective* (pp. 1-9). Washington, DC: Smithsonian Institution Press.

Dent, H. S. (1993). *The Great Boom Ahead: Your Comprehensive Guide to Personal and Business Profit in the New Era of Prosperity*. New York, NY: Hyperion.

Dent, H. S. (2004). *The Next Great Bubble Boom: How to Profit from the Greatest Boom in History, 2005-2009*. New York, NY: The Free Press.

Doktor, R. (1983). Culture and Management of Time: A Comparison of Japanese and American Top Management Practice. *Asia Pacific Journal of Management, 1*(1), 65-71.

Dumont, L. (1986). *Essays on Individualism: Modern Ideology in Anthropological Perspective*. Chicago, IL: University of Chicago Press.

Dychtwald, K., & Kadlec, D. J. (2005). *The Power Years: A User's Guide to the Rest of Your Life*. New York, NY: Wiley.

Edgeworth, M. (1990). Analogy as Practical Reason: The Perception of Artifacts in Archaeological Practice. *Archaeological Review from Cambridge, 9*(2), 243-251.

Edgeworth, M. (Ed.). (2006). *Ethnographies of Archaeological Practice: Cultural Encounters, Material Transformations*. Lanham, MD: Altamira Press.

Epperson, T. W. (1990). Race and the Disciplines of the Plantation. *Historical Archaeology, 24*(4), 29-36.

Fabian, J. (1983). *Time and the Other: How Anthropology Makes Its Object*. New York, NY: Columbia University Press.

Fabian, J. (2006). The Other Revisited: Critical Afterthoughts. *Anthropological Theory, 6*(2), 139-152.

Fabian, J. (2011, February 4). Huxley Memorial Lecture: Cultural Anthropology and the Question of Knowledge. London: Backdoor Broadcasting Company for the Royal Anthropological Institute. Retrieved from http://backdoorbroadcasting.net/2011/02/johannes-fabian-cultural-anthropology-and-the-question-of-knowledge/

Fagan, B. (2002). Epilogue. In B. Little (Ed.), *Public Benefits of Archaeology* (pp. 253-260). Gainesville, FL: University of Florida Press.

Falk, L. (Ed.). (1991). *Historical Archaeology in Global Perspective*. Washington, DC: Smithsonian Institution Press.

Fallers, L. A. (1973). *Inequility: Social Statification Reconsidered*. Chicago, IL: University of Chicago Press.

Flannery, K. (1982). The Golden Marshalltown: A Parable for the Archaeology of the 1980's. *American Anthropologist, 84*(2), 265-278.

Fogel, R. W. (2000). *The Fourth Great Awakening and the Future of Egalitarianism*. Chicago, IL: University of Chicago Press.

Ford, J. A. (1954). The Type Concept Revisited. *American Anthropologist, 56*(1), 42-53.

Freeman, D. (1984). *Margaret Mead and Samoa: The Making and Unmaking of an Anthropological Myth*. London: Penguin book.

Funari, P. P., Hall, M., & Jones, S. (Eds.). (1999). *Historical Archaeology: Back from the Edge*. London: Routledge.

Galenson, D. W. (2006). *Old Masters and Young Geniuses: The Two Life Cycles of Artistic Creativity*. Princeton, NJ: Princeton University Press.

Gero, J. M. (1996). Archaeological Practice and Gendered Encounters with Field Data. In R. P. Wright (Ed.), *Gender and Archaeology* (pp. 251-280). Philadelphia, PA: University of Pennsylvania Press.

Gillespie, S. D., & Nichols, D. L. (Eds.). (2003). *Archaeology Is Anthropology*. Washington, DC: American Anthropological Association, Archaeological Papers No. 13.

Gilmore, K. P., Tate, M., Chenault, M. L., Clark, B., McBride, T., & Wood, M. (Eds.). (1999). *Colorado Prehistory: A Context for the Platte River Basin*. Denver, CO: Colrado Council of Professional Archaeologists.

Glassie, H. (1975). *Folk Housing of Middle Virginia*. Knoxville, TN: University of Tennessee Press.

Gmelch, G., & Gmelch, S. B. (1999). An Ethnographic Field School: What Students Do and Learn. *Anthropology and Education Quarterly, 30*(2), 220-227.

Godfrey, W. S. (1949). The Newport Puzzle. *Archaeology, 2*(3), 146-149.

Godfrey, W. S. (1951). The Archaeology of the Old Stone Mill in Newport, Rhode Island. *American Antiquity, 17*(2), 120-129.

Godfrey, W. S. (1955). Vikings in America: Theories and Evidence. *American Anthropologist, 57*(1), 35-43.

Goodwin, C. (1994). Professional Vision. *American Anthropologist, 96*(3), 606-633.

Gordinier, J. (2008). *X Saves the World: How Generation X Got the Shaft But Can Still Keep Everything from Sucking*. New York, NY: Viking Press.

Gore, A. (2007). *The Assault on Reason*. New York, NY: Penguin Press.

Gorer, G. (1964). *The American People: A Study in National Character* (Revised ed.). New York, NY: Norton.

Gould, S. J. (1987). *Times's Arrow, Time's Cycle: Myth and Metaphor in the Discovery of Geological Time*. Cambridge, MA: Harvard University Press.

Grant, L., Preissle, J., Beoku-Betts, J., Finlay, W., & Fine, G. A. (1999). Fieldwork in Familiar Places: The UGA Workshop in Fieldwork Methods. *Anthropology and Education Quarterly, 30*(2), 238-248.

Gruen, E. S. (2010). *Rethinking the Other in Antiquity*. Princeton, NJ: Princeton University Press.

Gunn, G. B. (1979). *The Interpretation of Otherness: Literature, Religion, and the American Imagination*. New York, NY: Oxford University Press.

Guralnick, E. (Ed.). (1982). *Vikings in the West*. Chicago, IL: Archaeological Institute of America.

Gusterson, H. (1997). Studying Up Revisited. *Poltical and Legal Anthropology Review, 20*(1), 114-119.

Guthe, C. (1967). Reflections on the Founding of the Society for American Archaeology. *American Antiquity, 32*(4), 433-440.

Haag, W. G. (1985). Federal Aid to Archaeology in the Southeast, 1933-1942. *American Antiquity, 50*(2), 272-280.

Hall, E. T. (1976). *Beyond Culture* . New York, NY: Doubleday.

Hall, M. A. (2004). Romancing the Stones: Archaeology in Popular Cinema. *European Journal of Archaeology, 7*(2), 159-176.

Hall, M., & Silliman, S. W. (Eds.). (2006). *Historical Archaeology*. Maxwell, MA: Blackwell Publishing Ltd.

Hamada, T. (1985). Corporation, Culture, and Environment: The Japanese Model. *Asian Survey, 25*(12), 1214-1228.

Handsman, R. G. (1983). Historical Archaeology and Capitalism, Subscriptions and Separations: The Production of Individualism. *North American Archaeologist, 4*(1), 63-79.

Hannerz, U. (1969). *Soulside: Inquiries into Ghetto Culture and Community*. New York, NY: Columbia University Press.

Hardesty, D. (1999). Historical Archaeology in the Next Millennium: A Forum. *Historical Archaeology, 33*(2), 51-58.

Hazan, H. (2009). Essential Others: Anthropology and the Return of the Old Savage. *International Journal of Sociology and Social Policy, 29*(1-2), 60-72.

Head, F. A. (1992). Student Teaching as Initiation into the Teaching Profession. *Anthropology and Education Quarterly, 23*(2), 89-107.

Headley, S. C. (1983). Recognising God in Another Culture. *International Review of Mission, 72*(285), 75-80.

Hennigh, L. (1981). The Anthropologist as Key Informant: Inside a Rural Oregon Town. In D. A. Messerschmidt (Ed.), *Anthropologists ar Home in North America* (pp. 121-132). New York, NY: Cambridge University Press.

Henry, J. (1965). *Culture Against Man*. New York, NY: Vintage Books.

Herzfeld, M. (1989). *Anthropology through the Looking-Glass: Critical Ethnography in the Margins of Europe*. New York, NY: Cambridge University Press.

Hicks, D., & Beaudry, M. C. (Eds.). (2006). *The Cambridge Companion to Historical Archaeology*. New York, NY: Cambridge University Press.

Ho, K. (2009). *Liquidated: An Ethnography of Wall Street*. Charlotte, NC: Duke University Press.

Hodder, I. (1986). *Reading the Past: Current Approaches to Interpretation in Archaeology*. New York, NY: Cambridge University Press.

Hodder, I. (1991a). Interpretive Archaeology and Its Role. *American Antiquity, 56*(1), 7-18.

Hodder, I. (1991b). Postprocessual Archaeology and the Current Debate. In
    R. W. Preucel (Ed.), *Processual and Postprocessual Archaeologies: Multiple
    Ways of Knowing the Past* (pp. 30-41). Southern Illinois University at
    Carbondale, Il: Center for Archaeological Investigations,
    Occaisional Paper No. 10.

Hodder, I. (Ed.). (2000). *Towards Reflexive Method in Archaeology: The Example
    at Çatalhöyük.* Cambridge: McDonald Institute for Archaeological
    Research Monograph #28.

Hodder, I. (2003). Archaeological Reflexivity and the "Local" Voice.
    Anthropological Quarterly, 76(1), 55-69.

Holtorf, C. (2005). *From Stonehenge to Las Vegas: Archaeology as Popular Culture.*
    Lanham, MD: Altamira Press.

Holtorf, C. (2007). *Archaeology is a Brand! The Meaning of Archaeology in
    Contemporary Popular Culture.* Walnut Creek, CA: Left Coast Press.

Honerkamp, N. (1988). Questions that Count in Historical Archaeology.
    Historical Archaeology, 22(1), 5-6.

Horgan, J. (1996). *The End of Science: Facing the Limits of Knowledge in the
    Twilight of the Scientific Age.* Boston, MA: Addison Wesley Publishing
    Company.

Horn, J. P. (1988). "The Bare Necessities": Standards of Living in England
    and the Chesapeake, 1650-1700. *Historical Archaeology, 22*(2), 74-93.

Howe, N., & Strauss, B. (1993). *13th Gen: Abort, Retry, Ignor, Fail?* New
    York, NY: Vintage Books.

Howe, N., & Strauss, W. (2000). *Millennials Rising: The Next Great Generation.*
    New York, NY: Vintage Books.

Hsu, F. L. (1973). Prejudice and Its Intellectual Effect in American
    Anthropology: An Ethnographic Report. *American Anthropologist,
    75*(1), 1-19.

Hsu, F. L. (1979). The Cultural Problem of the Cultural Anthropologist.
    American Anthropologist, 81(3), 517-532.

Hume, I. N. (1964). Archaeology: Handmaiden to History. *North Carolina
    Historical Review, 41,* 215-225.

Hymes, D. H. (Ed.). (1972). *Reinventing Anthropology.* New York, NY:
    Pantheon Books.

Ingstad, A. S. (1977). *The Discovery of a Norse Settlement in America.* Oslo:
    Universitetsforlaget.

Jacobs, J. (1974). *Fun City: An Ethnographic Study of a Retirement Community.* New York, NY: Holt, Rinehart, Winston.

Jacobs, J. (1984). *The Mall: An Attemped Escape from Everyday Life.* Prospect Heights, IL: Waveland Press.

Jenkins, R. (2000). Disenchantment, Enchantment and Re-Enchantment: Max Weber at the Millennium. *Max Weber Studies, 1,* 11-32.

Joffe, A. H. (2003). Identity/Crisis. *Archaeological Dialogues, 10*(1), 77-95.

Johnson, M. (1996). *An Archaeology of Capitalism.* Cambridge, MA: Blackwell Publishers.

Jones, T. L., & Klar, K. A. (2005). Diffusionism Reconsidered: Linguistic and Archaeological Evidence for Prehistoric Polynesian Contact with Southern California. *American Antiquity, 70*(3), 457-484.

Jordan, A. T. (2002). *Business Anthropology.* Long Grove, IL: Waveland Press.

Kaplan, D. (1974). The Anthropology of Authenticity: Everyman His Own Anthropologist. *American Anthropologist, 76*(4), 824-839.

Kaufman, E. P. (2004). *The Rise and Fall of Anglo-America.* Boston, MA: Harvard University Press.

Kehoe, A. B. (1998). *The Land of Prehistory: A Critical History of American Archaeology.* New York, NY: Rutledge.

Kehoe, A. B. (2003). The Fringe of American Archaeology: Transoceanic and Transcontinental Contacts in Prehistoric America. *Journal of Scientific Exploration, 17*(1), 19-36.

Kehoe, A. B. (2004). *The Kensington Runestone: Approaching a Research Question Holistically.* Long Grove, IL: Waveland Press.

Kehoe, A. B. (2010). Consensus and the Fringe in American Archaeology. *Archaeologies, 6*(2), 197-214.

Kelley, J. H., & Hanen, M. P. (1988). *Archaeology and the Methodology of Science.* Albuquerque, NM: University of New Mexico Press.

Kelso, W. M. (1984). *Kingsmill Plantations, 1600-1800: Archaeology of Country Life in Colonial Virginia.* Orlando, FL: Academic Press.

Kemenetz, A. (2006). *Generation Debt: Why Now is a Terrible Time to be Young.* New York, NY: Riverhead Books.

Kenny, B., & Murray, V. (2003). Creating Competent Customers of Historic Preservation. *Practicing Anthropology, 25*(4), 19-22.

Khare, R. S. (1990). Indian Sociology and the Cultural Other. *Contributions to Indian Sociology, 24*(2), 177-199.

Kim, C. S. (2002). *One Anthropologist Two Worlds: Three Decades of Reflexive Fieldwork in North America.* Knoxville, TN: University of Tennessee Press.

Kluckhohn, C. (1949). *Mirror for Man: Anthropology and Modern Life.* New York, NY: McGraw-Hill Book Company.

Kotlikoff, L. J., & Burns, S. (2005). *The Coming Generational Storm: What You Need to Know about America's Future* (Revised and expanded ed.). Boston, MA: MIT Press.

Krugman, P. (2007). *The Conscience of a Liberal.* New York, NY: W. W. Norton and Company.

Landy, J., & Saler, M. (Eds.). (2009). *The Re-Enchantment of the World: Secular Magic in a Rational Age.* Stanford, CA: Stanford University Press.

Lareau, A., & Shultz, J. (Eds.). (1996). *Journeys through Ethnography: Realistic Accounts of Fieldwork.* Boulder, CO: Westview.

Latour, B. (2004). *Politics of Nature: How to Bring the Sciences into Democracy.* Boston, MA: Harvard Univerity Press.

Latour, B., & Woolgar, S. (1979). *Laboratory Life: The Social Construction of Scientific Facts.* Beverly Hills, CA: Sage Publications, Inc.

Lave, J., & Wenger, E. (1991). *Situated Learning: Legitimate Peripheral Participation.* Cambridge, MA: Cambridge University Press.

Lavine, L. (1988). *Highbrow/Lowbrow: The Emergence of Cultural Hierarchy in America.* Boston, MA: Harvard University Press.

Leach, E. R. (1954). *Political Systems of Highland Burma.* London: Beacon Press.

Lende, D. (2010, December 1). *Anthropology, Science, and Public Understanding.* Retrieved March 10, 2013, from Neuroanthropology: http://blogs.plos.org/neuroanthropology/2010/12/01/anthropology-science-and-public-understanding

Lende, D. (2011, February 11). *A Vision of Anthropology Today--and Tomorrow.* Retrieved March 10, 2013, from Neuroanthropology: http://blogs.plos.org/neuroanthropology/2011/02/11/a-vision-of-anthropology-today-%E2%80%93-and-tomorrow

Leone, M. P. (1982). Some Opinions about Recovering Mind. *American Antiquity, 47*(4), 742-760.

Leone, M. P. (1986). Symbolic, Structural, and Critical Archaeology. In D. J. Meltzer, D. D. Fowler, & J. A. Sabloff (Eds.), *American Archaeology Past and Future: A Celebration of the Society for American Archaeology,*

1935-1985 (pp. 415-438). Washington, DC: Smithsonian Institution Press.

Leone, M. P., & Potter, P. B. (1988). Introduction: Issues in Historical Archaeology. In M. P. Leone, & P. B. Potter (Eds.), *The Recovery of Meaning: Historical Archaeology in the Eastern United States* (pp. 1-22). Washington, DC: Smithsonian Instution Press.

Leone, M. P., & Potter, P. B. (Eds.). (1999). *Historical Archaeologies of Capitalism.* New York, NY: Kluwer Academic/Plenum.

Levi-Strauss, C. (1963). *Structual Anthropology.* (C. Jacobson, & B. G. Schoepf, Trans.) New York, NY: Doubleday Anchor Books.

Lewis, H. S. (1999). The Misrepresentation of Anthropology and its Consequences. *American Anthropologist, 100*(3), 716-731.

Lightfoot, K. G. (1995). Culture Contact Studies: Redefining the Relationship between Prehistoric and Historical Archaeology. *American Antiquity, 60*(2), 199-217.

Lipe, W. D. (1996). In Defense of Digging: Archeological Preservation as a Means, Not an End. *CRM: Cultural Resource Management, 19*(7), 23-27.

Little, B. J. (Ed.). (1992). *Text-Aided Archaeology.* Boca Raton, FL: CRC Press.

Little, B. J. (1994). People with History: An Update on Historic Archaeology in the United Staes. *Journal of Archaeological Method and Theory, 1*(1), 5-40.

Little, B. J. (2006). *Historical Archaeology: Why the Past Matters.* Walnut Creek, CA: Left Coast Press.

Little, B. J., & Shackel, P. A. (1992). Introduction. *Historical Archaeology, 26*(3), 1-4.

Lovata, T. (2006). *Inauthentic Archaeologies: Public Uses and Abuses of the Past.* Walnut Creek, CA: Left Coast Press.

Lynch, M. E. (1985). *Art and Artifact in Laboratory Science: A Study of Shop Work and Shop Talk in a Laboratory.* London: Routledge and Kegan Paul.

Lynott, M. J., & Wylie, A. (Eds.). (1995). *Ethics in American Archaeology: Challenges for the 1990s.* Washington, DC: Society for American Archaeology.

Lynott, M. J., & Wylie, A. (Eds.). (2000). *Ethics in American Archaeology* (Second revised ed.). Washington, DC: Society for American Archaeology.

Madsen, R., Sullivan, W. A., Swidler, A., & Tipton, S. (1985). *Habits of the Heart: Individualism and Commitment in American Life.* New York, NY: Harper and Row.

Malinowski, B. (1989). *A Diary in the Strict Sense of the Word.* Palo Alto, CA: Stanford University Press.

Marcus, G. E., & Fischer, M. M. (1986). *Anthropology as Cultural Critique: An Experimental Moment in the Human Sciences.* Chicago, IL: University of Chicago Press.

McDavid, C. (1997). Descendants, Decisions, and Power: The Public Interpretation of the Archaeology of the Levi Jordan Plantation. *Historical Archaeology, 31*(3), 114-131.

McDavid, C. (1997). Towards a More Democratic Archaeology? The Internet and Public Archaeological Practice. In N. Merriman (Ed.), *Public Archaeology* (pp. 159-188). London: Routledge.

McGhee, R. (1984). Contact between Native North Americans and the Medieval Norse: A Review of the Evidence. *American Antiquity, 49*(1), 4-26.

McGilchrist, I. (2009). *The Master and His Emissary: The Divided Brain and the Making of the Western World.* New Haven, CT: Yale University Press.

McGimsey, C. R. (1972). *Public Archaeology.* New York, NY: Seminar Press.

McGimsey, C. R. (2006). Letter to the Editor. *The SAA Archaeological Record, 6*(4), 4.

McGovern, T. (1981). The Vinland Adventure: A North American Perspective. *North American Archaeologist, 2*(4), 285-308.

McGovern, T. (1990). The Archeology of the Norse North Atlantic. *Annual Review of Anthropology, 19*(1), 331-351.

McLoughlin, W. G. (1978). *Revivals, Awakenings, and Reform: An Essay on Religion and Social Change in America, 1607-1977.* Chicago, IL: University of Chicago Press.

McManamon, F. P. (1991). The Many Publics for Archaeology. *American Archaeology, 56*(1), 121-130.

Mead, M. (1942). *And Keep Your Powder Dry: An Anthropologist Looks at America.* New York, NY: Berghahn Books.

Merriman, N. (Ed.). (2004). *Public Archaeology.* London: Routledge.

Merton, R. K. (1957). *Social Theory and Social Structure* (Revised ed.). New York, NY: The Free Press.

Messerschmidt, D. A. (Ed.). (1981). *Anthropologists at Home in North America*. New York, NY: Cambridge University Press.

Meyer, K. E. (1992). Digging Berlin's Chamber of Horrors. *Archaeology, 45*(4), 24-29.

Minor, H. (1956). Body Ritual among the Nacirema. *American Anthropologist, 58*(3), 503-507.

Moeller, R. W. (2000). A Post-Apocalyptic View of Archaeology. *North American Archaeologist, 21*(4), 351-366.

Moffatt, M. (1992). Ethnographic Writing about American Culture. *Annual Review of Anthropology, 21*, 205-229.

Mooney, N. (2008). *(Not) Keeping up with Our Parents: the Decline of the Professional Middle Class*. New York, NY: Beacon Press.

Moore, L. E. (1986). *Patterns without Rhythm: Social Structure Ambiguity in an Archaeological Field Camp*. Master's Thesis, University of Montana.

Moore, L. E. (1992). Down in the Uplands. *Quarterly Bulletin of the Archaeological Society of Virginia, 47*(2), 129-139.

Moore, L. E. (1994a). Notes on the Prehistory of Dunn Loring, Virginia. *Quarterly Bulletin of the Archaeological Society of Virginia, 49*(1), 25-31.

Moore, L. E. (1994b). The Ironies of Self-Reflection in Archaeology. In I. Mackenzie (Ed.), *Archaeological Theory: Progress or Posture?* (pp. 43-56). Brookfield, VT: Avebury/Ashgate Publishing Company.

Moore, L. E. (1994c). Getting Back to Work: Reply to Mackenzie. In I. Mackenzie (Ed.), *Archaeological Theory: Progress or Posture?* (pp. 61-65). Brookfield, VT: Avebury/Ashgate Publishing Company.

Moore, L. E. (1995). Studying the Modern Period: Expanding the Perspective of Historical Archaeology. *Journal of Middle Atlantic Archaeology, 11*, 119-124.

Moore, L. E. (2001a). Hoaxes and the Norsemen of Canada. *All Points Bulletin, 38*(3), 1-2.

Moore, L. E. (2001b). The Misplaced Trowel. *North American Archaeologist, 22*(4), 387-402.

Moore, L. E. (2002). Prehistoric Sites and Settlement Patterns in the Ken-Caryl Valley, Jefferson County, Colorado. *Southwestern Lore, 68*(1), 1-22.

Moore, L. E. (2005a). A Forecast for American Archaeology. *The SAA Archaeological Record, 5*(4), 13-16.

Moore, L. E. (2005b). Social Change and Oklahoma Public Archaeology. *North American Archaeologist, 26*(4), 361-369.

Moore, L. E. (2006a). CRM: Beyond Its Peak. *The SAA Archaeological Record, 6*(1), 30-33.

Moore, L. E. (2006b). Going Public: Customization and American Archaeology. *The SAA Archaeological Record, 6*(3), 16-19.

Moore, L. E. (2006c). Toward a Still and Quiet Conscience; A Study in Reflexive Archaeology. *North American Archaeologist, 27*(2), 149-174.

Moore, L. E. (2007a). The End of Prehistory. *Society for Historical Archaeology Newsletter, 40*(1), 26-28.

Moore, L. E. (2007b). Archaeology's High Society Blues: Reply to McGimsey. *The Archaeological Record, 7*(4), 11-14, 22.

Moore, L. E. (2009). Nomads and Commanders: Welcoming Generation X. *The SAA Archaeological Record, 9*(5), 33-36.

Moore, L. E. (2013). Letter to the Editor. *SAA Archaeological Record, 13*(4), 3.

Moore, L. E., & Busch, R. (2003). The Hogback Valley and Its Relation to Denver Area Prehistory. *Southwestern Lore, 69*(3), 1-25.

Moore, L. E., & Hurst, G. J. (2005). Medicine for the Troops: Glass from a Civil War Encampment in Centreville, Virginia. *Quarterly Bulletin of the Archaeological Society of Virginia, 60*(3), 150-176.

Moore, T. (1992). *Care for the Soul: A Guide for Cultivating Depth and Sacredness in Everyday Life*. New York, NY: Harper Collins.

Mrozowski, S. A. (1993). The Dialectics of Historical Archaeology in a Post-Processual World. *Historical Archaeology, 27*(2), 106-111.

MSNBC. (2007, January 24). Japan Marine Park Captures Rare Shark on Film: "Livinging Fossil" Species has Changed Little since Prehistoric Times. *MBCNews.com*. Retrieved March 16, 2013, from http://www.nbcnews.com/id/16785254/?GT1=8921

Murphy, R. F. (1980). *The Dialectics of Social Life: Alarms and Excursions in Anthropological Theory* (Morningside ed.). New York, NY: Columbia University Press.

Myerhoff, B., & Ruby, J. (1982). Introduction. In J. Ruby (Ed.), *A Crack in the Mirror: Reflexive Perspectives in Anthropology* (pp. 1-35). Philadelphia, PA: University of Pennsylvania Press.

Nadel, S. F. (1957). *The Theory of Social Structure*. New York, NY: The Free Press.

Nash, D. (1964). The Ethnologist as Stranger: An Essay in the Sociology of Knowledge. *Southwestern Journal of Anthropology, 19*, 149-167.

Nash, D. (1970). *A Community in Limbo*. Bloomington, IN: Indiana University Press.

Ndlovu, N. (2006). The Role of Archaeology in the 21st Century: A Personal Journey. *Paper presented at the 39th Annual Chacmool Conference*. Calgary: Alberta.

Nielson, R., & Wolter, S. F. (2005). *The Kensington Rune Stone: Compelling New Evidence*. Eden Prairie, MN: Outernet Publishers.

Nietzsche, F. (1967). The Birth of Tragedy. In W. Kaufman (Ed.), *The Basic Writings of Nietzsche* (pp. 1-144). New York, NY: The Modern Library.

Ntarangwi, M. (2010). *Reversed Gaze: An African Ethnography of American Anthropology*. Urbana, IL: University of Illinois.

O'Brien, M. J., & Lyman, R. L. (2000). Darwinian Evolutionism is Applicable to Historical Archaeology. *International Journal of Historical Archaeology, 4*(1), 71-112.

Orser, C. E. (1988). Toward a Theory of Power for Historical Archaeology: Plantations and Space. In M. P. Leone, & P. B. Potter (Eds.), *The Recovery of Meaning: Historical Archaeology in the Eastern United States* (pp. 313-343). Washington, DC: Smithsonian Institution Press.

Orser, C. E. (1994). Toward a Global Historical Archaeology. *Historical Archaeology, 28*(1), 5-22.

Orser, C. E. (1996). *A Historical Archaeology of the Modern World*. New York, NY: Plenum.

O'Shaughnessy, L. (2008, June 27). Debt Squeezed Gen X Saves Little. *USA Today*. Retrieved March 16, 2013, from http://usatoday30.usatoday.com/money/perfi/retirement/2008-05-19-generation-x-retirement_N.htm?loc=interstitialskip

Pachinco, J. (1997). *Swamp*. Berkeley, CA: Superstition Street Press.

Partnership for Public Service. (2005). *Where the Jobs Are: Continuing Growth of Federal Job Opportunities*. Retrieved March 16, 2013, from http://media.newjobs.com/opm/www/usajobs/pdf/WHERE_THE_JOBS_ARE.pdf

Patterson, T. C. (1986). The Last Sixty Years: Towards a Social History of Americanist Archaeology in the United States. *American Anthropologist, 88*(1), 7-26.

Patterson, T. C. (1989). History and the Post-Processual Archaeologies. *Man, 24,* 555-566.

Paynter, R. (1988). Steps to an Archaeology of Capitalism: Material Change and Class Analysis. In M. P. Leone, & P. B. Potter (Eds.), *The Recovery of Meaning: Historical Archaeology in the Eastern United States* (pp. 407-433). Washington, DC: Smithsonian Institution Press.

Pearson, M., & Shanks, M. (2000). *Theater/Archaeology: Reflections upon a Hybrid Genre.* London, Routledge.

Pelias, R. J. (2003). The Academic Tourist: An Autoethnography. *Qualitative Inquiry, 9*(3), 369-373.

Peters, S. (2001). *Gen X in the Newsroom: Expectations, Attitudes Don't fit Traditional Culture.* Evanston, IL: Northwestern University, Media Management Center.

Peterson, P. G. (2004). *Running on Empty: How the Democratic and Republican Parties are Bankrupting Our Future and What Americans Can Do About It.* New York, NY: Straus and Giroux.

Pokotylo, D., & Guppy, N. (1999). Public Opinion and Archaeological Heritage: Views from Outside the Profession. *American Antiquity, 64*(3), 400-416.

Porterfield, A. (2001). *The The Transformation of American Religion: The Story of a Late-Twentieth Century Awakening.* New York, NY: Oxford Univerity Press.

Potter, D. M. (1964). American Women and the American Character. In J. A. Hague (Ed.), *American Character and Culture: Some Twentieth Century Perspectives* (pp. 65-84). Deland, FL: Everatt Edwards Press.

Potter, P. B. (1991a). What's the Use of Plantation Archaeology? *Historical Archaeology, 25*(3), 94-107.

Potter, P. B. (1991b). Self-Reflection in Archaeology. In R. W. Preucel (Ed.), *Processual and Postprocessual Archaeologies: Multiple Ways of Knowing the Past* (pp. 225-234). Carbondale, IL, Southern Illinois University, Occasional Paper No. 10.

Praetzellis, A. (2004). A Ten Minute History of Everything or 30 years of Historical Archaeology in California. *Proceedings of the Society for California Archaeology, 17,* pp. 11-13.

Praetzellis, A., & Praetzellis, M. (Eds.). (1998). Archaeologists as Storytellers. *Historical Archaeology, 32*(1).

Prechter, R. R. (2003). *Conquer the Crash: You Can Survive and Posper in a Deflationary Depression* (Expanded and Updated ed.). New York, NY: John Wiley and Sons.

Preucel, R. W. (1991). Introduction. In R. W. Preucel (Ed.), *Processual and Postprocessual Archaeologies: Multiple Ways of Knowing the Past* (pp. 1-16). Carbondale, IL: Southern Illinois University, Occasional Paper No. 10.

Pyle, R. E., & Koch, J. R. (2001). The Religious Affiliations of American Elites, 1930 to 1990s: A Note on the Pace of Disestablishment. *Sociological Focus, 34*(2), 125-137.

Rabinow, P. (1977). *Reflections on Fieldwork in Morocco*. Berkeley, CA: University of California Press.

Ramos, M., & Duganne, D. (2000). *Exploring Public Perceptions and Attitudes about Archaeology*. Washington, DC: Harris Interactive for the Society for American Archaeology.

Rathje, W., & Murphy, C. (1993). *Rubbish! The Archaeology of Garbage*. New York, NY: Harper Perennial.

Redding, G. S. (1987). Research on Asian Cultures and Management: Some Epistemological Issues. *Asia Pacific Journal of Management, 5*(1), 89-96.

Redfield, R. (1963). *The Primitive World and Its Transformation*. Ithica, NY: Cornell University Press.

Reed-Danahay, D. (1997). *Auto/Ethnography: Rewritting the Self and the Social*. Oxford: Berg Publishers.

Reid, J. J., Rathje, W. L., & Schiffer, M. B. (1974). Expanding Archaeology. *American Antiquity, 39*(1), 125-126.

Richard, M. J. (2001). Novices in the Field: Filling in the Meaning Continuum. *Frontiers: The Interdisciplinary Journal of Study Abroad, 7*, 95-119.

Robertson, J. E. (2002). Reflexivity Redux: A Pithy Polemic on "Positionality". *Anthropological Quarterly, 75*(4), 785-792.

Rodriguez, T. (2006). Conjunctures in the Making of an Ancient Maya Archaeological Site. In M. Edgeworth (Ed.), *Ethnographies of Archaeological Practice: Cultural Encounters, Material Transformations* (pp. 161-172). Lanham, MD: Altamira Press.

Rorty, R. (1979). *Philosophy and the Mirror of Nature*. Princeton, NJ: Princeton University Press.

Roth, W. M., & Bowen, G. M. (2001). Of Disciplined Minds and Disciplined Bodies: On Becoming an Ecologist. *Qualitative Sociology, 24*(4), 459-481.

Roveland, B. E. (2000). *Contextualizing the History and Practice of Paleolithic Archaeology: Hamburgian Research in Northern Germany.* Amherst: PhD. Dissertation, University of Masschusetts.

Ruby, J. (Ed.). (1982). *A Crack in the Mirror: Reflexive Perspectives in Anthropology.* Philadelphia, PA: Pennsylvania University Press.

Russell, M. (Ed.). (2002). *Digging Holes in Popular Culture: Archaeology and Science Fiction.* Oakville, CT: David Brown Book Company.

Sahlins, M. (1981). *Historical Metaphors and Mythical Realities.* Ann Arbor, MI: University of Michigan Press.

Sandlin, J. A., & Bey, G. B. (2006). Trowels, Trenches, and Transformation: A Case Study of Archaeologists Learning a More Critical Practice of Archaeology. *Journal of Social Archaeology, 6*(2), 255-276.

Sangren, P. S. (2007). Anthropology of Anthropology? Further Reflections on Reflexivity. *Anthropology Today, 23*(4), 13-16.

Sapir, E. (1924). Culture, Genuine and Spurious. *The American Journal of Sociology, 29*(4), 401-429.

Schechner, R. (1985). *Between Theater and Anthropology.* Philadelphia, PA: University of Pennsylvania Press.

Scheuerman, W. E. (2001). Reflexive Law and the Challenges of Globalization. *Journal of Political Philosophy, 9*(1), 81-102.

Schuyler, R. L. (1970). Historical and Historic Sites Archaeology as Anthropology: Basic Definitions and Relationships. *Historical Archaeology, 4*, 83-89.

Schuyler, R. L. (Ed.). (1978). *Historical Archaeology: A Guide to Substantive and Theoretical Contributions.* Famingdale, NY: Baywood Publishing Company.

Schuyler, R. L. (1988). Archaeological Remains, Documents, and Anthropology: A Call for a New Culture History. *Historical Archaeology, 22*(1), 36-42.

Schuyler, R. L. (1991). A Complete Curriculum: Historical Archaeology on the Undergraduate Level. In K. C. Smith, & F. P. McManamon (Eds.), *Archaeology and Education: The Classroom and Beyond* (pp. 33-

40). Washington, DC: U. S. Department of the Interior, Archeological Assistance Study No. 2.

Schuyler, R. L. (1995). Global Perspectives and Scales of Analysis in Historical Archaeology. *Paper presented at the annual meeting of the Society for Historical Archaeology.* Washington: DC.

Sellers, M. (1973). The Secret Notebook for the Practicing Archaeologist: With Preliminary Notes Towards an Ethnoscience of Archaeology. *Plains Anthropologist, 18*(60), 140-148.

Shackel, P. A., & Little, B. J. (1992). Post-Processual Approaches to Meanings and Uses of Historical Archaeology. *Historical Archaeology, 26*(3), 5-11.

Shanks, M., & McGuire, R. H. (1996). The Craft of Archaeology. *American Antiquity, 61*(1), 75-88.

Shi, D. E. (1985). *The Simple Life: Plain Living and High Thinking in American Culture.* New York, NY: Oxford University Press.

Smith, I. W. (1990). Historical Archaeology in New Zealand: A Review and Bibliography. *New Zealand Journal of Archaeology, 12*, 85-119.

Smith, M. E. (2010, December 3). *Science and the AAA: Five Problems with the Proposed Change.* Retrieved March 10, 2013, from Publishing Anthropology: http://publishingarchaeology.blogspot.com/2010/12/science-and-aaa-five-problems-with.html

South, S. (1977). *Method and Theory in Historical Archaeology.* New York, NY: Academic Press.

Spaulding, A. C. (1953). Statistical Techniques for the Discovery of Artifact Types. *American Antiquity, 18*, 305-313.

Spradley, J. P. (1970). *You Own Yourself a Drunk: An Ethnography of Urban Nomads.* Boston, MA: Little, Brown, and Company.

Spradley, J. P. (1980). *Participant Observation.* New York, NY: Holt, Rinehart, Winston.

Spradley, J. P., & Rynkiewich, M. A. (Eds.). (1975). *The Narcirema: Readings in American Culture.* New York, NY: Little Brown.

Spriggs, M. (Ed.). (1984). *Marxist Perspectives in Archaeology.* New York, NY: Cambridge University Press.

Star Tribune. (2006, October 17). A New Minority: Married Couples. *Star Tribune.*

Stocking, G. W. (1966). Franz Boas and the Culture Concept in Historical Perspective. *American Anthropologist, 68*(4), 867-882.

Strauss, W., & Howe, N. (1991). *Generations: The History of America's Future, 1584 to 2069.* New York, NY: William Morrow.

Strauss, W., & Howe, N. (1997). *The Fourth Turning: An American Prophecy.* New York, NY: Broadway Books.

Strauss, W., & Howe, N. (2001, October 29). Sept. 11 Tragedy Marks Another Turning Point. *USA Today.*

Taagapera, R. (1969). Growth Curves of Empires. *General Systems, 13*, 171-175.

Taagapera, R. (1978). Size and Duration of Empires: Systematics of Size. *Social Science Research, 7*, 108-127.

Taagapera, R. (1997). Expansion and Contraction Patterns of Large Polities: Context for Russia. *International Studies Quarterly, 41*(3), 475-504.

Tannen, D. (1990). *You Just Don't Understand: Women and Men in Conversation.* New York, NY: Random House.

Taylor, W. W. (1948). *A Study of Archaeology.* Washington, DC: American Anthropological Association, Memoir No. 69.

Tengan, T. P. (2005). Unsettling Ethnography: Tales of an 'Oiwi in the Anthropological Slot. *Anthropology Forum, 15*(3), 247-256.

Thomas, D. H. (1989). *Archaeology* (Second ed.). Chicago, IL: Holt, Rinehart, Winston.

Tilly, C. (1989). Excavation as Theater. *Antiquity, 63*, 275-280.

Tönnies, F. (2002). *Community and Society.* (C. P. Loomis, Trans.) Mineola, NY: Dover Publications.

Trencher, S. R. (1993). *Toward an Anthropology of American Anthropology: An Analysis of Fieldworker Ethnographies.* Washington, DC: Phd Dissertation, Catholic University of America.

Trencher, S. R. (2000). *Mirrored Images: American Anthropology and American Culture, 1960-1980.* Westport, CT: Bergin Garvey.

Trencher, S. R. (2002). The Literary Project and Representations of Anthropology. *Anthropological Theory, 2*(2), 211-231.

Trigger, B. G. (1991). Constrain and Freedom--A New Synthesis for Archaeological Explanation. *American Anthropologist, 93*(3), 551-569.

Trouillot, M.-R. (2003). *Global Transformations and the Modern World.* New York, NY: Palgrave Macmillan.

Turner, V. W. (1969). *The Ritual Process: Structure and Anti-Structure*. New York, NY: Aldine.

Utley, R. M. (1986). On Digging Up Custer Battlefield. *Montana: The Magazine of Western History, 36*(2), 80-82.

Van der Leeuw, S., & Redman, C. L. (2002). Placing Archaeology at the Center of Socio-Natural Studies. *American Antiquity, 67*(4), 597-605.

VanPool, C. S., & VanPool, T. L. (1999). The Scientific Nature of Postprocessualism. *American Antiquity, 64*(1), 33-53.

Varenne, H. (1977). *Americans Together: Stuctured Diversity in a Midwestern Town*. New York: Teachers College Press.

Vogt, E. Z. (1960). On the Concepts of Structure and Process in Cultural Anthropology. *American Anthropologist, 62*, 18-33.

Walker, I. C. (1970). The Crisis of Identity--History and Anthropology. *The Conference on Historic Site Archaeology Papers, 1968, 3*, 62-69.

Wallace, A. (1956). Revitalization Movements. *American Anthropologist, 58*, 264-281.

Wallace, A. F. (1972). Paradigmatic Process in Culture Change. *American Anthropologist, 74*, 467-478.

Wallace, J. (2004). *Digging the Dirt: The Archaeological Imagination*. London: Duckworth Publishers.

Wallace, M. T. (1999). Mentoring Apprentice Ethnographers through Field Schools. *Anthropology and Education Quarterly, 30*(2), 210-219.

Waselkov, G. A. (2001). Historical Archaeology, with Sails Set and Tacking into the Wind. *Historical Archaeology, 35*(2), 20-22.

Watkins, J. (2001). *Indigenous Archaeology*. Lanham, MD: Altamira Press.

Weber, M. (2009). *The Protestant Ethic and the Spirit of Capitalism*. New York, NY: Norton Critical Editions.

Whyte, W. F. (1955). *Street Corner Society: The Structure of an Italian Slum* (Enlarged ed.). Chicago, IL: University of Chicago Press.

Wilentz, S. (2005). *The Rise of American Democracy: Jefferson to Lincoln*. New York, NY: W W Norton.

Wilkie, L. A. (2005). Inessential Archaeologies: Problems of Exclusion in Americanist Archaeological Thought. *World Archaeology, 37*(3), 337-351.

Wilkinson, R. (1983). American Character Revisited. *Journal of American Studies, 17*(2), 165-187.

Wilson, C. (2006). Dis-enganging from the Institution and Re-engaging with the Community: Transformation of an Indigenous Student to an Indigenous Archaeologist. Calgary: Paper presented at the 39th Annual Chocmool Conference.

Winograd, M., & Hais, M. D. (2008). *Millennial Makeover: MySpace, YouTube, and the Future of American Politics*. Piscataway, NJ: Rutgers University Press.

Wolf, E. R. (1982). *Europe and the People without History*. Berkeley, CA: University of California Press.

Wood, M. C. (2002). Moving Towards Transformative Democratic Action through Archaeology. *International Journal of Historical Archaeology, 6*(3), 187-198.

Wylie, A. (2002). *Thinking from Things: Essays in the Philosophy of Archaeology*. Berkeley, CA: University of California Press.

Zeder, M. A. (1997). *The American Archaeologist: A Profile*. Walnut Creek, CA: Altamira Press.

Sorry, no Index

SENSE AND NONSENSE ABOUT THE AUTHOR

Larry Moore is currently an archaeologist with the Bureau of Land Management, Oklahoma Field Office, in Tulsa. In recent years, he was an archaeologist for Naval Air Station Whidbey Island, Washington, an environmental protection specialist for the US Army Garrison at the Presidio of Monterey, and an archaeologist with the Army Garrison at Fort Hunter Liggett. He also held archaeological contractor positions with the Southwestern Power Administration and the NRCS-Colorado. Further back, he worked in financial sales for several years. Even further back, as a young adult starting his career, he was a shovel bum and a sole proprietor consulting archaeologist, and then a staff archaeologist for Fairfax County, Virginia. All that covers about thirty years. His interest in the sociology of archaeology started in graduate school in the early 1980s and continues.

Back in the mid 1980s, he and Joe Baker were out on Koocanusa Reservoir, near Libby, MT, looking at, "monitoring", several archaeological sites revealed by the drawdown of lake waters by the Army Corps of Engineer. They did their work and returned to the Forest Service office only to be informed that a complaint had been made by some Kootenai who said that they had "desecrated" a site by urinating on it. Of course they urinated there--where else would they do their natural business? Where did the ancient ones do theirs? And wasn't flooding a site worse than what they had done? Didn't matter, they were scolded. Politics.

Another time he was digging a site in Northern Virginia on a cool winter day, with snow on the ground. The crew were bailing out water from the pits and a journalist was there, lovely lady in high heeled shoes, and a camera man. After the interview Moore returned to the crew and helped to discern soil layers on a profile. He joked about reading the soil, being one with it, you know, doing Zen archaeology. The next day the *Fairfax Herald* ran an essay about the project with Moore being the Zen Archaeologist. That wasn't part of the interview! She was eavesdropping on their conversations. So much for being a public archaeologist.

There are so many stories to tell. Truth is, he is a Tibetan Warrior who tries to live the Four Dignities: Relaxed confidence, perkiness, outrageousness, and inscrutability. Yes, number two has a long way to go.